The
Christmas
Chronicles

Nigel Slater is an award-winning author, journalist and television presenter. He has been food columnist for the *Observer* for twenty-five years. His collection of bestselling books includes the classics *Appetite* and *The Kitchen Diaries*, and the critically acclaimed two-volume *Tender*. He has made cookery programmes and documentaries for BBC1, BBC2 and BBC4. His memoir *Toast – the story of a boy's hunger* won six major awards and is now a film and stage production. His writing has won the James Beard Award, the National Book Award, the Glenfiddich Trophy, the André Simon Memorial Prize and the British Biography of the Year. He lives in London.

nigelslater.com
Twitter @nigelslater
Instagram @nigelslater

Also by Nigel Slater:

The Kitchen Diaries III: A Year of Good Eating

Eat

The Kitchen Diaries II

Tender, Volumes I and II

Eating for England

The Kitchen Diaries I

Toast – the story of boy's hunger

Appetite

Real Food

Real Cooking

The 30-Minute Cook

Real Fast Food

Nigel Slater

The Christmas Chronicles

**Notes, stories
& 100 essential
recipes
for midwinter**

Recipe photography by
Jonathan Lovekin

4th Estate | London

4th Estate
An imprint of HarperCollinsPublishers
1 London Bridge Street
London SE1 9GF

www.4thEstate.co.uk

First published in Great Britain by 4th Estate in 2017

1

A catalogue record for this book is available from the British Library

ISBN 978-0-00-826019-4 (hardback)

Design by David Pearson

Typeset by GS Typesetting

Printed and bound in Germany by Mohn Media Mohndruck GmbH

MIX
Paper from
responsible sources
FSC
www.fsc.org   FSC C007454

For James

Who once told me 'You can grow old, just make sure you never grow up.'

Acknowledgements

The seeds of this book were sown half a century ago, in the attic of my childhood home, where my parents kept our collection of Christmas decorations in cardboard boxes. It was there, amongst the faded baubles and skeins of silver tinsel, the boxes of magic tricks and impenetrable tangle of fairy lights that my enduring fascination with Christmas was born.

That my love of winter, its food and folklore, has made it to the printed page is due to the support of many, but none more so than Louise Haines, my publisher at Fourth Estate. I should like to thank Michelle Kane, Julian Humphries, Annie Lee and Louise Tucker for their collaboration and my thanks, once again, to Jonathan Lovekin and to David Pearson.

I will forever be in debt to Allan Jenkins at the *Observer* and to Ruaridh Nichol, Martin Love, Gareth Grundy and Debbie Lawson for their unfailing belief and support.

To my literary agent Araminta Whitley and everyone at LAW, and to Rosemary Scholar and all at United Agents. I am blessed to have you in my life.

I am hugely grateful to Charlotte Moore, Alison Kirkham and Catherine Catton at the BBC, and to Pete Lawrence for their continued support and encouragement.

Thanks and admiration to Dalton Wong and George Ashwell at Twenty Two Training, Timothy d'Offay, Takahiro Yagi, Katie Findlay, Robbie Johnson and to Rob Watson and Sam Jackson at ph9 and Richard Stepney at Fourth Floor. To Lyn Harris and Caroline Russell at perfumer h (perfumerh.com) for their invaluable advice and to all my followers on Instagram and Twitter for their kind words and inspirational pictures. I am also grateful to Louise Heard of that most magical of places, Benjamin Pollock's Toyshop, (pollocks-coventgarden.co.uk) for permission to reproduce Simon Seddon's beautiful Pantomime Feast Shadow Box.

It means a great deal to me that so many of those acknowledged here have been alongside me for a decade or more, and several for over twenty-five years.

It also has to be said that my books, journalism and television programmes would probably never see the light of day (and would be a lot less fun to do) without the dedication, inspiration and enthusiasm of James Thompson, business and creative partner, producer, collaborator and best friend. James, you are amazing. I can never, ever, thank you enough.

Introduction

The icy prickle across your face as you walk out into the freezing air. The piercing burn to your sinuses, like wasabi. Your eyes sparkle, your ears tingle. The rush of cold to your head is stimulating, vital, energising.

The arrival of the first snap of cold is invigorating, like jumping into an ice pool after the long sauna of summer. Winter feels like a renewal, at least it does to me. I long for that ice-bright light, skies of pale blue and soft grey light that is at once calm and gentle, fresh and crisp. Away from the stifling airlessness of summer, I once again have more energy. Winter has arrived. I can breathe again.

My childhood memories of summer are few and precious. Picking blackcurrants for pocket money. A vanilla ice cream, held between two wafers, eaten on the seafront with my mum, seagulls overhead. Sitting in a meadow, buttercups tickling my bare legs, eating ham sandwiches and drinking dandelion and burdock. Pleading with my parents to stop the car so I could get out and pick scarlet poppies, with petals like butterflies' wings that wilted before I could get them home. These are virtually the only recollections I have of those early summers. It is the winters that stay in my memory, carved deep as a fjord, as long and clear as an icicle.

It is as if my entire childhood was lived out in the cold months, a decade spent togged up in duffel coats and mittens, wellingtons and woolly hats. To this day, I am never happier than when there is frost on the roof and a fire in the hearth. I have always preferred snow underfoot to sand between my toes.

I love the crackle of winter. The snap of dry twigs underfoot, boots crunching on frozen grass, a fire spitting in the hearth, ice thawing on a pond, the sound of unwrapping a Christmas present from its paper. The innate crispness of the season appeals to me, like newly fallen snow, frosted hedges, the first fresh page of a new diary. Yes, there is softness in the cold months, too, the voluminous jumpers and woolly hats, the steam rising from soup served in a deep bowl, the light from a single candle and the much-loved scarf that would feel like a burden at any other time of year.

We all know winter. The mysterious whiff of jasmine or narcissus caught in the cold air; the sadness of spent, blackened fireworks the morning after Bonfire Night; a row of pumpkins on a frosted allotment spied from a train window; the magical alchemy of frost and smoke. Winter is the smell of freshly cut ivy or yew and the childish excitement of finding that first, crisp layer of fine ice on a puddle. It is a freckling of snow on cobbled pavements and the golden light from a window on a dark evening that glows like a Russian icon on a museum wall. But for each midwinter sunset, there is another side to this season. Like the one of 1962–3, when farmers, unable to negotiate deep snowdrifts, wept as their animals froze to death in the fields; the snap of frail bones as an elderly neighbour slips on the ice; the grim catalogue of deaths of the homeless from hypothermia. Winter is as deadly as she is beautiful.

A walk through the snow

It started with berries. Holly, rowan, rosehips. A project to record the plants, edible and poisonous, that we spotted on our walk to school. Two miles, in my case, of hedgerows to inspect daily. Hardly a project for me; I knew those hedgerows intimately, each tree and ditch, every lichen-covered gate. I knew which had wild sweet peas – *Lathyrus odoratus* – or primroses hidden by twigs and where to find a bullfinch's nest. When you walk the same route every day on your own, you get to know these things. A tree you must duck to avoid a soaking if it has rained during the night; the progress of a slowly decomposing tree stump among the grass; a bush that delights with a froth of white blossom in spring that by autumn is a mass of purple-black berries. You get to know the site of the sweetest blackberries and the exact location of the wild violets, white and piercing purple, that twinkle like stars in dark holloways.

Even then I knew that hedgerows were sacred, the homes of birds' nests and voles, hedgehogs and haws. I knew that the long, slim rosehips came from the single wild roses that are to this day one of my favourite flowers, along with the hawthorn. I knew too that my father's name for hawthorn was 'bread and cheese', an ancient reference to the usefulness of its leaves and

berries in winter. I also understood that the scarlet berries of yew and holly were never, ever, for consumption.

It was the berries left behind in the winter that held a special fascination for me. The darkening rosehips and hawthorn berries seen against a tapestry of frosty leaves; the solemn beauty of ivy and hypericum berries against a grey wall; a rosehip trapped in ice. Walking was part of my country childhood. A solitary one, but by no means lonely. Not that there was any choice. My father drove back to the Black Country during the week. We had just four buses, two on a Wednesday – one there, one back – and two on Saturday. A bike, you say? Not up the steep hills that surrounded Knightwick, with a gym bag and a leather satchel full of books. There were always books. We lived on the border of two counties. Home and school were in Worcestershire, the nearest shops in Herefordshire. The walks were wretched in summer, sweaty and hateful, full of stinging nettles and sunburn, but in autumn and winter each day was an adventure. I rarely got home before darkness fell. There was a moment, a patch of barely half an hour, when the sun would burn fiercely in the winter sky, just before it slid away, that I regarded as unmissable. Something I had to be outside for.

It was the walk to school that started everything. A life lived with the rhythm of the seasons. Not purely the food (miles from a supermarket or a greengrocer, we ate more seasonally than most), but the outdoors too, the landscape, the garden and the market. The sounds and smells that mark one season as different from another.

By the way, I kept that school project, neatly written in fountain pen, its berry-studded exercise books covered in dried leaves and curls of 'old man's beard', for almost twenty years. Like pretty much everything I owned, it was destroyed in a house fire shortly after I moved to London.

Getting to grips with the season

Winter is caused by the movement of the Earth, the dark winter months appearing when the Earth's axis is at its furthest point from the Sun. For all its bare twigs and pale, watery sunshine, winter is very much alive. Underneath the fallen leaves things are happening at a rate of knots; new life burgeons. Bulbs are sprouting, buds are bursting through grey bark, new shoots push their way to the surface. Many plants require vernalisation, a prolonged patch of low temperatures, in order to grow. Tulips, freesias, crocus and snowdrops, for instance. (I sometimes feel I do, too.) A secret world quietly doing what it does each year. A study in renewal, rebirth, new life.

Winter officially starts in Britain on December 21, the winter solstice, which is the shortest day. I feel this is slightly odd. You would expect the shortest day to be in the middle of winter, not the start, but it gets more complicated when you learn that the date varies from country to country. Sweden and Ireland, for instance, consider the start of winter as November 1, All Hallows' Day. Agriculturally, it is Martinmas, November 11, that is considered to be the beginning. Some cultures also measure winter by temperature rather than by the calendar. Others ecologically or astrologically. In the northern hemisphere we generally consider winter to mean the months of December, January and February. Just to throw a further wooden spoon into the works, this book includes much of November.

The winter light. Stars and shadows

The winter sky has a clarity and gentleness that I find more pleasing than the harsh, screaming colours of summer. Softer tones, those clean, arctic blues, the whisper-soft greys and pin-sharp paper whites, are the skies I want to live under.

The night sky is clearer in cold weather too, the stars infinitely more visible. During the months of December, January and February we are no longer facing directly into the heart of the Milky Way, whose brightness has the effect of making our view of the stars hazy and blurred. In winter, with the planet facing the galaxy at a different angle, we see fewer stars, which is why they seem clearer on a cold frosty night. A clear case of less is more. Standing in the garden, even in London, it is easier to read the sky on a frosty night.

Shadows are more interesting in winter too. More fuel for the imagination. As the Earth tilts away from the sun, the shadows become longer. This is why, perhaps, the walk home is more scary on a winter's night, because generally, shadows are seen as ghostly, eerie, even sinister. That said, it is true that most horror films and ghost stories are set on winter nights (if there is a summer ghost story, it has escaped my attention), where long shadows lend a suitably mysterious, spine-tingling atmosphere. I see them differently, thinking of shadows mostly as benign and fascinating. I often move lamps, furniture and plants in order to get a clearer, longer, more intriguing shadow.

The landscape

The stillness of winter. Snow on a twig. A berry imprisoned in ice. The quietness of a frozen lake. The bareness of the winter landscape allows us to get a better view of the world we inhabit. No long grass and canopy of green leaves to confuse the eye. No fluff of blossom to deceive us (their blossom gone, cherry trees surely get the prize for the most boring trees on the planet), just the clean lines of a winter landscape. The architecture is clear and crisp. The shape of a tree, the path of a river, the outline of a barn, as clear as if they were drawn on a map.

I was brought up with the mother of all 'views', which as an eleven-year-old I somewhat took for granted. From our back door, an undulating landscape of meadows, woodlands, rivers, against a backdrop of the Cotswolds and the Malvern Hills. Snowfall would stay untouched for days, sullied only by the footprints of birds, rabbits, squirrels and foxes. (As a child I imagined wolves and bears too.) Walking in the plantation of Christmas trees that backed on to our long, thin garden was like a trip to see Mr Tumnus. No lamplight, but we had the moon to illuminate the frost-like glitter on a Christmas card. The joy of the little forest of fir trees in the dell was that they stayed cool in the hottest of summers too. A place for a child to hide and play.

The move to the city has brought an altogether different winter into my life. Shorter (city snow is gone in a heartbeat); frosted pavements trashed by pedestrians and the warmth from buildings; snow in London is as rare as hens' teeth. I have lived in the city for thirty years now and have seen all too few proper winters. By proper, I mean those winters with snow deep enough to shovel. The bare trees, however, remain majestic.

I'm not sure you really know a tree until you have seen it without its leaves. Naked, so to speak. They are often at their most peaceful and romantic in winter, like watching a loved one asleep.

Without the diversion of leaves, deciduous trees take on a sculptural quality; we get the opportunity to see their bark more clearly, the dance and flow of their branches, their character and form. Large trees are bare for only four months before new leaf buds emerge, first as freckles, then as tiny, opening leaves. This is when I take them into the house; as large twigs break off the horse chestnuts in the street, I gather them up and stuff them, however large, into one of two capacious vases. The branches I value most are those that have a good horizontal, fluid form, large enough to leave a shadow across the table. As the season moves into spring, their leaves will often open, slightly ahead of those out in the cold. A gift.

Being out in the cold

Those who work outdoors probably have a different view of the winter landscape from someone like me, who simply plays in it. Fishermen, shepherds, road sweepers, farm workers, professional gardeners and those whose working life is spent mostly in the open air may have an altogether less rosy take on the season. Fair enough. Working in the fields, for instance, your fingers can soon become numb, your face raw.

Being outside in the cold is invigorating but we do need to keep moving. The body doesn't like being cold and still, which in extreme cases can result in hypothermia. It wants to maintain a steady temperature. We shiver simply because the brain is sending a message to the nerves all over our body to move quickly to generate heat. We should listen to it.

I am rarely happier than when working outside. Digging, sweeping, walking, all do it for me. I find manual work in the cold as energising and life-affirming as much as I find it (deliciously) exhausting. Short trips around the garden punctuate my day. I walk rather than use public transport to go shopping. Each morning, I will usually saunter around the garden, coffee in hand, rain or shine, frost or snow. I live in hope of that last one.

Coming in from the cold

It is just as good to come in. You stamp to shake the snow from your boots. The flakes of snow on your coat melt instantly. Your glasses steam up. You close the door and thank God you remembered to put the hall light on a timer.

You hang up your coat, tug off your boots and light the fire. You will probably put the kettle on or pour yourself a drink. Not so much as a way to get warm, more to welcome yourself home. Home means more to us in cold weather. Making ourselves comfortable is a duty. Making friends and family comfortable is an art.

'Come in.' Two short words, heavy with meaning. Step out of the big, bad, wet world and into my home. You'll be safe here, toasty and well fed. 'Come in.' They are two of the loveliest words to say and to hear.

Having suggested someone might like to enter, then it is up to us to make them feel welcome. The words alone aren't enough. And that is where the art comes in. There is almost nothing I enjoy more than welcoming visitors into my home. (Full disclosure, I quite like it when they go too.) But in between 'in' and 'out' I want them to feel wanted, comfortable (cosy even) and happy. Yes, warm, even in my rather chilly house, but also fed, watered and generally made to feel that all is well with the world. And yes, I know the world is a shit-storm at the moment, but we all need a safe harbour.

A welcome will invariably involve food, and never more so than at this time of year. No, I don't have a tray of warm mince pies waiting. I don't really live that sort of life, but I do like to have a cake of some sort in the house. Gingerbread in the biscuit tin (Lebkuchen if it's remotely near Christmas), or a fruit cake. I am one of those people who, even in the twenty-first century, still makes fruit cake. Guests only get something savoury if they arrive in the evening, when I'm eating anyway. This house is always in a state of flux, being an office, photography studio and workspace all in one. But it is first and foremost a home, and I have always been a bit of home-maker. (The only thing I ever made in woodwork lessons at school was a coffee table, because I hoped it would make my unhappy adolescent home more hospitable.)

Our lives cannot always be about other people, love them as we do. We need some time for ourselves. I am never, ever without a book, but I do read differently in the winter. My feet curled underneath me, a blanket over my legs. I will always put another layer of clothes on rather than turn the heating up. I dislike, intensely, an overheated room.

But I am getting ahead of myself. It is the months prior to the arrival of the winter solstice – on December 21 – that I look forward to as much as anything. That first nudge that the summer is finally exhausted and we are slowly sliding into the golden days of another autumn. The slide is often protracted, but last year I distinctly remember the moment. We had eaten lunch in the garden, the last in a long, good summer of eating outside; the dahlias were collapsing into the flower beds in a tangle of burgundy and brown; the leaves on the medlar tree had turned as yellow as a ripe quince; dinner had been, at the last moment, bolstered by a dish of roast potatoes. Suddenly, from nowhere, the smell of drifting woodsmoke, and yet not a garden fire in sight, followed in a heartbeat by the urgent need for a jumper, another glass of wine. The season had, in the space of an afternoon, turned.

You either 'get' the cheer of winter, or you don't. Some are rarely happy in fresh air. They only want to eat outside when the air is heavy and hot. But the mood is changing. We are, at last, seeing cafés hanging blankets and woollen throws over their outdoor seats for us to wrap ourselves in, as they do in Scandinavia. (Sadly, too many are often accompanied by the dreaded outdoor heaters.) I have happy memories of flasks of hot drinks on cold walks, of winter picnics of sugar-encrusted cardamom buns and hot coffee. And yet we have a long way to go before we see the cold the way some of our neighbours do.

The negative vocabulary of winter is well used. 'It's so cold' is almost always said in a negative sense. 'Yes,' I usually say, 'invigorating, isn't it?' A sentiment often met with a look of bafflement. We talk about 'fighting the cold', 'battling the elements', and 'cold comfort'. The dead are 'cold' and we give people the 'cold shoulder'. You can argue that statistically more people take their own life in cold countries. Yet those same countries, with their long winters and fewest hours of daylight, continually come out top in quality of life surveys. Go figure.

I pick a newspaper article about winter, totally at random, from the internet. Within the first three paragraphs the author trots out 'bitter, plummeting, battered, dire, freezing, awful, discontent', and then the ultimate – 'Snowmageddon'. Finally, with the vocabulary of negativity exhausted, we get 'Click to see our countdown of Britain's Worst Winters.' Not a single word in praise of an entire season of the year. Which is, in an average lifespan, over twenty years of our life. In my book, that is far too long not to enjoy ourselves.

Eating winter – The food of fairy tales

Gingerbread biscuits with icing like melting snow; steaming glasses of 'glow-wine'; savoury puddings of bread and cheese and a goose with golden skin and a puddle of apple sauce. There are stews of game birds with twigs of thyme and rosemary; fish soups the colour of rust and baked apples frothing at the brim. Winter is the time for marzipan-filled stollen, thick with powdered sugar, pork chops as thick as a plank, and rings of Cumberland sausage sweet with dates and bacon.

The flavours of winter come at us like paper-wrapped presents in a Christmas stocking. Ginger, aniseed, cardamom, juniper and cloves. The caramel notes of maple syrup, treacle, butterscotch and the damp muscovado sugars. Fruits dried on the vine, and preserved in sugar. Ingredients too that hold the essence of the cold months: red cabbage, russet apples, walnuts, smoked garlic, chestnuts, parsnips and cranberries. Winter cooking is clouds of mashed potato flecked with dark green cabbage, roasted onions glistening like brass bedknobs and parsnips that crisp and stick molasses-like to the roasting tin. The food of the cold months is fatty cuts of meat, the flanks, shins and cheeks that we can leave to braise unhindered in a slow oven, with onions and thyme, wine and woody herbs, plodding silently towards tenderness. Meat you could cut with a spoon. Winter cooking is ham with a quince paste crust; game birds with redcurrant jelly; treacle sponge and Lebkuchen, mince pies and marmalade tarts.

Winter food is about both celebration and survival. It is about feasting – roast turkey, plum pudding and fruit cake; frugality – bean soups and mugs

of miso broth; it is the food of hope – lentil soup for good luck on New Year's day and the food of love – the mug of hot, cardamom-spiced chocolate you make for a loved one on a freezing day.

There is a gleeful abundance to late autumn and winter shopping, and a feeling of urgency to gather up things while we can. The last of the late-fruiting raspberries and damsons well on their way to jam; the late white peaches and crisp-as-ice local pippins and russets; walnuts in their shells and green figs with their soft, powdery scent. Late on an autumn evening, as I turn the corner to do my vegetable shopping, the heavy, sweet ripeness of the season hangs in the air, the glowing melons and late plums, the pumpkins and the last of the runner beans. Tomatoes, green and orange, red and gold. This is as good as food shopping gets.

As the season slides into winter – you can feel the heavy, sweet air of autumn turning crisp and clean with each passing dawn – there is the return of chestnuts and sweet potatoes, almonds in their shells, cream-fleshed parsnips, fat leeks and muscat grapes with their scent of sugary wine and honey. There are squashes shaped like acorns and others that resemble turbans to bake and stuff and beat into piles of fluffy mash; pomegranates – I love to see one or two cut in half on the display so we know whether we are buying jewels or pith – and proper big-as-your-hat apples for baking.

The game birds are lined up at the butchers, their featherless breasts kept warm by fatty bacon and a bay leaf. Partridges, pheasants and quail to roast, pigeons to bring to tenderness slowly with red wine and onions, and quails to split, skewer and grill till their skin blackens and their bones crunch. As the winter wears on, we see the first of the turkeys dressed for the feast, fat ducks and hams ready to boil, bake and slice.

That said, I don't go wholly along with the idea of winter food as a source of comfort and cosseting, solace and warmth. I still want a crackling fresh salad, a plate of fruit to finish my meal, food that refreshes. I don't drop my need for a daily bowl of leaves and herbs lightly dressed just because there is frost on the ground and woodsmoke in the air. It is all here, by the way, in these pages.

Drinking winter – raising a glass

Nothing changes quite so dramatically with the seasons as what I drink. Gone the glasses of rosé in the garden as the evening light falls, the artisan gin, cucumber and tonic. Gone too the lemon verbena tea glistening like absinthe in its fragile glass pot. Winter brings a whole new type of refreshment. Hot cider in a thick glass, frothy cocoa in a mug, buckwheat tea smelling of toast and warm rice. The drinks of winter smell different, of cloves and cinnamon, honey and fruit, rice and smoke, damson and cardamom.

I make my favourite winter drink in early autumn, so it is ready for Christmas. Damsons, squirrelled away in a bottle of gin, as happy as a fruit could ever be. (The recipe, by the way, is in *Tender*, Volume II.) I make cocoa thick and creamy, beaten to a froth with a little whisk, and serve it in deep mugs to keep it hot right to the end. It is part of the ritual of drinking cocoa that the first sip scalds your lips. Cardamom seeds, crushed beneath the weight of a pestle and mortar, have much to offer to a mug of hot, dark chocolate.

Apple drinks abound. Hot juice, mulled with cinnamon sticks and cloves; steaming cider with orange peel; cider brandy, sugar and cream. For the feast there are frivolous, sparkly things, sometimes flushed with pomegranate or blood orange and, occasionally, a hot toddy in a glass dotted with condensation. Even tea changes with the weather. The light green teas I drink in summer, welcome at any time of year, take a step back while the roasted teas, full of smoky notes and the humble cosy notes of toasted rice, take their place.

The alcohol level rises as the temperature dips. It is the only time of year the eaux-de-vie come out, the fruit liqueurs whose potency hides under a cloak of fruit and syrup.

My winters start with sight of the first damsons in the shops, the first bonfire lit. They end in late March when I take off to the coldest place I can find. And then, in an attempt to hold on to it all, I end up in Japan, Iceland or Finland. I eat a cup of crab soup in a hut on the harbour in Reykjavik or a thoughtful, foraged meal at one of my favourite restaurants in Helsinki, where each meal is peppered with Douglas fir or shoots of young green spruce, rowan berries picked from a tree in the churchyard, or an ice cream made from the young, green berries of juniper. Chef's cooking, full of imagination and playfulness, and a world away from the simpler fodder I make at home. And then, full of the last tastes of winter, I step out into the cold for the last time.

The coldest winters

Some people remember summers. A holiday in Tuscany; a lunch outdoors that turned into dinner and ran long into the darkness; a picnic on the beach or the summer afternoon they lost their virginity.

I remember winters. I can trace my love of the cold months to one particular day. The winter of 1962–3, to be precise. Late afternoon, just as the sun went down and the sky slipped from apricot to scarlet to lavender. I was playing outside, a huge lump of snow that we had rolled down the silent street, getting larger and larger until we could roll it no further and which I then flattened to form a counter. I was playing shop, in duffel coat and mittens, with the food fashioned out of snow. A vast truckle of cheese from which I cut wedges to sell, a cake (of course) and snow sweets the size of pebbles. (There is a little shopkeeping in the family's blood: in Victorian times we had a dairy in Birmingham.) My friends bought the snow cakes and then hurled them at one another as snowballs. I remember my mother bringing me in when she realised that every other kid had gone in for tea and I was still there, tending my snow shop.

The winter of 1962–3 was the coldest since 1895. I was six. It had been a particularly foggy late autumn and snow first arrived on December 12. The heaviest snow came on Boxing Day and by the 29th had drifted in some places to twenty feet deep. We had eighteen inches in Staffordshire. Villages were without power, people were stranded in their cars, the sea froze in parts of Kent and temperatures as low as –19°C were recorded. The lowest since 1814. I can't ever remember having such fun as I did that winter, leaping into snowdrifts on my walk to school; building a snowman (carrot nose, lumps of coal for eyes) with my brother in the back garden; coming home soaked and freezing from having lost another snowball fight. It is no wonder that modern winters are something of a disappointment.

In truth Britain has had very few truly cold winters, especially in the south of the country. The coldest on record was 1684, the year the Thames froze over for two months and a fair was held on its frozen waters. The coldest of the last century have been 1940, 1947, 1963 and 1979.

Daily meteorological records began in the seventeenth century. Britain's coldest include 1739–40, when snow started on Christmas Day and lasted to February 17, with temperatures as low as -9°C. London, usually one of the least snowy areas of the country, recorded thirty-nine days of snow. Two full months where the average temperature was less than 0°C were recorded.

1836 was one of the coldest but also a winter of floods, avalanches and stranded rail passengers. 1927–8 was a white Christmas, and with one of the heaviest snowfalls of the twentieth century. In 1933, forty-eight hours of continual snowfall were recorded.

The north, which takes the brunt of winter weather, did so especially in 1940, and was particularly cold. Four feet of snow fell in Sheffield, and the Thames froze for the first time since 1880. An ice storm hit the south on January 28.

The long winter of 1947 began in late January and lasted until mid-March. Many villages around the country were snowed in and thousands were cut off for days. Not especially cold, but a good one for snow, with not a single area of the country that didn't record snowfall from January 22 to March 17. Many snowfalls measured 60cm or more, with Scotland recording drifts of seven metres. At one point the armed forces were brought in to rescue people.

1952–3 saw the highest winter loss of life this country has ever known during peacetime. The smog in London accounted for 12,000 deaths. 1962–3 is still the coldest I remember, and the coldest weather for 200 years. The sea froze in some parts of the country, and villages were cut off. Animals froze in their fields because farmers couldn't gain access. A temperature of -22°C was recorded in Braemar in Scotland. The mean maximum temperature in January was -2°C, making it the coldest month since the 1800s. The *Guardian* reported that a farm in Dartmoor was cut off by snowdrifts for sixty-six days, and the owners had to be rescued by troops. It wasn't until March that the temperatures climbed above -5°C. Glasgow recorded its first white Christmas since the 30s.

The scent of winter

Scent always seems particularly intense to me in winter. The smell of a toasted crumpet on a frosty morning. The sap from a branch, snapped in the garden, or of lemon zest grated in the kitchen, all seem especially vivid, heightened at this time of year. The cold air seems to illuminate scent.

Well, yes, and no. The cold actually reduces our ability to detect smells. Our body's capacity to pick up the scent of something reduces on cold days partly because our odour receptors, all three to four hundred of them, protect themselves against freezing by burying themselves deeper in the nose. They snuggle down and are less 'receptive'. It is like they can't be bothered to get out of bed.

There is also less to smell in the winter, because odour molecules, denser in the cold, move more slowly in the air in the cool weather. So we actually smell fewer things. This may explain why the smells we do notice, the smoke from burning leaves or of roasting nuts, of a pot of marmalade bubbling on the hob or the Christmas tree being brought into the house, is more pronounced. Our nose is less confused with other smells.

Some things actually smell cold. Snow, obviously, but also peppermint, cucumber, yoghurt, ginger and juniper. They make us feel cool. But there are also smells that don't actually smell of winter, but simply make us think of it, things that we connect with this season alone. A tray of mince pies in the oven; an orange studded with cloves; dumplings swelling in the damp wood of a Chinese steamer; or a shallow dish of potato Dauphinoise, calm and creamy, baking. There are the winter herbs, of course, bay, rosemary and thyme, the aromatics that weave their magic in stock or meat juices over time rather than the instant hit of torn basil or coriander. The comforting 'sugar smells' of warm treacle, toffee, butterscotch and liquorice. Of marmalade and caramel.

I don't like the smell of mulled wine, it reminds me of cheap pot-pourri. But the zest of an orange mingled with the warmth of cloves is certainly a part of any catalogue of winter scents. All the more when it comes in the form of a Seville orange. The lumpy, bitter sort needed for classic duck à l'orange and for marmalade. More pleasing, I think, is that of orange blossom, preferably caught on a breeze rather than from a bottle. (Too much, it reminds me of Savlon, and childhood grazes and cuts.) If ever you are in Sorrento in Italy in the winter, head for the nearest lemon tree, often overhanging the path, and its white, star-like blossom. There is an olfactory treat in store.

One of the loveliest things anyone has said about my home is that it always smells nice. I hardly ever notice it, to be honest, but thinking about it they are probably right. In winter there will almost certainly be woodsmoke and beeswax polish.

Most of the things designed to make our houses smell festive are uniformly nauseous. They are the very essence of the fake Christmas. Those 'Yule-scented' candles, usually red, that smell of cinnamon and orange, or plug-in room fragrances that smell like cheap air-freshener. Hideous. A real Christmas will smell of itself without us trying to evoke it.

The tree, of course. The scent of the tree will vary according to the variety. The smell comes from a cocktail of compounds, including a-pinene and ß-pinene, in which conifers are particularly abundant, and bornyl acetate, known as the heart of pine. Balsam, Douglas and Nordmann firs are particularly high in the balsamic and camphor compounds. The reason the tree smells so strongly when you first bring it into the house is because the sap continues to rise in a freshly-cut tree. As the cut tree ages, the sap stops moving and the smell fades.

There is a difference between the smell of winter and winter smells. The latter tend to be induced by us – the smell of a potato baking, of logs burning or of hot chocolate. But winter has its own smell: step outside on a frosty morning and you are smelling the cold. That scent of smoke we detect despite the lack of a fire nearby is due to the fact that smoke doesn't rise as well in cold air, so any there is will stay closer to the ground.

Evergreens, freshly cut, give subtle seasonal notes. Holly, mistletoe and laurels all work. Eucalyptus will make your home smell like granddad's chest rub. I would have to add the sweet, Barbara Cartland fragrance from a bowl of hyacinths too, though really only from a nostalgia point of view. My father always insisting on having a bowl of them ready in time for Christmas. He would force them in a dark cupboard under the stairs, then in the airing cupboard. He usually managed to get them to perform on cue.

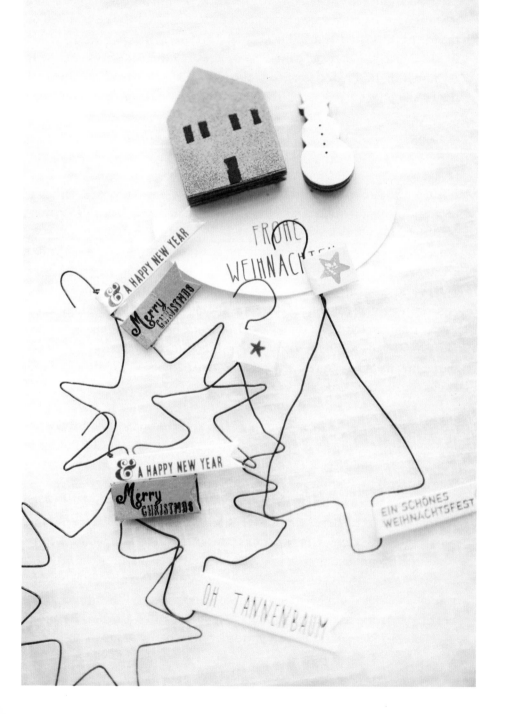

Bay shouldn't have come as a surprise to me, being one of the more fragrant evergreens, but I have only just realised its seasonal notes. The essential oil made from its leaves (I am talking bay laurel – *Laurus nobilis* – here) is rather like having a little bottle of Christmas around. A few drops on a saucer or an oil burner, or dribbled on to a few dry leaves and twigs in a bowl, will scent the house subtly for several hours. There are some good bay candles around too.

Fire

Fire has always been at the heart of it all. The place where everyone gathered, for warmth and for safety. Flames to warm us from the cold, but also to ward off danger. Flames to keep wild animals at bay. Flames to sit round and read, a place for conversation. Now a real fire is a rare and wonderful thing. It is hard work: the carrying of logs, the lighting of kindling and taking the ashes out, but nothing can match it.

A fire is a magical thing. There are those who worship them, literally. Zoroastrians, some Vedic branches of Hindu religion, the Romans and the Greeks have all at some time worshipped the fire or the hearth. The purity of the fire, its ability to render food from the inedible to the edible and the protection it affords, are all worthy of worship.

I have two fires burning at home. On a winter's night, the room changes the instant they are lit. Bricks and mortar transcend from house to home. The fire lit, the mood of the room changes too. Shoes are removed, feet are put up on sofas, we tuck ourselves up. In truth, after a day's work, we sleep too. Friends joke that within ten minutes of me lighting the fire, they are asleep. Cosy.

There is much to watch in the flames. We say they 'dance'. And with good reason. The flames flicker and wave, float and soar as the mood takes them. Sometimes the embers are even more beautiful than the flames. I could watch them for hours.

We shouldn't ignore the ashes. You can use a small amount of them on the garden. But they should be ashes from wood, not coal, and shouldn't be used near blueberries, azaleas or potatoes, which don't like a high pH. Burned wood doesn't contain nitrogen, but it is a source of potassium, phosphorus and calcium. Useful for raising the pH of the soil if it is low, by which I mean below pH 6.

There is a little Japanese onsen I visit. It takes a while to get there, as there is no rail connection. The wooden building is hidden in the hills, and is probably my favourite place on Earth. It is undeniably beautiful, with its lovingly polished wooden floors and moss-covered garden. What sets it firmly as the place where I want my ashes scattered is the constant scent of smoke. It filters through the house but also through the gardens – little trails of blue-grey cross your path as you walk along the stone paths, or warm the wooden arbours where you sit and read.

What we burn affects the smell of the fire and also the heat it gives. My parents burned coal and logs. I have never liked the smell of a coal fire, preferring to use logs. You need kindling to light a fire – thin, crisp sticks of wood that are, crucially, dry. A few sheets of newspaper rolled into loose balls tucked among them, and then some larger logs to burn slowly. The reason most fires go out is because the logs are too large, or there is not enough air. A loose arrangement of scrunched paper, kindling and small logs, no thicker than your arm, is a good start. Newspaper lights more easily than the paper from glossy magazines. (My stepmother used to roll up newspaper, then tie a loose knot in each roll. Worked a treat.) A taper, if you have such a thing, is better, safer, than a match or a lighter.

Although my parents and grandmother kept a fire going, almost constantly, in the hearth, the idea is not a practical one for most of us. A wood-burning stove is one answer. The flames hidden behind glass, they can be left burning safely while you are out. They are clean and easy to deal with. They are the heart of many a Scandinavian and Japanese home, and are becoming popular in Britain too. A wood-burner has a constant glow, the low golden flame that greets and warms and toasts us. It is my next project.

Fire has always been precious, particularly when it was the only form of heating or cooking. Therefore taxable. In 1662, on May 19, a hearth tax was introduced, where householders had to pay two shillings for each hearth. Payment was twice a year, once at Michaelmas and again at Lady Day, March 25. The poor and charitable institutions were exempt. The tax was abolished by William III in 1689. Good for him.

For me the cold months are the best of times. And at the heart of those months lies Christmas.

Celebrating Christmas

Christmas is celebrated by Christians and non-Christians alike. It is a cultural event as much as a religious one, and its history is confused. Many of the festival's observances date from pre-Christian times, and those who celebrate it as a purely religious event might be surprised to find how much of the festivities hails from pagan times. We celebrated winter long before we celebrated Christmas. (Saturnalia was the Roman festival in honour of the God Saturn, with feasting lasting from December 17 to the 23rd.) Happily atheist, I celebrate Christmas as much as anyone, with food and gifts and, yes, carols, but I fully accept that much of my own celebration has a religious history.

I go along with the religious details of Christmas because they have become interwoven with the cultural side of the festivities. The Nativity is as much a part of Christmas as Santa Claus and the pagan habit of bringing holly and mistletoe into the house. It is almost impossible to separate the pagan from the pious, and why would I want to anyway when December 25 was chosen simply because it landed in the middle of what was already a pagan festival?

Christmas is a vast steaming pudding of Christianity, folklore, paganism, tradition and commerce. Those of us who are part of a tolerant, open-minded and intelligent society can make our Christmas whatever we want it to be. To put it another way, we can have our cake and eat it.

The best of Christmases, the worst of Christmases

We tend to remember Christmases with exemplary clarity. Something unusual that happens over these twelve days at the heart of winter is unlikely ever to be forgotten. Even the most innocent event is almost guaranteed to be re-lived with a certain annual glee. My own catalogue of unlikely Yuletide events has involved a Christmas Eve where I forgot to tell the family I was coming home, only to find they had left for the week (I was taken in, waif-like, by generous neighbours). The year the cake sat half-iced because I had run out of icing sugar. The Christmas morning I realised the goose was too long for the oven and had to be cut in half. Then there was the time the cats pulled the ten-foot tree on to the floor, smashing my much-loved collection of decorations (and frightening the life out of themselves into the bargain). Then there was the Christmas Mum died.

For me Christmas is the heart and soul of the cold months, the jewel in the crown of midwinter, a time to feast and to give. But it is, after all is said and done, just a few days that sit at the heart of the season. Three months of our year in which to offer warmth, welcome and something good to eat to all.

A toast to the winter solstice

'What can I get you to drink?' Never has a simple question been so bursting with delicious possibilities. The word 'welcome' put instantly, joyously into motion.

It is true, I do love pouring someone a drink. In my time I have worked in a country pub (all gumboots, roaring fires and golden labradors) and behind the bar of a grande dame five-star hotel. You probably didn't know that. Whether it is as simple as a cup of coffee, a beer served in a small, ice-cold glass or a home-made fruit liqueur that has been steeping in my pantry for six weeks, I get quite a buzz handing someone a glass of 'welcome'.

Drinks are different in winter. I often want something sweeter, darker and more alcoholic when the weather is cold. This is the only time of year I have a fancy for sweet wines, by which I mean the muscats and Pedro Ximénez sherries, the fruit-based eau-de-vie of quince and plum and the sloe gin that light up the drinks cupboard like the stained-glass window at Midnight Mass.

There are drinks I make especially for a winter's night. A tiny glass of apricot brandy, glowing like a candle, the fruit steeping quietly for a month with orange zest and star anise. A liqueur made with dried figs and fennel seed, and another of sticky prunes in sweet wine. Served very cold, in diminutive glasses, the drinks warm, soothe and delight. The other contenders are the hot drinks, the mulled ciders and spiced mixtures. Drinks that will melt anybody's frost.

The best known of cold-weather tipples is probably the least well regarded. I speak of mulled wine. I like the idea of this ancient winter ritual (the instant bonhomie of sweet spices, rosy cheeks and hot red wine) more than the drink itself. Wonderful, I think, is a spiced punch of hot cider or apple juice. This is the drink whose cinnamon-scented fumes fill the air on Guy Fawkes Night, Hallowe'en and in many of Europe's Christmas markets. The stir-up of ingredients – baked apples, brandy, cider, cloves, cinnamon and allspice – actually makes sense. A drink with a winter nose and too good to be left for wassailing. I shall start right here.

A hot apple drink for a cold night

Slice an apple in half, then into quarters, discard the core and pips, then cut each piece of apple into two thick segments. Warm 3 tablespoons of apple juice in a shallow pan, add 2 tablespoons of brown sugar and lower in the apples. Let them cook until soft, stopping before they fall apart. Remove from the heat.

In a deep, stainless steel saucepan put 100ml of brandy, 400ml of cloudy apple juice, a clementine, 3 cloves, a stick of cinnamon, 3 allspice berries gently bashed with a heavy weight and bring to the boil. Reduce the heat, so the cooking continues at a gentle bubble for fifteen minutes. Ladle into four glasses, dropping a few of the cooked apple slices into each drink.

A welcoming drink, may I suggest, is not just about other people. Something good in a glass can be a rather lovely way to welcome our own arrival home. God knows, we deserve it. Finding a rare moment of peace and quiet, there are surely few greater joys than pouring ourselves a drink as we curl up on the sofa with a book after a long hard day. It might only be a stolen few minutes, but I regard this time as deeply grounding. Something that, just for once, is about no one but ourselves.

I was brought up in a family that drank sherry. Not a chilled manzanilla with a dish of crisp, salty almonds or an amontillado the colour of amber, but Bristol Cream sherry, sweet as fudge. We drank it from a glass called a schooner and had it with Twiglets (in the days when Twiglets were long and thin, rather than dumpy and puffed up with air as they are now). Occasionally there would be a bottle of Italian fizz and at Christmas my father would make snowballs with advocaat and maraschino cherries for everyone. To this day I would hardly call myself much of a drinker, but pouring something into a glass for someone remains one of life's pleasures.

This week seems a prudent time to put drinks down for Christmas and the chilly weeks that follow. There are few fresh fruits, save the pear and the quince, that will make a fruit liqueur dazzling enough to show its face in candlelight at Christmas. So I turn to the store cupboard, and especially to the stoppered jars of dried fruits, the 'Christmas pudding fruits', to make drinks that will shine a light on the dark nights.

The suggestions that follow are meant for any cold night but are particularly useful at Christmas. I also include uses for the fruits that remain after the liquor has been drunk. Fat, alcohol-soaked little fruits, each one pissed as a newt, that can be served as dessert.

Three dried fruit drinks for winter

Apricot, orange and anise

Deep, golden fruit notes here. Rather delightful after dinner, with crisp, dark chocolate thins.

Enough for 20 small glasses
dried apricots – 500g
an orange
whole star anise – 4
brandy – 300ml
granulated sugar – 150g
sweet white wine – 300ml

Put the apricots into a stainless steel saucepan. Using a vegetable peeler, slice thin strips of zest from the orange and drop them into the pan. Add the star anise, brandy and sugar and bring to the boil. Stir until the sugar has dissolved.

Into a sterilised preserving jar, spoon the apricots and star anise, then pour in the liquor (breathing in at this point is highly recommended) and top up with the sweet white wine. Seal and place in a cool, dark place for a good fortnight (better still, a month) before pouring the golden liquor into glasses.

The fruit

Once the ravishing, honey-hued liqueur is finished (and you have dried your tears) you will no doubt want to use the plumped-up fruits for something. My first suggestion is to serve them, whole and fat with alcohol, in a beautiful glass with a jug of cream at their side. Even better, perhaps, is to serve a thick, strained yoghurt with them and a scattering of toasted, flaked almonds.

Figs with maple syrup and anise

Christmas pudding in a glass. Though perfect for Guy Fawkes too if you start it early enough. The remaining fruit – little bundles of joy, soft as a pillow, juicy as a xiaolongbao dumpling – should not be wasted.

> *Enough for 20 small glasses*
> granulated sugar – 250g
> maple syrup – 100ml
> dry white wine – 750ml
> dried aniseed – $\frac{1}{2}$ teaspoon
> dried figs – 500g
> vodka – 250ml

Put the granulated sugar into a medium-sized, stainless steel saucepan and add the maple syrup, white wine and aniseeds. Cut half the figs in half, then put all the figs into the pan. Bring to the boil, then lower the heat and let the figs simmer for twenty minutes, until soft and plump and bloated with wine.

Spoon the figs into a sterilised storage jar, then pour over the liquor. Pour in the vodka, then seal and store in a cool, dry place for three or four weeks, or better still, until Christmas.

The fruit

Later, once the liquid is gone, you would be wise to use the alcohol-laden figs for something. Two or three hidden in the depths of an apple crumble are fun, as they would be in an apple pie. (I often have one or two, straight from the jar, as a treat when I have finished the ironing.) They also make a fine addition to a slice of plain cake, taken with coffee, mid-morning, and served as a dessert with a spoonful of deepest yellow clotted cream. The thick sort you can cut with a knife.

Muscat prunes

You can most certainly drink the mahogany-coloured liquor here, but I really make these marinated fruits as a little extra, something to serve alongside chocolate mousse or milky panna cotta.

Serves 6
prunes – 250g
golden sultanas – 125g
muscat or moscatel – 750ml

Put the prunes and sultanas into a sterilised jar, then pour over the muscat or moscatel. Seal tightly and leave for a month before drinking.

A treat in store

Once you have poured the liquor into glasses, you are left, happily, with a jar full of delicious detritus. You could put the sultanas and prunes into an elegant glass and serve them with a spoonful of vanilla-scented whipped cream and a tiny silver spoon. Or you could spoon the fruit over vanilla ice cream, or frozen yoghurt, letting its syrup trickle down the frozen ice. I wouldn't exactly say no to finding a pile of these sodden fruits sharing a plate with some fluffy ricotta cakes hot from the frying pan on a Sunday morning.

We can get more adventurous with our little fruit bon-bons, using them to shake up a dish of stewed apple for breakfast; serving them alongside a slice of sugar-crusted sponge cake or with home-made vanilla custard. The wine-drenched fruits can be tucked into the almond filling for a frangipane tart or used in a trifle of layered crumbled amaretti, custard and mascarpone.

Possibly the best idea of all came about quite by accident. After a long day of photography for the book, James and I sat down with a glass of the apricot and fig liqueurs, accompanied by the plumped-up fruits. On the table was some blue cheese – a Gorgonzola, though it could just as well have been Stilton, Stichelton or any of the other blues. We nibbled. The marrying of the blue cheese and the velvety, wine-filled fruits was quite simply gorgeous.

The joy of stuffing

Goose-fat roast potatoes aside, I consider stuffing to be the most delicious of all accompaniments to the Sunday roast. A sausage meat stuffing made with browned onions, bacon, thyme and dried apricots; a couscous version with red onion, rosemary and raisins; another with minced turkey, lardo – the cured, herbed strips of pork fat from Italy – fennel seed and cranberries. I like my stuffings rough-edged, generously seasoned and deeply savoury. A little sweetness from dried fruits perhaps, but onions and herbs, much lemon zest and black pepper are essential.

There are two ways of cooking stuffing: inside and outside the bird. Each way has its disciples. Roasting the mixture inside the cavity of the turkey or goose means that the juices of the meat trickle down through the forcemeat as it cooks, imbuing the stuffing with the essence of the bird. The downside is that in order to cook the stuffing properly, it may mean overcooking the bird, and, should you pack it in too tightly, the heat will never penetrate fully, thus risking neither the inside of the bird nor the stuffing cooking thoroughly. Dare I mention salmonella?

Cooking the stuffing outside the roast, in the same roasting tin, means there won't be enough of it, and its presence interferes with the gravy and roast potatoes. It's pretty much a non-starter. The third way is to cook it separately in another dish. It works from a safety point of view, and you will get tantalising, crusty nuggets on the stuffing's surface, but this method loses the opportunity of soaking it with the juices from the bird as it cooks. I get round this by spooning some of the fat and flavouring from the roasting tin over the stuffing as it cooks.

Stuffings, forcemeats, call them what you will, have gone out of fashion. I suggest that this is a disgraceful state of affairs. Imagine the flavour in a ball of sausage meat that you have seasoned with sweet golden onions, thyme and rosemary, lemon zest, chopped bacon and juniper, then spooned goose fat over as it roasted. Or a tray of stuffing made with minced turkey, bacon, lemon, parsley and Parmesan you have left rough on top, so the ridges and furrows brown crustily.

I would give up the sprouts, the chestnuts, even the little sausages and bacon of the extended family roast rather than go without generous amounts of stuffing. It is also the icing on the big fat cake that is Christmas dinner. The bit which, if I am completely honest, I prefer to the meat itself.

And, of course, there should be plenty, that goes without saying. But this is not gluttony – there should be enough so that we can eat it cold the next day, cut like a cake and layered with sliced chicken, goose or turkey in a sandwich on chewy bread. And further, I need some to eat with slices of cold roast meat, a potato and spring onion salad and bright purple pickles.

Turkey, lardo and fennel seed stuffing, cranberry orange sauce

On this late autumn night, wet and cold from sweeping up leaves from the garden paths, I make plump rissoles of minced turkey with lardo and chilli flakes for supper. As we tuck in around the kitchen table, we decide that they would make an excellent stuffing too, to be baked around the bird or, more conveniently, in a separate tin. We bought the lardo, the silky white fat that is such a treat served on rough toast with a trickle of olive oil and some crumbled rosemary, from an Italian grocer's. It's not difficult to track down. Buy it in a block so you can grate it. Failing that, get it in thin slices and chop them finely. The gorgeous fat will melt and moisten the turkey meat, which has no real fat of its own.

Enough for 4
fennel seeds – 2 teaspoons
minced turkey – 500g
dried chilli flakes – 2 teaspoons
dried breadcrumbs – 60g
lardo – 150g
olive oil – 2 tablespoons

For the sauce:
cranberry jelly or sauce – 3 heaped tablespoons
orange juice – 50ml
orange zest – 2 teaspoons
cranberries, fresh or frozen – 100g

Toast the fennel seeds for a couple of minutes in a dry frying pan, then tip them into a large mixing bowl. Put the turkey mince, chilli flakes and breadcrumbs into the bowl, then coarsely grate in the lardo. Season generously with both salt and black pepper, then mix thoroughly.

Shape the stuffing mixture into 8 large balls, then place them on a tray and refrigerate for twenty-five minutes. Set the oven at 180°C/Gas 4.

To make the sauce, put the cranberry jelly or sauce into a small saucepan and place over a moderate heat, then add the orange juice and zest and the cranberries and bring to the boil. Turn down the heat so the mixture simmers gently and leave for five or six minutes, until the berries have softened a little. You should be able to squash them easily between thumb and forefinger. Remove from the heat and leave to settle.

Warm the olive oil in a shallow pan and fry the stuffing balls, moving them round as each side browns, until they are golden brown all over. Transfer the balls to a baking dish, sitting them snugly together, then spoon over the cranberry sauce. Bake for thirty minutes.

Pears, clove and orange granita

Carried away with their quiet beauty, I seem to have bought rather a lot of pears. I do this with peaches too. And avocados. Damsons as well. Fruits or vegetables caught at a perfect moment. Sometimes, I simply cannot resist. (We will be feasting on pears for a week.)

Today, a refreshing dessert, scented with sweet spices. The timing is tricky, with pears often taking anything from fifteen to fifty minutes to soften. I check them regularly with a skewer as they cook. Pears are often at their most delicious when on the edge of collapse. So tender they require a careful hand to transfer them to the serving plate.

Serves 4
orange juice – 1 litre
caster sugar – 100g
cloves – 4
half a cinnamon stick
pears, large – 2

Pour the orange juice into a non-reactive saucepan, add the caster sugar, place over a moderate heat and leave until the sugar has dissolved, stirring occasionally. Add the cloves and cinnamon stick and bring almost to the boil.

Peel the pears, slice each one in half from stem to base, then scoop out the cores using a teaspoon or, if you have one, a melon baller. Lower the pears into the juice in the pan and simmer gently until soft. Ripe pears will take about twenty minutes, hard fruit considerably longer. They are ready when they will easily take the point of a knife or skewer.

Lift the pears carefully from the pan with a draining spoon and place on a plate. Spoon over a little of the orange juice to keep them moist, then cover and refrigerate.

Chill the seasoned juice as quickly as possible. (Pouring the juice into a bowl, then resting it in a large bowl of ice cubes will speed up matters.) When the juice is cold, remove the cloves and cinnamon, pour into a shallow plastic freezer box and freeze for at least four hours.

When the juice is almost frozen, pull the tines of a table fork through it, roughing up the surface, then digging a little deeper, making large ice crystals in the process. Take care not to mash the crystals too much, leaving them as large as possible. Put the granita back into the freezer.

To serve, put a pear half on each dessert plate or shallow dish, pile some of the granita into the centre and serve immediately. You should have enough granita over for the next day.

5 NOVEMBER

Fire and baked pears

We have been lighting fires around this time for centuries. Since ancient times Celtic people have gathered around bonfires on October 31 and November 1 to celebrate Samhain, the end of the harvest and the beginning of winter. We burn candles in hollowed-out pumpkins on All Hallows, and since 1605 we have celebrated the failure of Guy Fawkes's attempt to blow up the House of Lords and the protestant King James by lighting fires and setting off fireworks.

The celebrations have changed since I was a kid. Hallowe'en has turned into a pantomime of extortion and petty vandalism dressed up as 'Trick or Treat'. The rickety piles of branches that stood quietly throughout the countryside, ready to be lit on November 5, are fewer. The back-garden firework parties have very much disappeared too. Spectacular displays and vast communal bonfires are now more organised and often run by local councils and bonfire societies. Traditional effigies are still displayed and burned, occasionally of Pope Paul V, head of the Catholic Church in the time of Guy Fawkes, but more often than not it is images of contemporary villains, Savile, Trump and Farage, which we now set alight. (There are so many I don't know which to choose.)

The climate seems different too. The remains of childhood fireworks, black with soot, were regularly rescued from spiky grass white with frost. Yet I can't remember the last time frost coincided with Bonfire Night.

In my part of London the fireworks start mid-afternoon. Barely visible against the milky grey sky, their startling beauty is wasted. At twilight, the cascades of pink, silver and green explode high above, sometimes to cheers of delight. I have never quite understood the draw of fireworks, it all seems a bit of a waste of money to me, but a bonfire is a different matter. The smell and crackle of dry twigs, the flames, smoke and glowing embers have always held a certain magic for me, and I am never happier than when there is a fire in the hearth.

There is no party tonight, no fire lit in the garden, just the occasional glances at a particularly extravagant cascade of lights over the East End. Instead, we sit round the fire eating fat Italian sausages, creamed leeks and beans, and to follow, a bowl of ice cream with searingly hot marmalade pears, whose glowing bittersweet sauce tastes like cinder toffee.

Leeks, beans and Italian sausage

This is one of those good-natured recipes that can be multiplied successfully for large parties, or made earlier and reheated as necessary.

Serves 2
leeks, medium – 3
butter – 30g
water – 100ml
olive oil – 2 tablespoons, or a little pork fat
plump sausages – 4 (400g)
vegetable stock – 250ml
cannellini or haricot beans – 1 × 400g tin
parsley, chopped – a handful

Cut the leeks into rounds about 1cm in length and wash them in plenty of cold water. Bring the butter and water to the boil in a wide pan with a lid, then add the leeks. Cover with a piece of greaseproof paper, or baking parchment, and a lid. The paper will encourage the leeks to steam rather than fry.

Warm the oil or a little pork fat in a frying pan and cook the sausages, slowly, over a moderate heat. Let them brown nicely on all sides.

Leave the leeks to cook for eight or nine minutes, until they are tender enough to take the point of a skewer with little pressure. Pour the vegetable stock into the pan and continue cooking for two minutes, then tip the leeks and their cooking liquor into a blender and process until almost smooth. (It is important not to fill the blender jug more than halfway. You may need to do this in more than one batch.)

Return the leeks to the pan, drain and rinse the beans and fold into the leeks. Heat briefly, stir in the parsley, and serve with sausages.

Marmalade pears with vanilla ice cream

This truly gorgeous recipe is, I suppose, a new take on my baked pears with Marsala (*Tender*, Volume II) but with a deep, syrupy bitter-sweetness, reminiscent of old-fashioned black treacle toffee. The hot, translucent pears and the glossy apple and marmalade sauce are wonderful with vanilla ice cream. There is a point, after about forty-five minutes, when you need to watch the progress of the sauce carefully, lest it turn to toffee. A non-stick roasting pan is essential.

Serves 4
pears – 3 medium
apple juice – 200ml
orange marmalade – 150g
Marsala, sweet or dry – 1 tablespoon
honey – 1 heaped tablespoon
vanilla ice cream, to serve – 8 scoops

Set the oven at 190°C/Gas 5. Peel the pears (I think you should because the skin can be tough, but it is up to you), cut them in half, and scoop out their cores. Cut each half into three, then place them in a non-stick roasting tin. In a small saucepan, bring the apple juice, marmalade, Marsala and honey to the boil, then remove from the heat and pour over the pears.

Bake the pears in the preheated oven for twenty minutes, then turn them over. At this point they will look decidedly uninteresting, but carry on anyway. Let the pears bake for a further twenty minutes, then watch them carefully. The sauce will be bubbling now, the colour of amber and rising up the pears, almost covering them. Test them for tenderness – a small knife should slide through them effortlessly. They should be translucent and butter-soft. If they aren't quite ready or if the sauce isn't syrupy, give them a further five minutes.

Let them rest for five minutes. Serve them with the vanilla ice cream.

Making gnudi

I sweep up the leaves, most of which I recognise. My parents' gift of *The Observer Book of Trees* was clearly not lost on me. There are those of the fig, like giants' hands; the feather-like golden robinia; the oval greengage and the smaller Ouillins gage, whose tiny leaflets are brown-freckled, like its fruit. There are the green leaves of the Doyenne du Comice pear, with their lichen-like splodges of rust, and those of the Discovery apple that somehow manage to be larger than its fruit. The honeysuckles are crisp already, like the tiny pieces of pork crackling I used to find in a bowl on the butcher's counter as a kid. And the horse-chestnuts have already found their way over the rooftops from the lane in front of the house. Heaven knows how. Others will stay put for a while – those of the jasmine and rose and white lacecap hydrangeas.

Sweeping the leaves is a thankless task – there will be just as many tomorrow. But better that than the boredom of a lawn. They go into net sacks to rot down. Soaking them, just occasionally with the watering can, helps to speed up the process. Once crumbly, they will be put on to the beds. Leafmould is treasure to a gardener, a bag of gold with which to treat his plants. There is a little science to it, and a wee bit of gardener's law. Hornbeam, oak and birch, lime and cherry leaves will rot down within eighteen months; horse-chestnut, beech, magnolia, hawthorn, maple and sycamore will take longer because of their high fibre content. A shredder would speed up the composting process, but I really don't have the room.

After Christmas, there will be the tree to get rid of. Pines and conifers take a good couple of years to rot down and so shouldn't be mixed with the others. They need to be left in the open and turned regularly with a garden fork. That done, they are best used only to mulch other acid-loving plants such as heather. Having not an inch of garden to spare, it might be more prudent to leave my tree out for the council, who collect and compost them for us.

It is too early, but I have been mulling over what to give the vegetarians for Christmas lunch when we are tucking into our grilled scallops. (I know it's going to be that because I did it last year, with pancetta and a smooth pea purée, and everyone loved its lightness and savour.) The vague plan is to serve a light pasta dish first, the little pillows of ricotta and Parmesan known as gnudi. My vegetarian friends are not hardcore, so I don't have to worry about mixing up their Parmesan with my Parmesan.

The gnudi take minutes to make, but absolutely must be dried on a tray in the fridge overnight, snuggled down in a deep snowdrift of fine cornmeal. Skip that stage (always a temptation) and they will dissolve in the cooking water. You will have no gnudi, no dinner. I choose them because they are light, simple and special. They are not hard to make but they do require a light hand. I make them myself because I enjoy shaping them and lowering the flattened balls into the cornmeal almost more than anything else, and anyway, you can't buy a decent commercial version of them for love nor money.

Gnudi require the hands of an angel. You must treat the mixture of fresh, white ricotta and grated Parmesan as delicately as if it were a Christmas bauble, which in this case I suppose it is. This is cooking with the utmost respect and care, and I love it.

The usual accompanying sauce is something with cheese and cream, though I have had others. My thought is that such a recipe is too rich and heavy for purpose, so I am keen to have a go at something else. In my head are ideas for both a creamy spinach sauce and a sort of avocado sauce, made with lemons, basil and olive oil. The Hass variety of avocado – the one with the crocodile skin – is at its best in the winter. I shall make the gnudi today and have a go at the sauce tomorrow.

Gnudi

My heart sinks when I see a recipe that takes two days, but this is an exception. We are talking minutes of work rather than hours. My gnudi recipe is based on that of the wonderful April Bloomfield, whose own version has become a permanent and much-loved part of her menu at the Spotted Pig in New York. Mine have a little more Parmesan to ricotta than is the norm, and my impatience means they get only twenty-four hours in the fridge. April leaves hers for at least thirty-six (and in the quest for perfection, I'm sure she's right).

Makes 20 small gnudi, serves 4
ricotta – 250g
a little nutmeg
Parmesan – 40g
fine semolina – 250g or more

Put the ricotta into a bowl. Grate a little nutmeg finely over, then add a very little salt. Grate the Parmesan finely and gently stir in. Have a baking sheet ready, covered with a thick layer of the semolina.

Using a teaspoon, scoop up a generous heap of mixture and make it into a small ball, rolling it in your hands. (A dusting of semolina on your hands will help.) You can leave the gnudi round if you like, but I prefer to press them into a slightly oval shape. Drop the ball on to the semolina-lined tray, then roll it back and forth until it is coated. Continue with the rest of the mixture. You will have roughly 20 little gnudi.

Once they are all rolled, shake the remaining semolina over them, then put the tray in the fridge. Don't be tempted to cover them. Leave overnight.

None of this solves our own dinner situation. So we go out. I feel somewhat blessed (not to say a wee bit smug) that so many good restaurants seem to be opening up on my doorstep. A dozen cracking places to spend an evening and all within walking distance.

A trip to the forest, and those gnudi

A couple of Novembers ago I was asked to choose the Christmas tree for Trafalgar Square. Well, I helped. We filmed the occasion for television. We had taken the train to Flåm, in Norway, a small village and port at the end of Sognefjord, the world's deepest fjord. It is easy to worship this landscape, with its crags, forests and crashing waterfalls. By turns lush with forest, or stark in tones of charcoal, grey and white, it is both somehow melancholy and invigorating. The latter especially when you poke your head (stupidly) out of the carriage window and feel the bite of icy air on your face.

By the time we got to Myrdal snow had started to fall. The first that year, each flake as soft and white as goose fat. As the little train arrived in Flåm, the snow turned to heavy, wretched sleet. The crew unpacked their kit with rapidly numbing fingers and filmed for what seemed like hours. They filmed me trudging endlessly through the driving sleet; soaked through to the skin; slipping clumsily on the icy track; barely able to see two feet in front of me; my lips almost unable to move with cold. But mostly they filmed me getting quietly more and more pissed off. Snow is one thing. But driving sleet, especially when you wear glasses, is another thing altogether. I should add that none of that footage ever saw the light of day. Such are the joys of television.

Next morning, we woke to find most of the snow gone, the sun peeping shyly over the mountains, the sky as clear as iced water. We set off for the forest, to find the rangers and, hopefully, our tree. There is nothing accidental about choosing The Tree. You don't just stumble upon it and think, 'Oh, that'll do for Trafalgar Square.' This is an important tree, an annual gift from the people of Norway each year since 1947, a token of gratitude for our support during the Second World War. Possible candidates are marked when little more than saplings, then monitored for decades. The tree, a Norway spruce, must not be crowded, so lesser examples that get too close are removed, allowing the chosen tree's branches access to even light, the chance for all sides to grow symmetrically, its trunk to grow straight. As we walk through the forest we spot the trees that might grace Trafalgar Square in 2030 or 2035.

'Which one do you think is best?' I am asked. We pick one of the right age, height and girth. It's a tree casting session. I am given a choice from three or four that have been shortlisted, having been spotted like child prodigies and nurtured towards stardom. The chosen fir has been growing for about seventy years – this we check by drilling a long, pencil-thin sample from its trunk, as a cheesemaker might check the blueing progress of a truckle of Stilton. We count the growth rings one by one.

Next, there follows a phone call to the mayor for permission – a courtesy – then the rangers set about felling. Next time I see it, on the first Thursday in December, the vast tree has been shipped and manoeuvred into position outside the National Gallery and carols are being sung around it by the choir from St-Martin-in-the-Fields, barely a cassock's throw away. The Norwegian Ambassador is there, as are the mayors of Oslo and Westminster. The tree is lit in traditional Norwegian style, with five hundred simple white lights, its base now garlanded, delightfully, with poems specially commissioned by the Poetry Society.

A few weeks later, just before Twelfth Night, my beloved tree is removed, chipped and composted.

And two sauces for the gnudi

I rescue yesterday's gnudi from the fridge. I pat them, tenderly, to check their firmness.

Watercress and avocado pesto
avocados, ripe – 2
a lemon
pine kernels – 50g
basil leaves – a handful (about 10g)
olive oil – about 8–10 tablespoons

watercress – 50g
Parmesan (if you wish. I don't.)
gnudi – 20, small

Halve, stone and peel the avocados. Halve and juice the lemon. Put the pine nuts into a food processor and blend briefly, until they are coarsely crushed, then add the avocados and basil leaves and process, adding as much olive oil and lemon as you need to produce a loose, bright green paste.

Wash the watercress and remove any tough stalks. Grate the Parmesan finely if you are using it.

Bring a pan of water to the boil, deep and generously salted, as you would to cook pasta. Carefully lower the gnudi, a few at a time, into the boiling water. When the balls float to the surface they are ready. This is generally between three and five minutes.

Add the watercress to the sauce, folding it gently through the green paste, then spoon into a serving dish. Lift the gnudi from the water with a draining spoon, place them on the avocado sauce and serve, should you wish, with grated Parmesan on the side.

Spinach and pecorino
spinach – 150g
double cream – 350ml
pecorino romano – 100g, grated
pea shoots – a handful

Wash the spinach and soften it briefly in a large pan with a lid, letting the leaves cook for a minute or two in their own steam, turning them once or twice. When the spinach is bright green and wilted, remove from the pan, squeeze almost dry, then chop it quite finely.

Warm the cream in a saucepan, add the finely chopped spinach and the grated pecorino, then spoon over the gnudi and serve with a scattering of pea shoots.

8 NOVEMBER

A seat at the pantomime

There are lads in tights, girls in breeches, elderly men with pancake make-up, and bare-chested boys in baggy pants. There are dwarfs and giants, fairies and wizards, a puss in boots and babes in a wood. There are death threats and dreams, genies in lamps, a witch, a princess, and pumpkins that turn into stagecoaches. Pantomime is a gorgeous cacophony of comedy, music, cross-gendering and high jinks.

As a child I was mesmerised by the slightly sinister, dream-like quality that runs through pantomime. I revelled in being slightly scared while all the time knowing I was in a safe place. The cross-dressing, the psychedelic costumes and the sexual innuendo appealed to a boy sitting in the company of the straightest of parents. The colours, comedy and costumes were more of a draw than the stories, which I always found slightly confusing. Take *Aladdin*. Is it South East Asian, Middle Eastern or East End? Answer, all three.

Most of the political and satirical references were there to amuse the accompanying adults, but not much went over my head. I often found the music terrifying. Especially in *Aladdin*. Rimsky-Korsakov's *Scheherazade* has always sent shivers up my spine. I always went accompanied by adults, Mum and Dad, an aunt or uncle. I adored the way that pantomime, like fairy tales, made me comfortably uncomfortable. It has an effect on the imagination no television or film ever could. Although I have to say the slapstick didn't appeal then, just as it doesn't now. I have never found people falling over terribly funny.

Pantomime has been with us, in various forms, since the sixteenth century. The version familiar to us is influenced by the Italian Commedia dell'Arte, a style of travelling comedy that moved around Italy and France during the sixteenth and seventeenth centuries. Much of the act was improvised, a comedic performance that involved characters, often masked, always in

costume, which we would recognise today. The form took hold in Britain to become Harlequinade, with its main characters being a harlequin, a clown and a pair of lovers.

Panto in Britain was originally, as its name suggests, a mime. Silent comedy performed by mostly French actors escaping their own country's clampdown on unlicensed theatres, initially at the Theatre Royal, Drury Lane, and the long-departed Lincoln's Inn Fields Theatre. During the nineteenth century, as stage machinery became more sophisticated, the shows became increasingly spectacular. Trapdoors and trick scenery became an essential part of the story, and the slapstick element took hold. Pantomime developed into a cleverly synchronised tapestry of comedy, song, slapstick, mime and satire loosely based around a well-known fairy story.

The titles are firmly established, though new ones come up all the time. *Aladdin, Cinderella, Dick Whittington, Snow White and the Seven Dwarfs, Puss in Boots, Goldilocks and the Three Bears, Mother Goose* and *Peter Pan* are as popular now as they were a hundred years ago, though each performance will have its own signature. No two versions are alike.

The season for pantomime is short, and tickets sell out like chocolate cake at a village fête. It is now, well before a single mince pie is baked, that you might like to sit down, go online and search what pantos are coming up this year. This may seem all very early, but once word gets round that something is going to be special, seats suddenly disappear.

Tonight, I make a dish of lentils with cream and basil. Essentially a frugal autumn dish, a baked aubergine with a knubbly mound of creamed lentils heady with basil.

Aubergine with lentils and basil

Serves 4
aubergines – 2 large or 4 small
olive oil – 6 tablespoons
a lemon
onions, medium – 2
garlic – 4 cloves
thyme sprigs – 8
rosemary – 6 sprigs
chestnut mushrooms – 200g
Le Puy or other small lentils – 400g
double cream – 250ml
parsley, chopped – 3 tablespoons
basil – a good handful of leaves
Parmesan, grated – 75g

Halve the aubergines lengthways, then score the cut surfaces in a lattice fashion, slicing deeply into the heart of the flesh but without piercing the skin. Place them skin side down on a baking sheet, trickle generously with some of the olive oil, and season lightly. Halve the lemon and squeeze over the juice. Place under a hot grill, a good way from the heat source, and cook until deep golden-brown. The flesh should be soft and silky.

Peel and roughly chop the onions. Warm the remaining olive oil in a shallow pan, then add the onions, stir, and leave them to cook over a moderate heat. Peel and crush the garlic, then stir into the onions. Pull the leaves from the thyme sprigs. Remove the needles from the rosemary, chop finely, then stir, together with the thyme leaves, into the softening onions.

Quarter the mushrooms, combine with the onions and leave to soften and colour. Season with salt and a little black pepper, then leave to simmer, very gently, over a low heat, partially covered with a lid.

Cook the lentils in a saucepan of boiling water for about fifteen minutes, until tender but with a slight nuttiness to them, adding salt about five minutes from the end of cooking. Drain the lentils, then stir into the onion and mushrooms. Pour in the cream, bring to the boil, then fold in the parsley, torn basil leaves and grated Parmesan and check the seasoning. It might need a little more pepper.

Serve the lentils in shallow bowls or plates, with a halved aubergine on top, or two if they are small.

9 NOVEMBER

The Christmas list and a fig tart

The row of notebooks, black, brown, indigo, fat with bookmarks and held together with tape, gets ever longer. The handwritten books where I scribble not just notes and recipes, but my endless, obsessive lists. This morning, while it is still dark, I sit at the kitchen table, get out the current little black book and start this year's Christmas list.

I have never felt Christmas should be run like a military operation, but I do need some sort of order at this time of year. Life isn't all art and poetry. There is so much to do and so many details to consider if the season is to be a joy rather than a chore. Occasionally, just occasionally, I need to put my practical hat on. Anyway, I actually like making lists, I have done it all my life. No need to stop now.

There are cards to be bought, gifts to consider, food to prepare and events to be scheduled. No, I don't know what sort of cheese is going to be on my kitchen table until I go shopping, but I do need to know I have remembered to buy sticky tape. Anyone who has wasted an hour of their life trying to find the bloody Sellotape will know what I mean.

A list, not only written but actually referred to, constantly, like a recipe, will make my Christmas easier. A present list (who will get what). A food and drink list (what will be on the table). The domestic list (is there enough Champagne and coffee beans?). A list of events, teas, and visits to the theatre. Do I need another row of Christmas lights or more candles? If you are the sort of person who makes lists but never looks at them again, fine, it is still worth doing. It will jog your memory. I envy those who feel they don't need to make any sort of plan and still don't find themselves short of matches to light the pudding. There is no delight in setting the family's plum pudding aglow on Christmas Day with a cheap plastic lighter.

Nothing sucks the joy out of receiving a gift than to have been asked, 'What do you want for Christmas?' If you know them well enough to ask that question, then you should probably know what they would like anyway. Yes, it's a practical idea, in as much as you don't risk disappointing the recipient with the wrong present, but I would rather somebody take that risk than be asked what I want.

My lists will develop slowly over the next couple of weeks, with details added as I think of them. Right now, it's the basics. I also decide to try out a couple of recipes that may be good to have around over Christmas, and certainly to enjoy over the winter. I start with a sweet tart.

Note to self: buy candles.

Dried fig and Marsala tart

There are two tricky moments in the preparation of any sort of upside-down tart and both involve the caramel. First the making of the sugar and butter sauce without burning or crystallising it, and second, restraining said hot sauce from pouring out over your fingers as you upend the tart on to its serving plate.

The caramel is something I have been playing with, on and off, for years. I have finally decided not to make it in the traditional manner. It is far easier, I find, to make one from sugar and a little sweet wine (in this case Marsala), then drop cubes of butter into it and let everything come together in the oven. The fruit helpfully soaks up most of the caramel, leaving just the right amount of buttery stickiness. Use a tarte Tatin mould or a metal-handled frying pan, or, as I do, a shallow-sided tart tin.

Serves 8
dried figs – 500g
golden sultanas – 50g
dry Marsala – 100ml
golden caster sugar – 100g
butter – 50g

For the pastry:
cold butter – 175g
plain flour – 225g
golden caster sugar – 2 tablespoons
large egg yolks – 2

To serve:
double cream
ice cream
crème fraîche

You will also need a 24cm round Tatin tin or shallow, non-stick cake tin with a fixed base.

Set the oven at 200°C/Gas 6. Put the figs and sultanas into a mixing bowl, pour over the Marsala and leave to stand for forty-five minutes, stirring occasionally.

Make the pastry: cut the cold butter into small cubes and rub into the flour, either with your fingertips or using a food processor. Work until you have what looks like coarse, fresh breadcrumbs. Stir in the sugar.

Add the egg yolks to the butter and flour. Mix together until you have a soft dough, then turn out on to a floured board and knead briefly, for just a minute. Shape the dough into a smooth, fat cylinder. Wrap it in greaseproof paper or clingfilm and leave to rest in the fridge for thirty minutes.

Make the caramel: place the Tatin mould or a frying pan over a moderate heat. (If you will be baking the tart in a cake tin, use a frying pan to make the caramel, otherwise you will damage your tin.) Add the Marsala from the dried fruit, leaving the fruit behind in the bowl, then add the sugar. Bring to the boil and leave to form a thin caramel. If you are using a Tatin mould, remove from the heat. If you are using a cake tin, pour the caramel from the frying pan into the tin.

Cut the butter into small cubes and scatter it over the caramel. Place the plumped-up figs on the base of the tin in a single layer (neatly or not, as you wish), then scatter over the sultanas, pushing them into any gaps.

Roll out the pastry a little larger than the Tatin mould or cake tin. With the help of the rolling pin – it is very fragile – lift the pastry into the mould or tin, pressing it gently into place over the figs. Tuck in any overhanging pastry.

Bake in the preheated oven for about thirty minutes, until the pastry is golden. Remove from the oven and leave to settle for ten to fifteen minutes. Place a large serving plate on top of the tart, then, using oven gloves, hold the tin and plate firmly and carefully turn them over, leaving the tart to slide out on to the plate. Serve warm with cream, ice cream or crème fraîche.

A sweet preserve with a savoury past

A glossy paste of currants and raisins, brown sugar and cinnamon, mixed spice and citrus zest. There is candied peel, and the comfort of Bramley apples and suet. A preserve, sweet, spicy, fruity, whose history goes back to the Middle Ages, and whose smell is redolent of the happiest moments of my childhood.

One of the more pleasing aspects of social media is learning just how many people still make their own mincemeat. I enjoy seeing (and, if I'm honest, am slightly envious of) their proud results after an afternoon spent stirring dried fruits, apples, cinnamon and cloves in the kitchen. Rows of glossy jars, plump as Friar Tuck, are displayed complete with handwritten labels. Presumably so that, come July, the contents won't be mistaken for chutney.

Disclosure: I don't always make my own mincemeat. The romanticism appeals, but in practice I often end up buying it, usually from a posh shop or a village fête. A jar whose contents lie somewhere between the syrupy offerings of commerce and something I could have made myself. The years I do have a go are memorable, not only for the day itself, the smell, the bubbling pot of stickiness, but for the lavishness with which I use the results. Mincemeat for cakes, for sandwiching between slices of hot toasted panettone, for steamed puddings and for baking in crumbly biscuits to be eaten mid-morning with a pot of coffee.

Mincemeat hasn't always been sweet. The clue is in the name. Early recipes, some of which go back to the sixteenth century, contain minced beef and its fat, vinegar and spices. Our little mince pie seems, at one time, to have been almost entirely savoury. A pasty.

The earliest recipes also bring with them a warm breeze from the Middle East, with their familiar marriage of sweet fruits and meat. Thomas Tusser, chorister, poet, musician, author and farmer, lists a recipe (1557) for mince or 'shred' pies that was considered standard Christmas fare. Lady Elinor

Fettiplace (1570–1647) describes them in more detail, showing them to be more akin to a pasty, listing mutton and beef suet as well as orange peel, raisins, ginger and mace (a spice I have only ever used in meat terrines: Heaven only knows how old my glass jar in the larder is) and rosewater.

The Good Housewife's Jewel by Thomas Dawson (1598) tempts its readers with a recipe using deer offal (the 'umbels' that gave their name to the phrase 'to eat umble pie'), salt, cloves, currants, almonds, dates and fat. The mince is baked, then boiled with sugar and spices. A long way from the syrupy jam in the present-day Robertson's jar.

Mincemeat takes a turn away from its savoury route in the seventeenth century. The writer and poet Gervase Markham, whose most famous work is *The English Huswife Containing the Inward and Outward Virtues which ought to be in a Complete Woman* (a title for which he surely deserves a bat round the head with a frying pan), has a recipe that is almost entirely devoid of meat. As the preserve continues its journey, it ditches not only the mutton, beef and salt, but also the passing whiff of the Middle East.

By the beginning of the twentieth century the minced meat had departed from most recipes, but the practice of adding beads of grated suet lives on to this day, though most used in commercial preparations is made from hydrogenated fat. As sugar becomes less of a luxury, the filling gets steadily sweeter until we arrive at today's sugar-laden, glistening goo. Most modern recipes have even ditched the tiny pearl-like nuggets of suet that twinkled in their dark, syrupy depths.

For those of us making our own mincemeat, the difficulty is getting our hands on a decent lump of fresh suet to grate. (Go for the whitest, creamiest beef fat your butcher can offer you.) My feeling is that if you use the packet stuff, creamy white specks in a nostalgic blue, red and yellow box, you might as well buy your mincemeat ready-made.

A classic brandy mincemeat

Today, November 10, I make this year's batch. It's a bit late, according to Mary Berry, who recommends a maturing time in the jar of six months. (Delia has kept hers for three years with no ill-effects, as I'm pretty sure my mum did.) Six glistening jam jars sit on the counter, each having had a ride in the dishwasher, then ten minutes in the oven at 180°C/Gas 4 to sterilise them. Their labels are already written, in fountain pen, waiting patiently for my Christmas jam.

Despite the long ingredients list, mincemeat is a doddle. I spend more time weighing the dried fruits, spices and sugar than I do cooking. Even then, the task takes barely an hour. I spin it out because I like the smell that is filling the kitchen. The scent of Christmases, past. Better than that, of Christmas to come.

Makes about 1.5kg, enough for 36 (ish) mince pies
shredded suet – 200g
dark muscovado sugar – 200g
sultanas – 200g
currants – 200g
prunes, stoned – 200g
dried apricots – 200g
cooking apples – 750g
skinned almonds – 50g
a lemon
ground cinnamon – 1 teaspoon
ground cloves – $\frac{1}{2}$ teaspoon
nutmeg, grated – $\frac{1}{2}$ teaspoon
brandy – 100ml

Put the suet, sugar, sultanas and currants into a large saucepan. Roughly chop the prunes and apricots and stir them in. Peel and core the apples, cut them into small dice, then add them to the other fruits. Place over a moderate heat and bring to the boil. Finely chop the almonds, finely grate the zest of the lemon, then stir both into the fruit with the cinnamon, cloves and nutmeg. Squeeze the lemon juice into the mixture and continue cooking for about fifteen minutes. Allow to cool, then stir in the brandy.

Spoon the mincemeat into the sterilised jars, seal with a tight lid and label.

Quince and cardamom mincemeat (without suet)

I feel a little sorry for those impervious to the charm of a mince pie. I want to offer them something. Calling the recipe that follows 'mincemeat' is stretching it a bit, but it still contains the fruits and spices of the original (many early recipes include quince in place of apple), and it smells like the classic as it cooks. But it has another appeal, that of no suet, or indeed fat of any kind. Think of it as Christmas jam. The colour is gold rather than black. It is rather good with cheese too, in the way a slice of Cheshire is good with fruit cake. Oh, and can I suggest grinding the cardamom seeds at the last minute – the ready-ground stuff loses all its magic.

Makes 3 × 400g jars
caster sugar – 100g
water – 1 litre
the juice of a lemon
quinces – 500g
green cardamom – 8 pods
mixed spice – 1 teaspoon
ground cinnamon – $\frac{1}{2}$ teaspoon
golden sultanas – 200g
raisins – 200g
currants – 200g
dried apricots – 200g
light muscovado sugar – 100g
brandy or quince liqueur – 100ml

You will also need 3 × 400g jam jars, sterilised.

Put the caster sugar into a medium-sized saucepan, add the water and bring to the boil. Pour the lemon juice into the syrup. Peel the quinces, cut them into quarters, remove the core, then lower them into the pan. As soon as the syrup comes back to the boil, lower the heat to a simmer, partially cover the pan with a lid and leave for forty minutes, or until the quinces are soft but far from collapsing. Take off the heat.

Break open the cardamom pods, scrape out the seeds and crush them quite finely, using a pestle and mortar or spice mill. Put them into a capacious saucepan with the mixed spice and ground cinnamon. Add the golden sultanas, raisins and currants, then roughly chop the dried apricots and stir them in. Pour in 400ml of the quince cooking liquor and add the brown sugar. Simmer, stirring from time to time, for twenty minutes. Cut the quinces into small dice and add to the mincemeat. Pour in the brandy or liqueur, simmer for a further five minutes, then spoon into sterilised jars and seal.

Martinmas, a ham dinner and a citrus cake

For centuries this has been a feast day. The date marked the end of the agricultural year, the harvest was well and truly in, the livestock were ready for slaughter, wine was ready for drinking. It is officially the beginning of winter. In medieval times, such an important feast was celebrated by eating a goose for those who could afford it, duck or chicken for those who couldn't.

The celebration began in France, then spread to the Low Countries, Eastern Europe and then to Britain. It is still celebrated in Germany, with goose, dumplings and red cabbage. In parts of Scandinavia too, though to a much lesser extent, with lantern processions and singing, church services and, of course, feasting. In Britain we have traditionally eaten our goose on Michaelmas Day, September 29. But reading Martinmas in my diary does get me thinking about Christmas dinner and what will be on the table.

By now, many a working-class Victorian family like mine would have had a healthy collection of coins in their local Goose Club. This was a way of saving up for your festive food by stashing away as much as you could afford each week during summer, autumn and early winter, to help dilute the horror of the cost of Christmas. Each member of the clubs, which were run by publicans, groups of friends and butchers, would eventually get a goose and possibly some other treat into the bargain. Goose Clubs live on in the form of Christmas Clubs, though one usually only hears of them when they go bust, and everyone loses their hard-saved cash.

Today is, of course, Remembrance Day, Poppy Day, when we remember those who have died in the line of duty. I have breakfast at the Wolseley in London's Piccadilly, where, on the dot of eleven, a full minute's silence is observed by staff and customers. Hush falls on the enormous, high-ceilinged room; the staff stands still, not so much as a teaspoon tinkles in a saucer. I am moved almost to tears.

I have cooked a ham around this time of year for as long as I can remember. A practice run for the ham I will need over Christmas, that eternally useful cut-and-come-again joint for lunch, supper, sandwiches.

I usually take the route of simmering the rolled and tied joint in water or apple juice with peppercorns, cloves, celery, carrots and onions, then draining and baking it. The poaching keeps it moist, and the baking ensures a sticky crust, the surface of the ham usually having been spread with marmalade, apricot jam or honey.

This year I take the same route, but decide on quince paste – membrillo – as the sweet spread for the crust. The quince jelly is a good idea; it stays put in the oven, which is more than you can say for maple syrup or apricot jam, which you painstakingly paint over the meat only to find it slides off into the tin. The fruity-tartness is welcome with the sweet pink ham.

Ham with quince paste, cauliflower and dill

Serves 6 hot (with enough for a further 6 cold)
gammon, rolled and tied – 2.5kg
quince paste – 250g
dry Marsala or medium dry sherry – 4 tablespoons

For the stock:
an onion
cloves – 5
a cinnamon stick
black peppercorns – 10
bay leaves – 3

For the cauliflower:
cauliflower – 1.3kg
dill – 25g

Put the gammon into your largest saucepan or stockpot. Peel and halve the onion, then add it to the water along with the cloves, cinnamon stick, peppercorns and bay leaves. Bring to the boil, then turn down the heat and remove any froth from the surface of the liquid with a draining spoon. Partially cover with a lid and leave to simmer, gently, for an hour and a half. After an hour's cooking, turn the meat over.

When the ham is ready, remove it from the cooking liquor and place it in a roasting tin, reserving the stock. Heat the oven to 200°C/Gas 6. Mix the quince paste and the Marsala or sherry in a small saucepan, letting it bubble briefly until it melts. Spread the paste over the ham. Bake for twenty-five to thirty minutes, or until the glaze has set. Remove and loosely cover with foil to keep warm.

While the ham bakes, break the cauliflower into florets and place in a saucepan. Ladle enough of the hot ham stock into the cauliflower pan to cover the florets, then bring to the boil – no need to add salt. Let the florets simmer until tender, about twenty to twenty-five minutes.

Remove half the cauliflower with a draining spoon and place in a warm, shallow dish. Put the remaining cauliflower and 200ml of the cooking stock into a blender with the dill (do not overfill – you may need to do this in two lots). Pour the cauliflower and dill purée over the cauliflower florets.

Serve the ham, carving it thinly, with the cauliflower. You will have plenty of ham left for tomorrow. Serve it with the apricot and tomato chutney recipe (see December 12, page 249).

Orange poppy seed cake

It is also useful to have a cake that will keep in fine condition for several days. This soft, moist, citrus-scented loaf cake has the crunch of poppy seeds running through it.

Serves 8
soft butter – 225g
golden caster sugar – 225g
grated zest of an orange
grated zest of a lemon
plain flour – 110g
baking powder – generous $\frac{1}{2}$ teaspoon
ground almonds – 115g
eggs – 4
poppy seeds – 20g

For the topping and syrup:
candied orange and citron peel
juice of the orange and lemon above
caster sugar – 75g
poppy seeds and golden sugar – 1 tablespoon of each

You will need a deep-sided, rectangular cake tin, 22cm × 12cm × 7cm deep, lined on the base and sides with baking parchment.

Set the oven at 180°C/Gas 4. Cut eight thin slices of the orange and citron peel, no thicker than 5mm, and the right size to sit on top of the cake, and set them aside. Put the butter into the bowl of a food mixer, add the caster sugar, and cream for a good five minutes until soft and fluffy. Add the orange and lemon zest. Sift together the flour and baking powder, then stir in the ground almonds.

Break the eggs into a small bowl and beat lightly with a fork to combine. With the beater at a moderate speed, add the eggs, a little at a time, to the butter and sugar. If the mixture appears to curdle slightly, add a spoonful of the flour and almond mixture. Continue adding the flour until thoroughly creamed. Mix in the poppy seeds.

Transfer the mixture to the lined cake tin, gently smoothing the surface flat. Place the slices of citrus peel on top of the cake. Bake for forty-five to fifty minutes, until a skewer, inserted into the cake, comes out without any raw cake mixture attached. Leave the cake to cool for ten minutes.

Make the syrup: put the orange and lemon juice into a saucepan and add the sugar. Bring to the boil, stirring until the sugar has dissolved. Still in its tin, pierce the cake in about twenty places with a metal skewer or a fine knitting needle. Spoon the citrus syrup over the surface, letting it trickle through the holes. Scatter the surface with poppy seeds and, if you wish, golden sugar crystals.

A pot-roast partridge

We never had Champagne. At least not the real stuff. All that mattered was that a cork went pop and there were bubbles in our glasses. No one minded that what we drank was tummy-twistingly acidic and had bubbles the size of Maltesers. The point was noise and fizz. Asti Spumante had it with brass knobs on.

For a family on the quieter side – Mum, softly spoken as ever, with her calming there-there tone; Auntie Fanny, deaf as a post, who just sat and hummed to herself; and me, the little boy too scared to speak lest he upset his father – we nevertheless managed to make quite a bit of noise at the Christmas table. Dad was unusually loud, Mum got the giggles, brothers and aunties and grandmas were animated and chatted excitedly. Even the docile, flatulent golden retriever would run in circles around everyone's legs. It never occurred to me that the table came to life because everyone was slightly pissed. We appeared, for once a year at least, like any other vast, happy family.

The year I was seven, Dad opened a bottle of the Italian fizz at the table, the cork flew across the room – a trajectory aimed at nowhere special – and contrived to hit one of my mother's precious painted birds that lived on the wall over the fireplace, knocking the poor thing into an explosion of blue and yellow feathers. Mum laughed, yet I could see she was quietly fuming. The dog was coughing up feather-balls for weeks afterwards.

Birds pepper my winter eating like currants in a garibaldi. The goose or turkey at Christmas, of course, but weeks before that, the pheasants, grouse, a roast duck with apple sauce, maybe a quail or two. I like the deep flavours of game birds, the toasty bits in the bottom of the roasting tin; the accompaniments of redcurrant jelly, bread sauce and tiny sausages. I also relish the chance to tear my food apart with my hands. Much has to do with the shooting season, but the flavours are appropriate to the time of year, particularly when small birds are roasted with suitable vegetables, onions, mushrooms, parsnips and Jerusalem artichokes. And that medlar jelly you didn't make, well, that is just the accompaniment for a roast pheasant or partridge too.

The most expensive of the birds is grouse and is something I tend to leave to restaurants. But the partridge does it for me. Expensive without being prohibitive, neat, lean and sweet-fleshed, they have a sense of jollity to them that I suspect comes from the carol. (There are no songs about a guinea fowl.) It is too early to think of partridges in pear trees but it is almost impossible to think of them without the rumbustious little tune coming into my head. The idea that one should be served on the first day of Christmas doesn't really work, as we need a bigger bird for the attending family, so they are better pre or post Christmas.

The rhyme, 'The Twelve Days of Christmas', starts with a modest bird on Christmas Day and carries on through French hens and milking maids, getting grander with each of the twelve verses until we get to the leaping lords on Twelfth Night. An accumulative song – each verse builds on the previous ones – it was first published in Britain in 1870 and is thought to be of French origin. No one really knows how it started but it is generally considered to be a children's game of memory and forfeit. I love the idea that the best-known version appeared in a children's book called *Mirth without Mischief* (oh, for simpler times).

I have a pear and partridge recipe in *Tender*, Volume II. I take a more savoury route today, browning parsnips and onions before cooking them with a pair of little partridges and some chicken stock.

The clever trick and indeed the point behind pot-roasting is the small amount of liquid added to the casserole. Under a tight lid, the moisture produces steam that keeps the flesh of the birds juicy, circumnavigating the lack of fat that can make a traditionally roast bird dry. The roast partridge, by the way, is a tidy little dinner for one, and carries with it a faintly festive air. I eat them from early September (they come into season from the 1st) until early February (last shoot is the first day of Feb), often as a plain roast. Covered with bacon and smeared with dripping, they will roast to rose-tinted perfection in twenty-five minutes at 230°C/Gas 9. I tend to remove the bacon after ten minutes to give the breasts a chance to burnish. I throw in a chipolata or two if I'm feeling frivolous, or a slice or two of black pudding for the final ten minutes of cooking. Cabbage is a splendid accompaniment.

Pot-roast partridge with parsnips and smoked garlic

I am pot-roasting today's birds with parsnips, juniper and smoked garlic.

Serves 2
banana shallots or small onions – 3
parsnips, medium – 2
smoked garlic – 4 cloves
olive oil – 3 tablespoons
partridges – 2
chicken stock – 250ml
thyme – 6 sprigs
juniper berries – 10
double cream – 125ml

Set the oven at 180°C/Gas 4. Peel the shallots and slice them in half lengthways. Peel the parsnips and cut them into chunks the length of a wine cork. Peel the garlic.

Warm the olive oil in a casserole for which you have a lid, lightly brown the shallots, parsnips and garlic in the hot oil, then remove. Season the birds with black pepper, then brown lightly in the oil. Remove the birds, pour in the stock and bring to the boil, scraping at any delicious debris in the pan and stirring it into the stock.

Return the birds and vegetables to the pot, tuck in the sprigs of thyme, and season with a little salt. Lightly crush the juniper berries and add them too. When everything returns to the boil, cover tightly with a lid and place in the oven for forty minutes. Remove the partridges, wrapping them in foil to keep them warm, then place the pot over a high heat and reduce the volume of liquid by half – it won't thicken but will instead give you sweet, creamy juices. Stir in the cream, check the seasoning, then make sure all is thoroughly hot. Serve the birds in shallow bowls or deep plates, spooning over the vegetables and the juices. You will need a spoon as well as a knife and fork, and something with which to wipe your fingers.

Maple syrup and fig terrine

The garden has skeletons – hydrangea, hornbeam and beech – holding their leaves even now. The pale walnut browns are smart and crisp against the green of the high yew hedges. Blue tits feast. Leaves, yellow, grey, black, lie frozen to the garden table, silver with frost. The space is tidy, but beneath the neatness lie worries. Two much-loved trees in the garden require major surgery, a third lost its leaves in the summer. The white jasmines, normally survivors in any garden, have suffered from a mysterious fungus. (This could well be due to their location, a curiously warm, damp courtyard where frost gets no hold, an enclosed space warm enough for pelargoniums to spend their winter unprotected.)

The garden needs a fierce snap of cold and so do I. The frost adds a touch of fairy-tale sparkle to the hedges and trees but it is still warm enough to venture out without a coat. I long for snow, for frost-ferns on the windows, for ice on the water butt.

I have been gardening long enough to know that there is much happening underground. Narcissi and tulips sprout, muscari and crocus are waking up. I feel this happening too. I feel in need of a prolonged cold patch to stir my own energy. Where some see a garden in repose, a sleeping beauty, I see what lies beneath, the garden's hidden spirit, waiting to emerge.

This morning, after a couple of hours at my desk, I take out the secateurs and cut back the white roses, removing their spindly growth and confusion of crossed stems. Standing back to admire my work, I feel the roses can breathe once more. I come in, make coffee and set about sorting the larder – discarding and tidying. A sort of culinary pruning and removing of dead wood.

There is method in my madness. Even though this is the busiest time of year, I like to spend a day sorting out the food cupboards. A seasonal stock-take. A snapshot of what I have a little too much of (lentils, beans, coconut milk, maple syrup) and what I don't have at all (light soy sauce, hoisin, honey and, crucially, dried yeast.) An inventory now means a slow picking up of necessities over the next few weeks rather than the horror and panic of a 'big shop' during Christmas week, when the rest of the country will be at it too.

There is only one way to tidy a kitchen cupboard and that is to take everything out. Everything. Moving things around from shelf to shelf and side to side doesn't work. You need to see what you have, so I spend the rest of the morning with bottles, cans and storage jars spread over the floor. The shelves get cleaned, then everything goes back (or at least most of it), starting with the top shelf (dried beans and lentils), then working down.

I rather enjoy finding the oldest sell-by date, but the haul is a disappointment this time. A jar of chestnuts from two Christmases ago, a twelve-month over-the-date bag of prunes and a bottle of oyster sauce that seems magically to have escaped at least three previous stock-takes isn't enough to satisfy me. I genuinely relish finding that box of coconut-flavoured sugar or jar of piccalilli that is old enough to have gone down on the *Titanic*.

A surfeit of maple syrup annoys me, though. It is one of the most expensive ingredients in the kitchen and I cannot imagine how I have ended up with three bottles. I put it down to the bottles being slim and stored sideways, thus becoming almost invisible, like a book in a bookshop with the spine facing out. This find does, however, give me the opportunity to try out an ice that may well end up on the table at Christmas.

Fig, maple syrup and Marsala ice cream

If you have an ice cream machine, churn the custard, syrup and yoghurt mixture first, then stir in the chopped fig and chocolate at the end. To prevent the custard from curdling, keep the heat low and, as it starts to thicken, remove from the heat, pour into a chilled bowl over ice or in a sink of cold water and beat firmly and continuously until most of the steam has gone and the custard is smooth. I like to serve the ice in chunks, like fudge, rather than in one large slab.

Serves 6
egg yolks – 4
caster sugar – 2 tablespoons
double cream – 450ml
vanilla extract – a few drops
maple syrup – 240ml
figs – 3
dark chocolate – 100g
thick, strained yoghurt – 200g
figs and physalis, to serve

Put the egg yolks and caster sugar into the bowl of a food mixer and whisk until light and fluffy. Warm the cream in a saucepan, switching the heat off just before it comes to the boil, then stir in the vanilla. Pour the warm cream on to the eggs and sugar and stir to mix. Rinse the saucepan, then pour in the egg and cream mixture and return to a low to moderate heat. Warm the custard, stirring regularly, until it starts to thicken slightly on the spoon, then pour into a cold bowl and stir or beat with a whisk to remove some of the heat. Leave to cool a little.

Pour in the maple syrup and combine. Chop the figs into small pieces, crushing them slightly as you go, then chop the chocolate into small, thin shards with a large knife. Stir the yoghurt, figs and chocolate pieces into the custard, then tip into a plastic freezer box and freeze for a good four hours, or overnight. Turn the ice cream out, then cut into large chunks and pile on to a chilled serving plate, perhaps with a few physalis and more slices of fig.

Dinner is a green and humble soup. The flavours are simple, the method is straightforward and the ingredients are everyday. Recipes like this, gentle, warming, unshowy and, it should be said, meatless, are the backbone of my eating. Yes, there is plenty to dazzle both plate and palate, but sometimes it is this sort of food I need, food without frills or fuss, calming, restorative and just a little bit nannying. Oh, and it has a flotilla of cheese and toast on top.

Cauliflower and leek soup with toasted cheese

I use whatever cheese is around for this sort of thing. Tonight, it is a mixture of Gorgonzola and Taleggio that needs using up, the two melting harmoniously over the pieces of toast. Use whatever you have.

Serves 4
leeks, medium – 3
butter – 30g
olive oil – 2 tablespoons
cauliflower – 1kg
vegetable stock – 1 litre
bay leaves – 2
parsley leaves – a good handful (10g)
sourdough bread – 4 slices
cheese (any good melting type) – 100g

Discard the coarse part of the green leaves from the leeks and roughly chop them. Warm the butter with the olive oil in a deep pan. Add the leeks and cover with a lid. Cook over a low to moderate heat, stirring and checking their progress regularly, until the leeks are soft but without browning them.

Trim and thickly slice the cauliflower and add to the leeks. Stir briefly, then pour in the vegetable stock and bring to the boil. Add the bay leaves and a little salt, then lower the heat and leave the leeks and cauliflower to simmer for fifteen to twenty minutes, until soft. Process half the mixture in a blender until really smooth. Add a handful of parsley to the remainder and process in the blender to a thick, rough-textured consistency. Mix the two together and check the seasoning, adding salt and ground black pepper as you think fit.

Spread the sourdough bread with a little butter or olive oil and place under a hot grill, toasting one side to a light crispness. Turn the bread over and cover the other side with thick slices of cheese, then return to the grill until melted. Divide the soup between shallow bowls and float the cheese toasts on top.

Candlelight and roast cabbage

I wake early, sit at my desk and write. A daily ritual which if missed sets my world briefly off its axis. For the best months of the year, it will still be dark, a prickle of cold in the air, the slightly-too-long arms of my sweater (my writing jumper, a dear old friend) slipping softly over my fingers as I type, as if I was wearing fingerless gloves.

I do most of my early morning writing by candlelight. There is a warmth to the light given by a single flame that no electric filament bulb can ever match, and shadows that flicker grey on white. Occasionally, in winter, the candles will gutter, the flame weaving a little as it burns, a flash, a hiss and a spit, as if someone has walked past, and then it steadies itself once more.

My love of candlelight has its history in the light given by a particular candle that would be burned at home, unfailingly, over Christmas, then put away again until the following year. A heavy, square, rough-sided candle, each side framing a paper stained-glass window. To this seven-year-old child, it seemed like a magic lantern, each window a door to a world in which wonderful things happened, but also a place of safety and warmth. A hollow in which to disappear, like a rabbit-hole or a wardrobe with a magical world past the fur coats.

There were other candles too, including those which, once lit, sent tiny brass horses spinning round a pole, and others huddled in a bunch whose wax slowly welded together as they melted, achieving a glowing island. The candles disappeared from our Christmas under the instruction of my stepmother, who thought they were dirty things, producing smoke and dripping wax on her lovingly polished tables. A somewhat strange decree, coming, as it did, from a lifelong chain-smoker.

A candle is not just for Christmas. Turn the lights off on a winter's night and light a candle or two instead. Instantly, the smell of cordite, and soon the scent of beeswax. Shadows to feed the imagination, flickers of flame, perhaps the scent of woodsmoke by which to read a book. None of this would I wish to live without. At home, we light them even during summer, though they tend to be in tall glass jars on the long garden table, lit as the night starts to fall.

Whale sperm and beeswax

The heart and soul of a candle is the wax from which it is made; it is what glows and produces a pillar of warm light in the room, but this hasn't always been so. The fat from nuts and trees, from bay berries and even rice was used long before the introduction of wax. In the West it was tallow, basically rendered beef fat, which is softer than the wax we know today and gave off much dark, acrid smoke, rather like beef fat on a griddle. There is evidence that candle makers – chandlers – went from house to house, making saved beef fat into useable candles.

In the Middle Ages, we progressed to beeswax. Cleaner and with a warming, honeyed fragrance, they were more expensive to make and initially the preserve of the wealthy and of churches, where they were an integral part of religious ceremonies. Cheaper candles were made from spermaceti, a waxy substance obtained from the spermaceti organ found in the head of a sperm whale. Spermaceti candles, also known as standard candles, were the ones used for measuring candlepower, the unit, no longer used, that measures the luminous intensity of a candle. You can get 500 gallons of spermaceti from a large whale. Is this book useful or what?

Wax for candles is obtained from a variety of sources, stearin (purified animal fats), paraffin, cinnamon, soya and palm being among the most common, but the most valued is the traditional beeswax. Even unscented they are capable of creating, almost instantly, an atmosphere of calm, welcome and humble bonhomie.

The wick

The wick that lies at the heart of the candle is made of braided cotton or linen. Occasionally a stiffener, in the form of copper wire, is used. As the wick burns, the heat travels downwards, melting the wax that supports it. The wax vapours rise around the wick, catch light and burn, feeding the flame. The wax is fuel to the burning wick. The thicker the wick, the larger the flame. The liquid pool of wax around the wick is known to some as the bishop, though I have absolutely no idea why.

Trimming your wick

Candle wicks are treated to encourage them to burn more slowly. The wick should be kept trimmed – snip off any burned cotton with scissors before lighting. Too long a wick will encourage the candle to smoke. In some cases a long wick can collapse back into the wax. No one wants that. I often pinch the burned cotton between my fingers when I can't be bothered to go and fetch the scissors. If my fingers aren't covered in fountain pen ink, they are sporting smudges of candle soot.

A life lived by the light of a candle

This is an old house, and candlelight suits it. The wobbly walls, the floorboards that creak even when you are still, the draughts that seep from every window and door. Most rooms have a fireplace; three of them, including the kitchen, have two. The space comes alive when candles are lit, shadows are exaggerated, corners deepen, here and there walls show the outline of doors long blocked up. These rooms have stories to tell. In daylight or under electric lights, the house is like any other, a closed book.

At the table

Candlelight has the extraordinary ability to make any meal into a special occasion, even when it is simply a bowl of soup and some bread and cheese. The light it gives welcomes and warms, soothes and calms. Faces glow, details are accentuated. Our lines, scars and wrinkles are more beautiful than ever.

Scented candles for Christmas

Much as I appreciate the purity of an unscented beeswax candle, scented candles can be interesting. They can be charming or hideously overpowering, depending on the type of scent used.

Scents come in every possibility, from wet cloisters to toasted brioche, wax floorboards to freshly ironed linen, and every imaginable flower, leaf and spice. I have to hold my hands up here and admit that I may not be a food snob but I am most certainly a candle snob. Cheap scented candles are simply disgusting. They smell of air freshener. Here are a few I recommend for burning at Christmas. All are subtle, and I promise they are not going to make your house smell like a cheap gift shop or a massage parlour.

Carmelite by Cire Trudon

A favourite of mine, often to be found burning in my basement kitchen, and whose 'wet' scent seems appropriate for the old stone floors, low ceilings and rough white walls. A deeply peaceful scent, of mossy stone and water. Not for Christmas Day, but for quiet moments before everyone gets up. There are the faintest notes of orange and clove, with heart-notes of violet and cardamom. Or, as the creator puts it, 'the black and white silhouettes of nuns, walking through the silence of a ritual mass'. Which is probably why it seems so appropriate in this house.

Spiritus Sancti by Cire Trudon

'Splinters of crimson, gold and olibanum,' says the creator, 'under the nave of a cathedral, the jubilant choir and holy scents rise into the souls.' There is magic in this scent, the perfect candle for Christmas Day. A fleeting note of incense too.

Santa Maria Novella

In 1221 Dominican friars built a monastery, just outside the city gate in Florence, and began to experiment with herbs grown in their gardens. Initially intended for the monastery's infirmary, the pharmacy opened to the public in 1612, and the Dominicans officially started selling their 'curative and ephemeral products'. To this day they sell their fragrances around the world. Their Melograno soap has been a permanent feature of my bathroom for many years. Their pale ivory Melograno candle is said to bring good luck and fortune for the coming year.

Ash by Perfumer H

A mixture of carde (a relative of the juniper plant), frankincense and amber. This is the candle I have burning pretty much permanently in my house on winter mornings. Understated, like the company that makes it, gentle and haunting, a scent as old as time.

Diptyque produce some fine fragances too, especially Ivy and Bay, both perfect for winter. And yes, they all cost a small fortune but let's be honest, the 'Christmas candles' that smell of cinnamon and mulled wine are particularly unpleasant. I will walk a mile to save a penny, but when it comes to candles, I think we should go for broke.

Candle myths and tips

Storing

There is a candle shelf in the larder, next to my collection of balls of string. (I have string for every occasion, some as fine as cotton thread, and some for the garden that smell of tar. It's a borderline obsession.) Like Christmas pudding, I buy candles one year for the next. I have been led to believe that the older and drier the wax, the longer they will burn. If you keep the lid on the box, the scent will not disappear for a good year or more. Aged candles seem to last longer. Candle experts disagree. This is distinct from curing, ageing a candle for a few weeks before it is first used, a process by which the wax and the perfume bond. Maybe I just like storing candles.

Bloom

Candles that have been in store sometimes develop a powdery coat, like a damson. This can be wiped off with a soft, dry cloth.

Burn rate

Look for candles with a long burn rate. It is usually marked on the box. This will tell you roughly how long a candle should burn for if burned continuously. Burning the candle in a draught will reduce its life.

A smoking candle

Occasionally a candle will produce plumes of black smoke. This is usually because the flame is being disturbed by a draught, causing the natural teardrop of light to distort and flicker. Rather appropriate if you happen to be reading a ghost story on a winter's night. Annoying if not. Which is why candles on window ledges often burn less evenly than those on a table in the centre of a room.

Chilling your candles

I was brought up to believe that candles should be stored in the fridge, as a cold candle burns more slowly. Sadly, although based on truth, the wax warms so quickly once lit that the practice is somewhat pointless.

Incidentally, Fortnum & Mason department store, one of the capital's prettiest Christmas sights, is, as Tom Parker Bowles says in *The Cook Book*, 'a company built on spent wax'. William Fortnum, footman to Queen Anne, was allowed to keep the spent candles, which he then successfully sold on, before eventually teaming up with Mr Mason to open their eponymous Piccadilly store. Their selection of dinner candles remains dazzling to this day.

Roast cabbage with cheese sauce

Happy tweets and emails have been coming in today about my recipe for roast cabbage. There is something particularly heart-warming about this, especially as I wasn't initially sure about the idea. I make it again, tonight, and sure enough, the readers are right, it is really good for a cold night. The Parmesan and old-fashioned sauce ensure its frugality goes unnoticed.

Serves 4
garlic – 2 cloves
olive oil – 2 tablespoons
lemon juice – 2 tablespoons
a small cabbage
Parmesan – 55g
milk – 500ml
bay leaves – 2
half an onion
butter – 30g
plain flour – 30g
bread, open-textured, such as ciabatta – a thick slice
smoked paprika – a pinch (optional)
sprouted seeds

Preheat the oven to 200°C/Gas 6. Peel the garlic and crush to a paste with a little salt. Put the paste into a small mixing bowl and stir in the olive oil and lemon juice. Season with a generous grinding of black pepper.

Slice the cabbage into discs about 3cm thick and place them, just touching, on a baking sheet. Spoon the garlic and lemon juice dressing over the cabbage and roast for twenty-five to thirty minutes. Turn the cabbage over, dust the top of each piece with a heaped tablespoon of grated Parmesan, and continue cooking for fifteen minutes.

While the cabbage cooks, bring the milk to the boil with the bay leaves and onion, then remove from the heat and leave to infuse. Melt the butter in a saucepan, stir in the flour and cook over a moderate heat for a couple of minutes. Add the milk, strained through a sieve, stir until smooth, then leave to simmer over a very low heat for fifteen minutes, barely bubbling, while the cabbage roasts. Tear the bread into small pieces and grill or fry until crisp, brushing or trickling them with a little oil as they cook.

Finely grate the remaining Parmesan into the sauce and season to taste with a little salt (you won't need much), some black pepper and, if you like, a little smoked paprika. Lift the cooked cabbage on to plates, spoon over some of the cheese sauce, and finish with the fried bread and some green sprouted seeds.

Frost fairs and braised brisket

I ache for snow. The last generous fall in this garden was in January 2013, when the yew hedges tilted drunkenly with its weight. I ache for silence, for the sound of my own muffled footsteps as I walk up the garden path. But most of all I ache for icicles. When I was seven or eight, icicles hung from every gutter on the house. Long glass stalactites hung down from the greenhouse roof like trickles of icing on a gingerbread house. They shone in the late afternoon sun. I snapped off the longest as a rapier for a mock fight with an imaginary friend, and galloped across the snow-covered lawn in a one-man jousting match. Before I went in for tea the other icicles met their fate, as a unicorn's horn, a fencer's épée and lastly a shimmering javelin.

I remember a winter in Paris when the fountains froze. One close to my tiny attic room near the Sorbonne had set into a vast, sparkling ice sculpture that stopped me in my tracks on the treacherous walk to cooking school. How I would have loved to be in London for the frost fairs on the River Thames.

Frost fairs were held on the river on several occasions – the Thames froze over twenty-six times between 1408 and 1814. In 1536 King Henry VIII travelled along the river from London to Greenwich by sleigh. Queen Elizabeth I practised shooting on the ice in the winter of 1564, and carnivals were held on the frozen river. The first recorded frost fair was in 1608 but it was the last one, held in 1814, that saw an elephant led across the frozen river near Blackfriars Bridge, and stalls, shops and funfairs set up on the ice. There was bull-baiting and horse-racing, carousels and puppet shows, skating and football matches. The fair held in the winter of 1683–4 saw the Thames frozen over for two months, complete with a shopping street built on the eleven inches of ice.

The cold winters were far from one big carnival. The ice on the river thawed unexpectedly on several occasions and many drowned. In January 1789 the melting ice dragged a riverside public house into the water, crushing five people. The winters were unimaginably cold, animals and birds died, plants and trees froze solid, people choked on the smoke trapped by the cold air and the homeless froze to death.

There is little likelihood of the Thames ever freezing again. The river was shallower then and flowed more slowly, the winters were considerably colder and any idea of global warming inconceivable. Yet the notion of a vast frozen river on which one could skate, roast a whole pig and travel downstream on a sleigh is still something I dream of seeing. Just as I dream of climbing through the back of my wardrobe into a snow-covered wood.

No sign of snow yet, but I need something warming today. A dark braise of a favourite cut of beef.

Braised brisket with porcini and onion gravy

You'll need a spoon. The broth surrounding the beef has been in the oven for four hours, along with a handful of caramelised shallots, black peppercorns, thyme sprigs and bay leaves. I could have used beef stock, but preferred to make a broth out of dried mushrooms. A dark-coloured, bosky liquor in which to coax a cheap cut of meat towards tenderness. The brisket was bargain enough, as you would expect from a cut situated at the front of the belly, a piece of meat that works hard throughout the animal's life. I asked the butcher to leave the fat on my brisket in place, so that it would soften to a quivering mass and slowly enrich the gravy during its long sojourn in the oven.

I cut the meat into thick, wobbly slices and laid them in wide, shallow dishes, the sort you might use for pasta, then spooned the shiny, mahogany-coloured broth round the meat. There was a temptation to add soft, pale dollops of creamed parsnips or mashed butter beans, but instead I voted for swede, mashing it to a cream with a ridiculous quantity of butter and black pepper. Ideally, there would have been a thick fog outside, or better still a howling storm crashing at the windows. But you can't have everything.

What we did have was enough silky brown meat for the next day, which I pulled into jagged strips and tossed with vinegar-crisped cabbage, finely shredded kale (yes, that again) and some sprouted radish seeds from the wholefood shop. I dressed it with a cool dill and mustard-seed-flecked cream dressing. If you want a quick fix, eat an expensive cut of meat, but if you crave homely warmth and bonhomie, the feeling that all is well with our world (especially when it isn't), it's the cheap, fat-rich cuts you should head for. The ones that enrich their cooking liquor to a point where you can feel the goodness seeping through to your soul with every mouthful. You're going to need that spoon.

The dried porcini will add about three quid to the cost of this dish, but you get a lot of flavour for your money.

Serves 6-8
dried porcini – 25g
beef brisket, rolled and tied – 1.5kg
banana shallots – 6
small carrots – 350g
black peppercorns – 12
bay leaves – 4
thyme sprigs – 6
mashed swede, to serve (see page 95)

Put the kettle on. Set the oven at 230°C/Gas 9. Put the dried porcini into a heatproof bowl, then pour boiling water over them, cover with a plate and leave to soak for twenty-five minutes. This will give you a deeply flavourful broth.

Place the rolled and tied brisket in a large casserole, then put it into the oven and roast for twenty-five minutes. Peel and trim the shallots and halve them lengthways. Scrub the carrots and halve them lengthways. Add them both to the casserole together with the porcini and their broth, the peppercorns, bay leaves and thyme, then cover with a lid. Lower the heat to 160°C/Gas 3 and bake for four hours.

Remove the brisket from its broth and leave to rest for ten minutes. Put the casserole over a high heat, bring the contents to the boil, and leave until reduced by about one-third. Slice the brisket into thick pieces, dividing it between deep plates, then spoon over the broth and vegetables.

And mashed swede to serve

Peel a large swede and cut it into large chunks, then pile them into a steamer basket or colander and cook over a pan of boiling water for twenty minutes, until soft. Tip into a bowl and crush thoroughly with a potato masher. Add a thick slice of butter (about 30g) and lots of quite coarsely ground black pepper. Beat firmly with a wooden spoon until fluffy. Serve in generous mounds, in the broth that surrounds the beef.

Pork and panforte

Just as I might eat a wedge of butter-soft panettone with shudderingly bitter coffee on a winter's morning, or break a marzipan-scented slice of stollen after an afternoon spent sweeping up leaves in the garden, I too get a fancy for a tiny triangle of chewy panforte. Looking forward to the gentle slap of sweet spice as much as I do that of Lebkuchen or gingerbread, I am more than a little ashamed that I had yet to warm to its honeyed tone when I visited its rust-red hometown, Siena. With hindsight, I probably thought the slim, white packages piled high in every shop were soap.

Night-time, after dinner, is when this treat comes out in our house. My version of my parents' habit of bringing out a box of After Eight mints. Except the mints got more takers. The chewy disc of nuts and dried figs, honey and spice is best consumed in a room glowing with candlelight and served in a tiny wedge at the foot of a small glass of equally glowing vin santo. To eat it straight from its white paper wrapper in daylight is to indulge only in its curiously chewable compounded figs and nuts. You need a certain sense of occasion to understand its charm, which is probably why it only really comes out at Christmas. Much the same could be said of advocaat.

Panforte has been made in Siena for centuries. Think of it as compressed fruit cake. And made to a secret recipe. I can't imagine anything like as much gets eaten as is brought back in suitcases. Tradition has it that panforte must be made of seventeen ingredients, one for each of the small districts, the contrade, of Siena. Panforte means strong bread, referring to the spices in the recipe. Dating from the early thirteenth century, it once contained so much pepper it was known as 'panpepato'. References to the Crusaders carrying it with them for sustenance are probably true, as it is a compact way of carrying high-energy, imperishable survival food. Like a medieval Kendal mint cake.

Between its compacted icing sugar crust or sheets of snowy rice paper are sugar, honey, hazelnuts, almonds, candied peel, cinnamon, nutmeg, ginger, cardamom, salt, cocoa powder, cloves, dried figs, raisins, flour and occasionally walnuts. Recipes abound – it is a doddle to make despite the everlasting shopping list – and many of them are worth making, but none seem to have quite the same chewy, seed- and nut-laden texture as that commercially made in Siena. There is also something ancient about this shallow, fudge-coloured sweetmeat. As if you are chewing a medieval manuscript.

After all the sweetness, something for dinner that has brightness and spirit, a welcome antidote.

Pork, miso and pickled pears

Strips of pork belly, sold without the bone, will work nicely here. I look for those with plenty of fat to meat. I use white miso for the dressing. Use dark miso if that is what you have, but expect the flavour to be saltier and more intense.

Serves 4
pork belly strips, without bones – 700g
liquid honey – 2 tablespoons
white miso paste – 3 tablespoons
grain mustard – 2 tablespoons
salad leaves – a handful

For the pears:
white wine vinegar – 4 tablespoons
black peppercorns – 8
caster sugar – 1 tablespoon
salt – 1 teaspoon
pears – 2

Put the vinegar, black peppercorns, caster sugar and salt into a saucepan with 100ml of water and bring to the boil. Peel the pears, halve them, then cut out the cores with a teaspoon. Lower the pears into the pickling liquid, lower the heat and leave the pears to cook until tender to the point of a knife. Remove from the heat, cover with a lid and leave to rest. Set the oven at 200°C/Gas 6.

Place the strips of pork on a shallow grill pan, season with salt and black pepper, and roast for thirty minutes, until golden and sizzling. In a large shallow pan, warm the honey, white miso paste and mustard until you have a thick paste.

Tear the pork into short, finger-width strips, then toss with the hot dressing. Return the dressed meat to the oven for seven to ten minutes, until the surface is sizzling and starting to caramelise. Wash and dry the salad leaves and place them on a serving plate, then pile the pieces of hot pork on top. Place half a pickled pear on each plate.

Toasted mincemeat sandwich

I am not going to make my own panforte. That would feel a bit like doing something just to prove you can. The stuff in the shops, straight from Siena, is what the Italians eat. And if it's good enough for them...

Instead, James has an idea to make a mincemeat-stuffed panettone, the soft cake sliced and stuffed with mincemeat, then toasted. We eat it, slightly too hot for everyone's lips, with vanilla ice cream. A jug of old-fashioned double cream would no doubt have hit the spot too.

mincemeat – 10 heaped tablespoons
panettone – 2 thick slices, 2cm thick, from an 18cm diameter cake
butter – 40g
icing sugar – 2 tablespoons

Warm the mincemeat in a small saucepan, stirring regularly. Place a slice of panettone on the work surface. Cover it with the mincemeat, then place the second piece on top and press gently to make a large, round sandwich.

Melt the butter in a small, non-stick frying pan. Place the sandwich in the pan and let it cook over a low heat for two minutes, checking the underside is turning gold by lifting it occasionally with a palette knife. As soon as it smells warm and buttery and the underside is golden and toasted, place a plate over the pan, turn the pan and plate over, firmly and confidently, let the sandwich turn out on to the plate, then slide it back into the pan to cook the underside.

Lift out, dust with icing sugar and cut, cake-like, into slices.

Surf and turf

It is a rare day when I don't make something to eat. If I am going out to dinner then I will make lunch, because I can't get all the way through to eight in the evening. My fishmonger has pieces of hot-smoked salmon cut from the thick end of the fillet. I bake them with new potatoes and dill.

While the oven is on, I test a quick recipe that I feel might be fun. A sort of toad in the hole for two, with chubby cocktail sausages and a handful of sour red cranberries from the freezer to offer a sharp contrast. A keeper.

Hot-smoked salmon, potatoes and dill

Serves 2
new potatoes – 300g
dill fronds – 2 heaped tablespoons
white wine vinegar – 2 tablespoons
olive oil – 4 tablespoons
hot-smoked salmon – 2 × 200g pieces

Set the oven at 200°C/Gas 6. Bring a deep pan of water to the boil, and salt it generously. Wash the new potatoes, cut in half lengthways, then cook them in the boiling water for fifteen minutes, until they are tender. Drain them.

Finely chop the dill fronds and put them into a small mixing bowl. Stir in the white wine vinegar, olive oil and a little salt and pepper. Put the potatoes in a roasting tin or baking dish, then add the dill dressing and toss them together. Bake in the preheated oven for fifteen minutes, until they turn pale gold. Place the hot-smoked salmon on top of the potatoes, spoon some of the dressing from the dish over the fish, then return to the oven for ten minutes and serve.

A new toad-in-the-hole

A nod, perhaps, to Thanksgiving. My butcher always uses the same herb-flecked recipe for his cocktail sausages as he does for his breakfast bangers. This isn't always the case when shopping in supermarkets, and the smaller the sausage the less likely it is to be of interest. If you can't find a decent one, use larger breakfast sausages cut into short lengths.

Serves 2
eggs – 2
full-fat milk – 300ml
plain flour – 125g
thyme – 5 sprigs
cocktail chipolatas – 350g
a little oil or bacon fat
marmalade – 2 tablespoons
cranberries – 100g
groundnut oil or dripping – 3 tablespoons

Make a batter by beating together the eggs and milk. Beat in a little salt and the flour. Don't worry about any small lumps. Pull the leaves from the thyme and stir them into the batter, then leave to rest for twenty minutes. Set the oven at 220°C/Gas 7.

Evenly brown the cocktail chipolatas in a little oil or bacon fat. When they are done, add the marmalade and the cranberries to the pan and toss the sausages in it to coat them evenly. Pour the fat, together with the groundnut oil or dripping, into a 22cm round metal dish or similar baking tin, add the marmalade-coated sausages and place in the oven to get hot.

When the oil and sausages are really hot, add the batter and return to the oven immediately. Bake for twelve minutes, until the batter is golden and puffed around the edges. Serve immediately.

Planting bulbs and a lamb boulangère

I have spent winters deep in the Worcestershire countryside, on the Cornish coast, the Yorkshire moors and in the Black Country. I have trudged through the snow in the Italian Alps, the Norwegian forests and the Icelandic lava fields. I have run from saunas to freezing ice pools in Finland and rolled in the snow after many a steaming hillside onsen in Japan. And yet it is still winter in the city that I find most entrancing.

London in the snow is breathtaking, especially if you can catch it before others wake. Ghostly footprints there will always be – a fox, a postman or a clubber returning home – but if you can rise before six after snow has fallen during the night you will see the city differently. A scene straight from Dickens. Amsterdam, Vienna, Kyoto and Bergen are enchanting blanketed by snow, as if made for deepest winter, but it is London that becomes a different city after a fall of snow.

People say that you only appreciate the cold if you are in the warm. They insist a snowy garden is at its best when viewed from the window of a toasty kitchen. I must disagree. Waking up on an icy morning, I can't wait to be outside. Showered, cup of coffee in hand, I am out of the kitchen door before a single word is written. My boots crunching on frosty gravel, the piercing air stinging my sinuses, the icy chill brings with it a sudden shot of energy.

As a teenager I had more than enough time to walk in the cold. The school bus couldn't make it up the hill on snowy mornings, and there was no choice but to walk an hour either way. I revelled in it, even then. Each branch, every snowdrift, each frozen puddle held a secret. Mittens were made to be frozen stiff. Wellingtons were invented to be filled with snow. Serene fields had to be stamped through. Frozen water, a pond, a stream, the water in a bucket all had to be shattered. (I was furious that the ice on the garden pond had to be thawed slowly, using hot kettles from the Aga, so as not to shock my Dad's precious goldfish.)

Winter gardens hold a spell all of their own. Roses frozen in bud, beads of glassy dew on the leaves of the hellebores, orange berries peeping from beneath a layer of sugar-snow. Today is the first morning cold enough to demand a sheepskin. There is plenty of work in the garden, medlar and chestnut leaves to sweep; a wayward rose bush to tame with the secateurs, bulbs to plant. It feels late to be planting tulips but I know others who leave it later. This year I plant Cairo, a soft orange-scarlet, like a tulip painted by Ambrosius Bosschaert, a tulip whose scent in early spring carries the sweetness of wallflowers. I plant them a good eight inches deep into the old green copper on the terrace. An idea borrowed from Sissinghurst. I dust the bulbs with chilli powder and cover them with netting in an attempt to thwart the light-fingered squirrels.

The time is right for a cheap, cold-weather potato supper.

Lamb belly boulangère

You could, of course, make this dish with boneless meat, but you would be missing the point. The slow pre-cooking of the lamb, with onions and stock, allows the bones to enrich the cooking liquor while at the same time adding succulence to the meat. This is one of my favourite ever recipes.

Serves 4–6
lamb breast, bone in – 1.6kg
a little oil
banana shallots – 4
rosemary sprigs – 6
thyme sprigs – 12
chicken stock – 1.5 litres
potatoes – 1kg

Set the oven at 180°C/Gas 4. In a very large pot, sizzle the lamb in a little oil over a moderate to high heat, until the surface is golden. Turn over and brown the other side, then remove from the pan.

Peel the shallots, cut into 1cm thick slices, then let them cook for ten minutes in the lamb pot, adding a little more oil if necessary, until they are light gold and translucent.

Return the lamb to the pan, add the rosemary and thyme, a seasoning of black pepper and the stock, then bring to the boil. Cover the pan with a lid and place in the oven, leaving it to bake for ninety minutes, until the lamb is tender.

Scrub the potatoes and cut into 5mm slices. Remove the pot from the oven, then take out the lamb and place on a chopping board. Tweak the bones from the meat – they should slide out effortlessly – then cut the meat and fat into pieces. Mix the meat with the shallots from the cooking liquor. Turn the oven heat up to 200°C/Gas 6.

Place a layer of potatoes on the bottom of a large baking dish, then spread a layer of the lamb and shallots over them, followed by a layer of potatoes. Continue layering potatoes and meat, seasoning with salt and pepper as you go, and finishing with a layer of potatoes.

Pour the stock over the potatoes, letting it run down through the layers. Bake for an hour to seventy-five minutes, until the potatoes are golden and totally tender.

A shining star. A pudding aflame

The last Sunday before Advent, the day on which we traditionally make the Christmas pudding, is known as Stir-up Sunday. The name sounds older, almost medieval, but like much of this festive lark, it is down to Queen Victoria and Prince Albert.

Of all the food we eat during the Feast of Christmas, none is quite so laden with religious significance as the Pudding. Stir-up Sunday, despite its kitchen connotations, takes it name from the collect, the general prayer, read on this day in Christian churches. The collect starts: 'Stir up, we beseech thee O Lord, the wills of thy faithful people.'

This prayer coincides neatly with the month or so the pudding needs in order to mature. I wonder how many times, as the assembled congregation kneels in prayer and the collect is read, someone has whispered, 'Oh God, the Pudding,' and then let their mind wander to the state of their larder. One probably shouldn't be thinking, 'Have I got enough currants?' at that particular moment.

So the day is usually either the third or fourth Sunday in November. Part of the movable feast that is the Christian calendar. I especially like the next, less well-known, line of the prayer: '. . . that they, plenteously bringing forth the fruit of good works, may of thee be plenteously rewarded; through Jesus Christ our Lord. Amen.' Words that clearly point us in the direction of pudding.

Like any 'ancient' ritual, Stir-up Sunday has its rules, the most important being that the whole family, or as many of them as possible, should be present at the kitchen table while the eggs, flour and fruit are mixed. The youngest member present is the first to wield the wooden spoon, the eldest giving the mixture its final stir. Oh, and it should be stirred east to west, celebrating the journey taken by the Three Wise Men to see the baby Jesus.

While working on this book, I have been amazed and delighted by how many keep up the tradition of Stir-up Sunday. As Yuletide days lose their meaning this is one that seems to be growing in popularity.

I feel a little disclosure necessary here. The last Sunday before Advent is not the only day I have been known to make my Christmas pudding. Publishers' copy dates and television filming schedules being what they are, I have occasionally been required to stir my pudding in the middle of summer. Usually on or around the hottest day of the year. It is part of the deal of doing what I do. Which is why I have also found myself denuding perfectly healthy trees of their leaves for a television show, and tying red berries to holly sprigs with invisible fishing wire under the summer sun. But let us not let too much daylight in on magic.

Folklore and superstition

Deliciously, pudding folklore and legend abound. How about this: the ingredients should number thirteen in total, to represent Jesus and his twelve disciples. The spices, once precious and expensive, are there as reminders of the myrrh and frankincense brought by the Wise Men to the Nativity. Charms or tokens, also known as favours, are tucked into the mixture before it is cooked. The charm was originally a single bean. (My guess is that so many people swallowed it unknowingly that something shiny and noticeable was needed to take its place.) But now a sixpence, a threepenny bit, a ring or a thimble is hidden at the heart of the pudding instead.

We all want to be the finder of the pudding charm, but we should be careful what we wish for. The finder of the thimble will remain single all year (not necessarily a bad thing). The holder of the coin will have good fortune all year. (Better still.) Finding a gold ring is a promise of marriage or wealth. (Cake and eat it.) The coin, by the way, should really be a silver sixpence, which went out of production in 1947. For most us any old sixpence will do.

The sprig of holly with which most of us decorate the finished pud is a reminder of the Crown of Thorns. We set the pudding alight, not just because it adds a faint taste of brandy, but because it takes us back to pagan times, though I have (sadly) yet to meet anyone who dances around the flames.

Folklore and religion do seem to have held their grip on this particular part of the feast, though I find my heart sinking at the pop-up on Google that says, 'People also looked for: "How long does it take to cook Christmas pudding in the microwave?"'

Probably the finest pudding in the world

As the vast, domed pudding is spooned into bowls and the brandy butter is passed around, the cry of 'Oh, none for me, thank you' must be one of the most depressing sounds of the season.

She carries with her a certain majesty. All sugar and spice and glistening with jewels, she is often more than a little tipsy, and is brought into the dining room aflame, sporting a sprig of holly like an evergreen fascinator. It is no overstatement to say that I adore this pudding above all others. It is the most sound of recipes, heavy with tradition. Unshakable. Its long list of ingredients is generally unsullied by the 'creative' cook, aka the interference of fools. The romance of dried fruits and spices once traded by the Venetians; the proud, steaming pudding and its sprig of red-berried, glossy leaves will forever be in my thoughts. I would be a happy man indeed should it turn out to be the last thing that passes my lips.

Of course, this is not only the Pudding of our Christmas lunch, but the finest winter pudding of all, and the only one I could eat every day of my life and never tire of. This is the one that beats steamed treacle sponge, Sussex pond or cabinet pudding. Better even than apple hat or jam roly-poly. Christmas pudding could knock spotted dick into a cocked hat.

The smell is beguiling as it cooks in its white muslin cloth. It is at once heart-warming and life-affirming. The steam carries notes of sugar, brandy and mixed spice with, to my nose at least, a hint of labrador that has come in from a walk in the rain. It is a smell by which you could set your clocks (it will most likely be either Stir-up Sunday or Christmas morning). I also associate the serving of this pudding with a feeling of being over-full, which might be the very essence of what we call a feast but is not a feeling I particularly like. Despite the worship, I am never entirely sure it is the right recipe at the right time. Maybe plum pudding should have a day of its own.

Above all, though, it is the jolliest of recipes, for bringing loved ones round the table, for seeking hidden treasure, for saying thank you. And for me it is also Boxing Day breakfast, but that is another matter.

A little history

Of course, it has not always been so. My beloved pud has its origins in a sort of fruit gruel. The original one having no form, no holly-crowned dome, no sixpence, no sugar. Our early pudding had neither charm nor charms.

The flaming, fruited globe has its feet in the boiled dinner of Roman times. A bubbling cauldron of beef, wine, herbs, onion and bread, sometimes seasoned with cinnamon and cloves, and for special occasions it seemed to have been sweetened with currants and spiked with wine. The eminent historian Maggie Black mentions the 'standing' pottage, where the fruited stew was thickened with egg yolks and breadcrumbs.

'Stewed Broth was, as near as possible, the direct forerunner of Christmas Pudding. We first hear of it in about 1420, as a standing pottage made with veal, mutton or chicken, thickened with bread, reddened with sanders (sandalwood) and rich with currants,' she writes in *History Today*, volume 31.

We have the Elizabethans to thank for the addition of prunes, and from where the plum pudding got its name. So popular were they that the name 'plum' became used to denote any dried fruit. Hence the introduction of the name 'plum pottage'.

It was not until the late 1600s that this fruit porridge, with or without the prunes, became associated with Christmas. It is only then that the bottle was uncorked and we see recipes for a Christmas broth with the addition of sack, the white Spanish wine that became the dry sherry we know today. As late as 1747 Hannah Glasse included a recipe for a beef-based 'Plumb-Porridge' (sic) for Christmas, recognisable from its ingredients and spiced with ginger and nutmeg.

Pottage turned to pudding rather later than we might imagine. According to *Elinor Fettiplace's Receipt Book*, published by biographer Hilary Spurling in 1986, ingredients including mace, eggs, bread and ox suet were boiled in a sheep's paunch. All of which makes me suspect it resembled a sweet, fruity haggis. Paul Levy points out that the porridge and the pudding 'served different purposes – one was a first course, the other a final course'. This makes me wonder if the simple beef consommé often suggested as a starter to our Christmas dinner (usually Lusty's, from a can) had its roots in those early beef porridges.

By the early 1800s we would recognise the recipe, producing a texture that was invariably solid rather than liquid, and being almost entirely sweet and eaten at the end, rather than the beginning, of the meal. The meat disappeared, spices lessened, and the sugar, now considerably cheaper, increased.

At this point our pud was not exclusive to this time of year, being made to celebrate anything from a birthday to the harvest festival. Eliza Acton, cook, poet and author of *Modern Cooking for Private Families*, and on whose recipe my own is loosely based, first referred to the recipe as 'plum' pudding in 1845. The Pudding feels much older.

1843 was the year the fruit-packed dome came centre stage, when Charles Dickens described it in *A Christmas Carol*. And in 1861 the redoubtable, prolific Isabella Beeton gave her recipe for 'A Christmas Plum Pudding' and it became a favourite of Queen Victoria.

The recipe

The bulk of the fruit is in the form of currants, allowing the mass to stick together more easily than if the fruits were larger. Currants are not, as I imagined when I was younger, dried blackcurrants. The word comes from Black Corinth, a type of small, dark-skinned grape. Originally shipped from Greece to Venice, they first appeared in Britain in the 1400s, where the sun-dried grapes were sold as Reysyns de Corauntz, Corinth being the Greek port from where most of them were shipped. Our dear little Eccles cake clearly has more exoticism to it than its name implies. Other fruits include sultanas and raisins, chopped candied peel, grated apples and orange zest and juice.

The fruits are held together as a sticky mass by eggs, breadcrumbs and flour, rather than suspended in the crumb as they are in a cake. The sugar is brown, usually a light or dark muscovado, and there is often a teaspoon or so of mixed spice and a tot of brandy.

Pushed annually to come up with variations, cookery writers and chefs endlessly tweak the recipe. With a doff of the hat to the old name of figgy pudding, my own recipe contains dried figs. Mary Berry introduces apricots to the recipe, giving a welcome touch of sharpness. Nigella Lawson's gorgeous recipe sees her soaking her fruits in Pedro Ximénez, 'the sweet, dark, sticky sherry that has a hint of liquorice, fig and treacle about it'. Jamie Oliver celebrates his Nan's version with cranberries, pecans and vin santo.

The lily is occasionally gilded. Bettys, the famous Harrogate tearooms, includes orange and chocolate; Bailey's adds glacé cherries and a healthy splash of their Irish Cream Liqueur. (I prefer mine in a glass with lots of ice.) Heston Blumenthal's inspired, fought-over version for Waitrose supermarkets includes a hidden candied clementine, an idea I would happily go along with were it not for the fact it robs me of a bit of my favourite pudding.

The delightful surprise for first-time cooks is how easy the recipe is to make. Ingredients assembled, it is simply a case of stirring them together, piling the mixture into a pudding basin and steaming it.

A few tips for the perfect pudding

· Check you have all the ingredients to hand. Obvious, I know, but there are so many you could easily forget to spot you are out of, say, mixed spice.
· Soak the vine fruits overnight. Unnecessary now that dried fruit is less hard than it used to be, but I believe a little snooze in brandy and fruit juice makes for a juicier result.
· Make a wish. Get the family, or as many as you can get together on a rainy afternoon in November, to stir the pudding and make a wish as they do so.

- Lightly butter the inside of the pudding bowl first – it will prevent the contents sticking. You may like to insert a small disc of baking parchment at the bottom of the bowl to further aid its easy removal.
- Time to sleep. Making the pudding a few weeks in advance will produce a better flavour, one that has had time to mellow and mature. This is not only something else ticked off your to-do list, but it means you can put the radio on, enjoy the stir-up of ingredients and the resulting fugged-up windows, rather than risk your pudding becoming yet another last-minute chore.
- Filling the bowl. Take the mixture almost to the top of the bowl, smoothing it level. It won't rise very much, but you should leave a couple of centimetres spare so it can breathe and swell.
- A standard 2–3 egg, 450–500g of fruit recipe (that's most of them) will feed eight and need a 1.5-litre bowl.
- The difference in cooking time between classic recipes varies enormously. I have seen everything from two and a half to eight hours for a 1.5-litre pudding. I remain unconvinced that any good will come from boiling your pudding for almost half a day. My timings, tested over and over, produce a very good result that will keep for months.
- Secure the lid. Perhaps the most crucial detail of all. Traditional recipes will suggest swaddling the pudding basin in sheets of greaseproof paper, balls of string and a layer of new muslin tied with a bow to aid lifting the pudding from the simmering water. I see no reason to depart from this tradition, but it must be said that the somewhat clinical alternative of a plastic bowl with a clip-on lid works a treat, ensuring the contents stay impenetrable to the water. The new way works all too well, and I take my hat off to the inventor, but it lacks the essential smell of warm linen and spice and the majesty of lifting the pudding from its water by its plump knot of steaming muslin.
- Check the water level. Constantly. I suggest every thirty minutes. If the pan boils dry, not only will the contents burn but you'll crack the bowl to boot.

My pudding

Light in colour – think honey rather than boot polish – and with the seedy crunch of dried figs, my little pudding first appeared in the *Kitchen Diaries* and has been the subject of many a delighted exchange. It was given top marks by the *Telegraph* newspaper (and it was up against the best of our living cookery writers), which I mention because I would imagine *Telegraph* readers take such matters more seriously than most. The recipe makes two, one for this year and one to put away on the top shelf for a birthday, Easter or even the following year.

Each pudding serves 8
sultanas – 350g
raisins or currants – 350g
dried figs – 150g, chopped
candied peel – 125g, chopped
dried apricots – 100g, chopped
dark glacé cherries – 75g, halved
brandy – 150ml, plus some for flaming
apples or, better still, quinces – 2, grated
the juice and zest of 2 oranges
eggs – 6
shredded suet – 250g
dark muscovado sugar – 350g
fresh breadcrumbs – 250g
self-raising flour – 175g
mixed spice – 1 teaspoon

You will need two 1.5-litre plastic pudding basins and lids, buttered, two old sixpences or two-pound coins, scrupulously scrubbed, two circles of greaseproof paper, buttered, large enough to cover the top of each pudding, with a single pleat folded down the centre of each.

Soak the sultanas, raisins or currants, figs, candied peel, apricots and cherries in the brandy overnight. The liquid won't cover the fruit but no matter – just give it a good stir now and again.

Mix the grated apples or quinces, orange juice and zest, beaten eggs, suet, sugar, crumbs and flour in a very large mixing bowl, then stir in the soaked fruit and the spice. Divide the mixture between the buttered pudding basins, tucking the coins in as you go. Cover with the greaseproof paper, folded with a pleat in the centre. Pop the lids on and steam in a large saucepan for three hours. Check the water level around the puddings every half hour or so – it should come halfway up the basins – topping up with boiling water from the kettle when necessary. Allow the puddings to cool, then remove the greaseproof paper, cover tightly with clingfilm and the plastic lids, and store in a cool, dry place until Christmas.

To reheat: steam the puddings for a further three hours. Turn out and flame with brandy.

A splendid new recipe, dark with sweet wine and liquorice notes

The lighter pudding, with its golden crumb and sweet figs, has been well received. I am happy, grateful even, that it has become so many people's go-to recipe. A recipe brought out year upon year for a family feast is more than any cookery writer could dare to ask. Yet I have a fancy to make a deeper-flavoured version, something with notes of black treacle or liquorice, sweet with notes of date and prunes. A recipe a little nearer the plum puddings of yore. Dark chocolate to the other's milk.

Earlier in the year there was a brief trial of a pudding with stout, yet even with the caramel sweetness of raisins and figs on board, it had a bitter backnote that didn't seem family-friendly. I was rather glad I only made a small one. Today I try it with a bottle of sweet sherry, a walnut-brown oloroso that has stood at the back of the fridge for months. The reason I have it now lost in time. James and I often have a glass of very cold fino or manzanilla after a day spent cooking, but the sweet stuff just sits there, like an aged aunt in a rocking chair.

The date syrup, dark with fruit and butterscotch notes, is available from large supermarkets and wholefood stores.

It turns out that sweet sherry is a resplendent addition to the recipe, gentle and rich, and well suited to the prunes and raisins. I do think soaking the fruit overnight is worth the trouble. Hot from the boiling water there is much to commend this pudding, and yes, it is as dark as I'd hoped, nicely risen, deeply, intoxicatingly fruity. Its caramel intensity, from the mixture of sherry and date molasses, should, I feel, be balanced with a simple jug of cream rather than brandy butter.

A dark, sweet and delectable 'plum' pudding

Large pudding serves 8–10
Smaller pudding serves 6–8
raisins – 350g
currants – 350g
dried figs – 150g, chopped
candied peel – 125g, chopped
soft-dried prunes – 100g, chopped
dark glacé cherries – 75g, halved
sweet sherry – 150ml
finely grated zest and juice of 2 oranges
date molasses – 5 tablespoons
apples – 2, grated
eggs – 6
butter – 125g, melted
dark muscovado sugar – 350g
brown breadcrumbs – 200g
ground cinnamon – 1 teaspoon
ground cloves – $\frac{1}{4}$ teaspoon
ground ginger – $\frac{1}{2}$ teaspoon
self-raising flour – 175g
brandy for flaming (later)

This recipe makes two puddings. One large pudding for Christmas and a second, smaller one for Easter, a birthday or what have you. You will need two buttered pudding basins, either plastic with a snap-on lid, or heatproof china; one that will hold 1.5 litres and another, smaller one that holds 1 litre. Also some baking parchment or greaseproof paper, muslin and string. Have ready a couple of good luck coins or charms, sterilised with boiling water. (Some cooks wrap them in foil too.)

In a large bowl, soak the raisins, currants, figs, candied peel, prunes and cherries in the sherry, orange zest and juice and the date molasses overnight. Turn the fruit over in the sherry every few hours.

Mix the grated apples, beaten eggs, melted butter, sugar and crumbs in a very large mixing bowl, then stir in the soaked fruit. Mix the cinnamon, ground cloves and ginger into the flour, then stir into the fruit, mixing thoroughly.

Divide the mixture between the buttered pudding basins. Push your sterilised and foil-wrapped coins or charms in as you go. Cover with the greaseproof paper, folded with a pleat in the centre. Pop the lids on and steam for three and a half hours for the small pudding, four for the larger one. Check the water level every half hour – it should be halfway up the basin. Top up regularly with hot water from the kettle. Allow the puddings to cool, then remove the greaseproof paper, cover tightly with clingfilm and the plastic lids and store in a cool, dry place until Christmas.

To reheat: steam the puddings for a further three and a half hours. Turn out and flame with brandy.

See also:
December 25: Steaming the pudding
December 24: Brandy butter

21 NOVEMBER

Fairies and Flammkuchen

Nine in the morning, church bells ringing, feet scurrying over the frosty cobbles. I'm warm with toasted rye bread and cherry jam, with Bircher muesli and sweet apple pastries, and have set out looking for decent coffee. The Christmas markets open at ten. Markets with canopies of twinkling lights and rows of starlit trees, stalls of painted wooden toys, nougat and Flammkuchen and later, much later, mugs of Glühwein to warm hands and souls.

The first of the markets is the one to the east side of the Kölner Dom, or, as it bills itself, seven thousand square metres of festive fun. There is stollen, whole loaves rolled in powdered sugar and also in neat two-bite cubes wrapped in crinkly cellophane bags. At the top of the steps, in the shadow of the Dom's blackened spires, are plates of raclette, which you eat standing next to a stuffed reindeer.

It is neither the busiest market, nor I think the best, but it has the advantage of the gorgeous bells from the Dom. Bells that shake your soul. It is worth picking up one of the printed programmes of entertainments, so at least you know if you are in for the gospel singers or Irina Ehlenbeck and her Christmas Hits. If you are lucky there will be carols by the sweet voices of St Stephen's youth choir. If not, you will get the Acoustic Christmas rock.

There are one hundred and fifty stalls. Stuffed crêpes, grilled Bockwurst, cookie-cutters. You know the sort of thing. The latter artfully nailed on to birch bark and tempting for being a step above the usual stars and Santas. They are well made. There are glove puppets and Glögg stalls, merry-go-rounds and mustards, angel workshops and sticks of liquorice.

Even over the baked potatoes and grilling sausages, the overriding scent is that of pine trees and aniseed. Christmas at a sniff. The atmosphere is jolly and the hot punch flows. There are glowing bottles of Bratapfel-Likör (tastes like baked apples), striped candy canes, and red felt shoes that wouldn't

look out of place on a goblin. Come to think of it, nothing here would look out of place on a goblin. Though, for me, the market is worth visiting for its Christmas tree alone, which still manages to stand magnificent, even when dwarfed by the Dom, spreading its strings of lights over the entire market like a shimmering festive cobweb.

I would recommend time spent at any nearby Brauhaus. Sit at the scrubbed wooden tables. Drink the lovely little beers in tall, thin glasses. Eat platefuls of black pudding, apple sauce and mashed potato.

Next day, I move on to the Kölner Altstadt, which is entered through fairy-tale illuminated columns complete with lighted candles and a hidden gnome. Here are stall upon stall upon stall of what looks like the usual craft-fair stuff. Gifts that people buy without anyone particular in mind. You know, that striped scented candle will do for someone. Then I take a closer look. I'm wrong. Intricate, laser-cut wooden tree decorations, like pieces of lace, hand-painted wooden soldiers and train sets in traditional colours, locally made chocolate with marzipan filling... The illuminated, half-timbered houses are beyond twee, but clearly made with love.

I pause at a brush stall. I have a thing for brushes, and have them for every possible occasion. Brushes for cleaning pelmets (I don't have pelmets), brushes for venetian blinds (I don't have venetian blinds), brushes for cleaning flower pots, tall thin glasses and the old stone floors of the kitchen. There are brushes here that I have never seen before, and finding out their specific purpose will require a better grasp of German than I possess. It strikes me that the young guy selling them, tall, slim, upright and with a carefully groomed tuft of beard sprouting from his long chin, clearly has the look of one of his own brushes.

The centre of the market is where 'events' take place. I generally avoid such things like the plague, but in the spirit of festive goodwill I attend the opening, in the presence of the mayor, or at least someone looking very much like a mayor, carol singers and a jazz band. I don't like live jazz bands in markets. Wrong music, wrong place. Yet I rather enjoy myself. This is still my favourite of the Cologne markets. I later visit the others, and they are worth the trip, but a bit craft-led for me. Too much knitting and coloured glass vases. The connection with Christmas often seems arbitrary.

Weihnachtsmarkt Kölner Altstadt has a warmly festive atmosphere. The stallholders are patient with picky customers like myself, and there are more locals than tourists. Which is always a good thing. It keeps everyone on their toes. Too few locals, and anywhere will slide into selling tat to tourists. I stop for Flammkuchen, the wafer-thin sheets of dough, like a pizza without the tomato-cheese glop, topped with translucent onions and nuggets of bacon. The dough is stretched in front of you, and served hot from the oven. You stand at scrubbed wooden tables. There might be a queue in the evening. You also might want to share one with a friend. Portions in Germany come as a surprise.

If you wander down to the far end of the market you will find a boy band of blacksmiths, hammering out a tune on lucky horseshoes in front of a burning fire, and then a passageway, lined with stalls that are worth a linger. It is here you may find antique Christmas decorations. Silver-painted glass walnuts in frail paper boxes, glitter-dusted fir-cones, with rusty metal clasps, and mercury glass balls in foxed silver and faded pink. They are not cheap and the packaging is usually as old and fragile as the hand-painted baubles themselves. Something for your hand luggage.

I'm still hungry and push my way through the crowds. Mind your pockets, your wallet, your bag, say the stallholders. There is ice-skating, a wooden beer hall rammed to its mistletoed eaves, and a nostalgic cream-painted carousel. The food is plentiful. A catalogue of carbs. Bread stuffed with sausages. Fried potato fritters – Reibekuchen – with apple sauce. Cheese oozing on to hot baguettes. Blackberry or chocolate strudel. I am not a fan of Currywurst but, from the queues, I look like the only one. You don't get far in Germany without seeing a sausage.

Markt der Engel feels new, like Covent Garden for gnomes. Bustling and booze-fuelled, with neat stalls with pointed roofs, like gingerbread houses. It is here I find roasted organic chestnuts, much Glühwein, and Flammlachs – sides of salmon grilled over open flames. I will not miss the latter, a soft bread roll stuffed with lettuce and hot salmon from the fire, for which I must join the queue. Well, I say queue. It's rather casual as queues go. You may need your pointiest elbow.

No glass cases of exquisite antique decorations here, but there are wooden snowflakes to hang from the tree. Good leatherwork, sauerkraut and

Bockwurst piled on to paper plates, and a magic kingdom of gaudy baubles ('No photographs,' snaps the security dragon). There is a particularly sinister Nativity scene in a glass case. Best of all, there is Käsespätzle, southern Germany's gloriously stringy answer to macaroni cheese. The 'little sparrows' of pasta, served with the mother of all Emmental sauces and crisped onions. I gorge on my third carb-hit of the evening.

While I'm in Cologne, I tuck into the famous Himmel und Erde – Heaven and Earth. As soon as I'm home, I make my own, rather tweaked, version of this black pudding and apple dinner.

Black pudding, baked apples and celeriac and mustard mash

If black pudding isn't your thing, try fat, herby butcher's sausages instead, but cooked whole rather than in slices.

Serves 4
celeriac – 750g
a lemon
potatoes – 350g
bay leaves – 3
dessert apples, small – 4
butter – 60g, plus a few extra knobs
black pudding – 500g
groundnut oil
parsley – a small bunch
grain mustard – 1 tablespoon

Set the oven at 180°C/Gas 4. Peel the celeriac, discarding the whiskery roots at the base. Cut the flesh into large pieces, then put them into a saucepan and cover with water. (A squeeze of lemon juice will prevent the celeriac discolouring.)

Peel the potatoes, cut them into similar-sized pieces to the celeriac and add them to the saucepan. Bring to the boil, add the bay leaves and a decent pinch of salt, then lower the heat and leave to cook at a gentle boil for about twenty minutes, until tender.

Score the apples round the middle, cutting just under the skin, then put them into a roasting tin. Place a knob of butter on each, and bake for fifteen minutes. Put the black pudding into the roasting tin next to the apples, place a knob of butter or a trickle of oil over each, then return to the oven for a further fifteen minutes, until the black pudding is sizzling and the apples are fluffed up.

Meanwhile, chop the parsley. Drain the vegetables, then tip them into the bowl of a food mixer fitted with a beater attachment. Add the butter, then beat until soft, light and creamy. Fold in the parsley, the grain mustard and a seasoning of black pepper.

Put generous scoops of the celeriac and potato mash on warm plates, add a slice of black pudding and an apple, and serve.

Gold, frankincense and myrrh

Off to see the golden tomb of the Three Wise Men at the Cathedral of St Peter, better known as the Kölner Dom. My adoration of the Magi, you could say. The glistening sarcophagus, made of wood overlaid with gold, pearls and images of Mary and Jesus and the Crucifixion, shines from the sepulchral darkness of the cathedral's high altar. It is said to contain the remains of the Three Kings. If it doesn't, I have just made a journey for nothing.

The bones are interred here due to being presented to the Archbishop of Cologne by the Holy Roman Emperor Frederick Barbarossa in 1164. A gift that resulted in the building of the largest Gothic cathedral in Europe – a feat that took 632 years to complete. Which sounds rather like the building of London's Crossrail. The sarcophagus, gilded to a fault by medieval goldsmith Nicholas of Verdun, is as impressive as you might expect, though it can hardly be called a resting place, the poor things being kept awake by the constant flashes from the cameras of the never-ending pilgrimage of tourists. If I am honest, I am as much here to pay my respects to Gerhard Richter's stained-glass window, though the floors, an unexpected treasure, get my attention too.

Of course, Cologne Cathedral is not the only place claiming to be the resting place of the Three Kings, but I'll go along with it as I'm here. As tombs go, this one is rather impressive, as is the cathedral, whose time-blackened stone has so far escaped the knee-jerk cleaning suffered by almost every stone building in Europe. An act of desecration that ensures even the most scarred of ruins is indistinguishable from a shopping centre in Bath.

A note for campanophiles: the bells of the Kölner Dom are as delightful as any I have ever heard, ringing copiously the entire time I am in the city and, somewhat whimsically, playing the nursery rhyme 'Oranges and Lemons, Say the Bells of St Clements' as I eat my breakfast. Sadly there is no marmalade today, but apricot jam on rye bread the colour of potting compost will do.

I have never quite got over not being chosen to play one of the Three Kings in the school Nativity play. I was a shepherd instead. I had to hold a broom, upside down, instead of a crook. I suppose I should be grateful I wasn't one of the sheep. Or Mary.

The Three Kings are also known collectively as the Three Wise Men. I prefer to call them the Magi. The Three Kings sounds a bit like an acapella group or a pub in Clerkenwell. Actually, it is a pub in Clerkenwell. According to Christian tradition, the Magi, who travel from the East to offer gifts to the baby Jesus, are three in number. In Eastern Christianity, there are twelve. Their place in the Nativity is mentioned only in the Gospel of St Matthew and even then he doesn't insist on an exact number. The idea of three wise men seems to have stuck. Details are confused, and will no doubt remain so. Depending on which branch of Christianity you choose to believe, their names vary too, but we seem to have settled on Balthazar, Melchior and Caspar.

The Magi were not kings, but most likely astrologers. Who else would follow a star? They were certainly scholars. Melchior is believed to have been Persian, Caspar Indian, Balthazar Ethiopian. Details are collated from the New Testament, and from manuscripts found (much) later. 'Characters based on', then. Every branch of Christianity has them down as something else. Their names, their nationality, their occupations. You choose.

The Magi knelt in front of the baby Jesus, signalling respect. A single act that may be responsible for our habit of kneeling in church. Caspar, white-bearded, was the eldest, Melchior was middle-aged, and Balthazar is generally depicted as young and black. Arguments continue, somewhat pointlessly in my opinion, to this day.

The gifts of the Magi

They brought with them gifts for the infant. An act borne out each year in the long tradition of giving presents to loved ones at Christmas. I find it interesting that two of the three gifts were fragrant, which may explain the habit of giving perfumes and cologne. Or it could just be that, like books, they are easy to wrap.

Myrrh

Balthazar is said to have brought myrrh, a smokily fragrant resin, probably in the form of oil, used then as incense and for embalming. (Joseph of Arimathea used it when wrapping Jesus's body after the Crucifixion.)

Myrrh is a gum extracted from the sapwood of a thorny-barked tree, *Commiphora myrrha*, and is used today, as throughout history, in perfume-making and medicine. The tree is native to Yemen and Ethiopia, which adds to the theory that Balthazar was from that part of the world. In quantity myrrh is intoxicating, and was apparently given to Jesus, dissolved in wine, before the Crucifixion. You can buy myrrh in the form of essential oil, and take advantage of its reputed cleansing and healing properties by adding it to toothpaste, using it as a moisturiser or for easing a sore throat. This is not a suggestion. It still intoxicates. Some believe a few drops will 'lift your mood'.

Gold

Caspar brought gold. The ancient version of giving a book token. Always precious, always welcome. Silver, white and gold are the predominant colours in this house at Christmas. (Visitors will notice a distinct lack of red, which I find a bit loud.) Gold often turns up in the most extravagant exchange of gifts between lovers, but it can be present in the cheapest gift-wrappings and ribbon too. Taking our cue from Caspar, gold has always been part of the celebrations: it is the colour of the 'star in the East' that the wise men followed and is the signature colour of warmth and light, a nod to the darkening days. Most often it is represented in the little bag of foil-wrapped chocolate coins that appears in children's stockings on Christmas morning.

Frankincense

Melchior brought the gift of frankincense. The word, particularly if whispered, conjures a certain magic. Like myrrh, it is a resin, collected by making a cut in the bark and sapwood of the boswellia tree, in particular *Boswellia sacra*, then letting the resin bleed and harden. The hardened lumps are called, somewhat poetically, tears.

There are several grades of frankincense, based on age, colour, purity and aroma. Many believe the older the better. Eighty per cent of it comes from Somalia. It has been used in religious ceremonies for centuries, for anointing and for burning as incense. It is also an essential ingredient of many perfumes and essential oils, and is said to have healing properties. I have heard tales of people who eat a tiny lump of it daily. The brittle rocks of resin can be broken into small pieces and chewed to alleviate arthritis and to settle the stomach.

Sometimes referred to as olibanum, the rocks of dried resin have a soft amber colour dusted with white. Like a precious stone that has been caught in a light frost. I carry a tear of frankincense around with me in my pocket (a gift from Lyn Harris, the London perfumier). I carry it not as a lucky charm, but simply as something to occasionally roll between the palms of my hands, where it warms and gives off a faint scent of rosemary, pepper and, to me, the smell of a freshly snapped branch from a pine tree. The ghost of Christmas.

The cake

I have been looking forward to this day for weeks. The one where I get to make 'the Cake'. It is, and it must always be, a day when I have little else on my plate. Baking a fruit cake that will feed twenty people is not something to shoehorn in between fifteen other errands. I usually put on some calming music or listen to the gentle babble of the radio, and today is no different. (Mitsuko Uchida, Mozart piano concerto, because it will help me concentrate on the lengthy ingredient list.)

No steaming pudding or simmering preserve can get the kitchen to smell quite so welcoming as does a baking fruit cake. Everything I want my home to be is here, in the smell of that cake. As baking days go, this is as good as it gets.

There is magic in a Christmas cake. The deep snowdrifts of white icing. The sprig of pagan holly. The crunch of bread knife on crisp frosting, followed by the soft sigh as you slice through the almond marzipan and richly freckled fruit beneath. And what a cake! The butterscotch notes of the soft crumbs. The dense huddle of currants, sultanas and sticky cherries. And always, always the temptation to clean the last few crumbs from your plate with your finger.

When you offer a slice of Christmas cake, you are handing over a box of jewels: the dried fruits that first came here with the Venetian traders, soaked in brandy and spices from the Orient. An edible version of the gifts the Three Wise Men offered to the infant. Or, if you prefer, think of it just as a piece of fruit cake. Your call.

From Toast: the story of a boy's hunger

'However much she hated making the cake, we both loved the sound of the raw cake mixture falling into the tin. "Sssh, listen to the cake mixture," she would say, and the two of us would listen to the slow plop of the dollops of fruit and butter and sugar falling into the paper-lined tin. The kitchen would be warmer than usual, and my mother would have that I've-just-baked-a cake glow. "Oh, put the gram on, will you, dear? Put some carols on," she would say, as she put the cake in the top oven of the Aga.

'Cake holds a family together. I really believed it did. My father was a different man when there was a cake in the house. Warm. The sort of man I wanted to hug rather than shy away from. If he had a plate of cake in his hand I knew it would be all right to climb up onto his lap. There was something about the way my mother would put a cake on the table that made me feel all was well. Safe. Secure. Unshakeable.'

I feel much the same about cake to this day. And no more so than at Christmas.

A thin slice of history

There is little or no history attached to the Christmas cake. As rituals go, the one of eating a decorated fruit cake around Advent is recent. Its beginnings lost in the chaos of celebration rather than the annals of time. Records of a baked cake eaten around this time of year mostly concern Twelfth Night cake, with its buried trinkets and beans to bring good luck in the coming year. A ritual that has, sadly, I think, fallen out of favour in Britain.

The iced and fruit-studded recipe as we know it is similar to that of the steamed Christmas pudding, which is descended from a fruit-laden plum porridge. The cake gathered momentum in Victorian times – the Queen was apparently a fan – and became popular for its ability to stay in perfect condition throughout the feast. An offering of welcome to anyone who arrived at your door. Something you couldn't say of a Victoria sponge.

We can probably thank the puritanical Oliver Cromwell for the fact we have a Christmas cake at all. Miserable sod that he was, he decided the much-loved Twelfth Night cake, traditionally baked to celebrate the end of the Christmas feast and eaten on January 6, was altogether too decadent. So he banned it. The consumption of a celebratory cake simply moved to Christmas Day.

Fruit cake has been attached to celebrations – weddings, christenings, picnics – for centuries. The arrival of a dark, fruity cake invariably marks a special occasion. To this day I smuggle a piece on to long train journeys.

Taking the cake to pieces

The sugar content alone should catapult our traditional Yuletide bake into the category of class-A drugs. At the very least it should qualify as a legal high. One lump of icing and marzipan would keep most of us going all night.

Does anyone actually eat it? One might well wonder, given the evidence returned on the flowery plates at teatime, each one with its own little pile of snow-white cement, nutty paste or painstakingly excavated sultanas. (I do wish people wouldn't do that.) In other words, no one eats THE ENTIRE CAKE.

Most of this splendid pièce montée, the one without which the feast is considered incomplete, seems to be eaten in stages. The layers of cake, marzipan and icing are carefully torn apart and eaten separately, with some being abandoned altogether.

Each layer has its fans. Some of us will nibble the cake in splendid isolation, snapping off and discarding the artistic handiwork that crowns it. Others peel the almond paste from the top in disgust, leaving it covered with fingerprints on the side of the plate. Few, it seems, take a bite of all three layers at once, which is surely how we are supposed to appreciate this marvel of the baker's art. My Auntie Fanny used to suck a wedge of the rock-hard frosting, then put it back on her plate, like a discarded set of false teeth. Which, considering the trouble my mother went to each year, seemed rather insensitive.

So, not for the first time, I find I'm slightly unusual. One of the few who eats the cake as it is designed to be eaten. That is, all three layers in one multitextured, festive bite. The crisp icing, so roughly plastered it hurts the roof of your mouth, the fudge-like layer of almond paste beneath, with its smear of apricot jam, and the soft, mahogany-hued, fruit-flecked cake itself. In my book at least, this is the Holy Trinity.

The ingredients

Sugar

Soft brown sugar, the sort that feels damp to the touch, is traditional in recipes for Christmas cake, imparting a deep toffee-like warmth but with the ability to keep the cake moist through weeks of storage. (Run your fingers through white caster sugar and it feels dry. Do the same with soft brown sugar and it is often so moist you can press it together, like a piece of fudge, or a snowball.)

Butter

I often use salted butter, or add a tiny pinch to unsalted, bringing out the sweetness of the cake. It is useful to soften the block slightly (an hour or so out of the fridge should do) before beating with the sugar to a latte-coloured cream. The two will whip up more quickly and lightly if the butter isn't used hard, straight from the fridge. Not to mention that it will stay in the mixing bowl rather than flying about all over the place. The best results seem to come from using a heavy worktop food mixer fitted with a flat paddle beater.

Vine fruits

Raisins, sultanas and currants, the dried grapes that give body and sweetness to our cake, are the heart and soul of the recipe and are used in such quantity that a single slice contains more fruit than crumb. In traditional recipes it is the pudding that gets the lion's share of the currants. The cake, originally the plaything of those who could afford ovens and the staff to seed the vine fruits, gets the plumper, juicier sultanas and raisins.

Grapes for raisins are now bred to have thinner skins and no seeds, which neatly dispatches the chore of removing the gritty pips before we use them in the cake. I have a vague memory of the task, sitting in the kitchen by the Aga, opening each one with my thumbnail and extracting the seeds within. The job was tedious beyond words, enough to put you off making a fruit cake for life. Such fruits are still available in posh food shops, usually attached to their curling, dried vines like a bunch of grapes someone has put in a flower press. Bring them to the table after dinner, when the sweet wines come out. The mix of intense musky sweetness and the crunch of the pips is curiously pleasing.

Sultanas sound altogether more interesting, with a hint of the Ottoman empire to their name. Many are made from the Kishmish grape, grown in Iran and Palestine, rather than the less exotic-sounding Thompson Seedless from California. They are golden rather than purple or brown, and in most cases appear more juicy. The reason is that they are generally steeped in potassium carbonate and vegetable oil to speed the drying process, keeping the colour bright. Raisins are dried without the solution, thus the process is longer and the fruit therefore darker. Preferring a lighter cake, I usually use more sultanas than raisins.

You can buy raisins in shades of anything from prune to mahogany and gold, and recently I have spied a rather dashing variety the colour of Beaujolais.

Whatever their size and colour, the dried fruits are traditionally reconstituted overnight in brandy and orange juice.

Candied peel

Proper candied peel: freshly cut from a full piece of candied citron bought from an Italian deli. (It appears in November, often hanging in crackly cellophane bags from the ceiling.) Your own peel chopped from a whole sugar-crusted fruit is juicier and far more interesting than the sour gravel sold in tubs as 'candied peel'. The colours are entrancing too, in shades of orange, champagne and gold, like stained-glass windows encrusted with frost. Peel introduces a slight marmalade bitterness to the proceedings.

Glacé cherries

You probably couldn't eat a glacé cherry if you tried. If the sticky, almost slimy syrup in which they are preserved didn't put you off, then the fruit's ability to be sweeter than sugar would certainly make you think again. Yet hidden in the velvety crumb of a rich Dundee-style fruit cake, snuggled up with other

preserved fruits, the 'clown's nose' cherry plays its part rather well, offering a juicy respite from the relentless raisins and currants. There are two types, the dark, black-red undyed fruits, and the almost luminous scarlet variety that has been artificially coloured. There are also green ones, which are really quite hideous.

Nuts

Nuts add a welcome change of step to the texture of a cake. Most popular are Brazils and almonds, the latter having to be skinned and toasted before being stirred into the cake batter. They are best chopped by hand, the ready-chopped sort available in bags invariably tasting curiously stale.

Spices

Spices have long been associated with luxury and expense. Wars have been fought over them. Fortunes made and probably lost. The spices introduce a depth of flavour and a little mystery and magic. They are always used very finely ground. No one wants to find a lump of allspice in their mouth. The presence of cinnamon, nutmeg and mixed spice represents the gold, frankincense and myrrh the Magi brought to the infant child. To add them to a cake recipe, quite unnecessary in most people's eyes, is what separates Christmas cake from a traditional everyday fruit cake. To hand a guest a slice of decorated cake is to offer them a gift, something unusual, expensive to make, and something you have given time to.

The method

A recipe becomes our own by altering the ratio of fruits to batter, the inclusion of nuts and brandy, or not, and the addition of some form of decoration that makes it special to us and to our family. But the method by which the cake is made is virtually universal. The sugar and butter are beaten to a cream, the mixture is turned to a batter with beaten egg, then thickened with a little flour before we stir in the fruits, nuts and spices. The cake is baked at a low temperature for several hours.

My cake

Inside, the crumb is golden, the colour of a toasted almond. Lighter than the one my mother made, which was dark as black treacle. The fruit is not so much currants, as golden sultanas, dried apricots and dark seedy figs. Bright fruits, each with a little more acidity than the sweetness of raisins. There are hazelnuts too, toasted, halved, and proper candied peel, pale citron and darker orange. Mine is a knubbly cake, crunchy with nuts and fig seeds.

The recipe has been made countless times, not only by me but by readers and friends. Each year I am sent photographs of the cake fresh from the oven, something that sparks a sense of happiness and the relief that all cookery writers probably get when someone other than themselves has success with one of their recipes. The lighter cake is growing in popularity, as people steer clear of molasses, the thick black treacle that is actually the waste product of the sugar trade. In cookery lessons at school, it was the only time Miss Adams permitted us to lick the spoon. Black treacle being apparently full of iron.

The recipe was first published, like so many, in the *Observer*. Then, a year later, in the first *Kitchen Diaries*. The recipe is based on Mum's, which was to be found, hand-written in biro, on a piece of blue, lined Basildon Bond, and kept in the bowl of the old Kenwood food mixer.

Lining the tin

You really must line the tin. And thickly too. The tin gets very hot during the long time in the oven and the outside crust can burn. A layer of paper, or, as my mum insisted, two layers, will protect the cake mixture from the hot tin.

Using the base of the cake tin as a template, cut a disc of baking parchment to fit neatly into the base. Now cut a long, wide strip that will fit not only around the inside of the tin, but a good 9cm above it. (For a 20cm cake tin that will be 66cm, for a 24cm cake, 73.) Place it around the inside of the tin.

Making the cake

Soaking the fruit
The counsel of perfection states to soak the dried fruit overnight in brandy and fruit juice. To be honest, I don't bother, simply because dried fruits are not as dry as they once were, being generally more juicy and soft than in years gone by. If you would like to do that, then put the vine fruits into a large mixing bowl, pour over the brandy and the orange and lemon juice, then steep overnight. An occasional stir will ensure as many fruits as possible stay in contact with the liquid.

A family cake

This makes a 20cm cake
butter – 250g
light muscovado sugar – 125g
dark muscovado sugar – 125g
shelled hazelnuts – 100g
dried fruits – ready-to-eat prunes, apricots and figs,
  candied peel, glacé cherries, 650g in total
large eggs – 3
ground almonds – 65g
vine fruits – raisins, sultanas, currants,
  dried cranberries, 350g in total
brandy – 3 tablespoons, plus extra to feed the cake
finely grated zest and juice of an orange
finely grated zest of a lemon
baking powder – $\frac{1}{2}$ teaspoon
plain flour – 250g

A large cake

This makes a 24cm cake
butter – 350g
dark muscovado sugar – 350g
shelled hazelnuts – 150g
dried fruits – ready-to-eat prunes, apricots and figs,
    candied peel, glacé cherries, 1 kg in total
large eggs – 5
ground almonds – 100g
vine fruits – raisins, sultanas, currants,
    dried cranberries, 500g in total
brandy – 5 tablespoons, plus extra to feed the cake
finely grated zest and juice of an orange
finely grated zest and juice of a lemon
baking powder – $\frac{1}{2}$ teaspoon
plain flour – 350g

You will need a deep, 20 or 24cm-diameter round cake tin with a removable base, lined with lightly buttered baking parchment.

Set the oven at 160°C/Gas 3. Using a food mixer and a flat paddle beater attachment, beat the butter and sugars until light and fluffy. Don't forget to push the mixture down the sides of the bowl from time to time with a rubber spatula. Toast the hazelnuts in a dry pan until light brown, then cut each one in half.

While the butter and sugars are beating to a cappuccino-coloured fluff, cut the dried fruits into small pieces, removing the hard stalks from the figs. Break the eggs into a small bowl, beat lightly with a fork, then add a little at a time to the butter mixture, beating continuously. (If it curdles, add a little flour.)

Slowly mix in the ground almonds, toasted hazelnuts and all the dried and vine fruits, the brandy and citrus zest and juice. Now mix the baking powder and flour together and fold them lightly into the mix. Scrape the mixture into the prepared tin, smooth the top gently, and put it into the oven.

Leave the cake for about an hour. Then, without opening the door, turn the heat down to 150°C/Gas 2 and continue cooking for one and a half hours for the small cake, two hours for the larger one.

Check whether the cake is done by inserting a skewer, or a knitting needle, into the centre. It should come out with just a few crumbs attached to it, no trace of raw cake mixture. Take the cake out of the oven and leave to cool before removing it from the tin.

Feeding the cake

If you make the cake early enough, or at least a month before you need it, you get the opportunity to 'feed it' with alcohol. Most people use brandy, though I have known those who prefer rum. The trick is to pierce the base of the cake several times with a skewer, then spoon brandy into the holes. I have never found a skewer wide enough so tend to prefer a thin, i.e. Japanese, chopstick.

My mum, incidentally, used a knitting needle, a number 8, which provided a suitably wide hollow. I suspect she did this to ensure enough alcohol was absorbed by the cake rather than in memory of Ambrogio Lorenzetti's 1345 painting of Mary, Joseph and the baby that clearly shows Mary clicking away on a pair of needles. One of a series of fourteenth-century paintings known as the 'knitting Madonnas'.

The idea is to keep the cake moist and to help preserve it. I have a suspicion that the task isn't really necessary, but the idea makes sense and I am happy to go along with it.

Once the cake is completely cool, remove the paper from the base and pierce all over with a skewer or knitting needle. Spoon over enough brandy to moisten the cake but not to make it soggy – I suggest three or four tablespoons at a time. Don't use your best cognac, but it's worth remembering that you can only take out what you put in. Wrap the cake in greaseproof paper and tin foil and store in a cake tin. Feed the cake every few days with the same amount of brandy.

Some useful stuff

Storing the cake

Let the cake cool completely before putting it away in a tin. Leave it in its paper, wrapped in clingfilm, foil or more parchment. Put the lid on tight and keep in a cool, dark place such as a kitchen cupboard. Like that, it will keep for three or four weeks.

A practical guide to cake 'faults'

I'm not sure any home-made cake should be thought of as having faults, only eccentricities and characteristics. Spin aside, there are details most of us would probably prefer to avoid.

The sunken cake: A cake whose centre has fallen into a deep hollow is not the end of the world, but in today's unforgiving and hypercritical world it does make you feel something of a failure. The dip in the middle is usually the fault of the mixture being too wet (it should fall slowly off the spoon without the need for a firm shake) or from too short a baking time. Putting the newly baked cake in a draught can also affect it, as can slamming the oven door during one of your several investigatory peeks.

The burned cake: A charred exterior is often the result of not lining the cake tin with a double layer of paper, allowing the crust to be in contact with the hot tin for too long. It might also be down to too high an oven temperature. Generally, I would bake at 160°C/Gas 3.

The soggy cake: We want a moist cake. I use the word without apology. There you go, moist. But there is a difference between moist and wet. A wet cake will be more like pudding than cake and is usually the result of too short a baking time or of a mixture that was too wet in the first place. The raw mixture should keep its shape on the spoon. You can correct this before baking by stirring in a little more flour, but that is your last chance.

The dry cake: Your ratio of wet ingredients to dry is out of kilter. Too few eggs or not enough liquid is usually the reason for a dry, mealy texture or an overly generous hand with the flour. Truth told, over-baking is more than likely to be at the root of it – the niggling desire to leave the thing in the oven just a little longer 'to make sure'. Often found in the same kitchens as jam or marmalade that is set too firmly.

The future of the cake

I fear the cake's days are numbered. If there is one piece of our beloved Christmas festival to be confined to history over the coming century, my money is on this one. To dispense with this little part of culinary tradition would free us from the trauma of the sunken middle, the dry crumb and the burned top. Not to mention the torture of getting the almond paste to stick to its sides. It might even relieve us of the ultimate guilt of serving a shop-bought cake. (And, no, 'It's from Waitrose' is not an excuse.)

And what exactly do we replace the traditional cake with? We must have something to cut and share, to show our solidarity as friends and family. Should it be the buttercream bark of the French chocolate log? The 'hunt the marzipan' stollen, so treasured by the Germans? An icing-sugar-dusted Victoria sponge? I feel sure some young Instagram star is already plotting to unleash a chia seed, spirulina and beetroot cake. Gluten-free, of course.

A few possibilities for Christmas cake refuseniks

The chocolate Christmas cake

White, of course. Otherwise it will just look like someone's birthday. Which, in a sense, I suppose it is. The French bûche de Noël, the chocolate log, has been increasing in popularity in Britain, not so much as a replacement but as an alternative. Let's have both. The practical will point out that, in matters of cake, more people like chocolate than fruit. The knowing will retort that the chocolate-buttercream-covered branch so beloved of the French is something you could eat at any time of year. Planting a plastic robin on a chocolate branch doesn't quite wash.

The healthy cake

The healthy option doesn't really fly either. Sans sugar, sans butter, sans icing, it is also sans Christmas. The whole point of the Christmas cake is that it is special, something we have only once a year. An event. Such a cake needs to be a celebration and an extravagance (no one actually needs a slice of Christmas cake). To try to turn it into something with all the joy of a bowl of muesli is rather to miss the point.

The tropical cake

However you choose to dress it up, a slice of cake is a little brown wedge of sweetness. You could introduce alternatives to the currants and raisins of the traditional recipe, with dried cranberries, sour cherries, golden and crimson sultanas, candied papaya and pineapple. Avoid mango, unless you still want to be chewing at New Year. The effect is to brighten the cake, and the flavour is a little sharper from the cherries, but it remains a brown, fruit-studded cake.

See also:
December 18: Making the almond paste.
December 21: Decorating the cake.

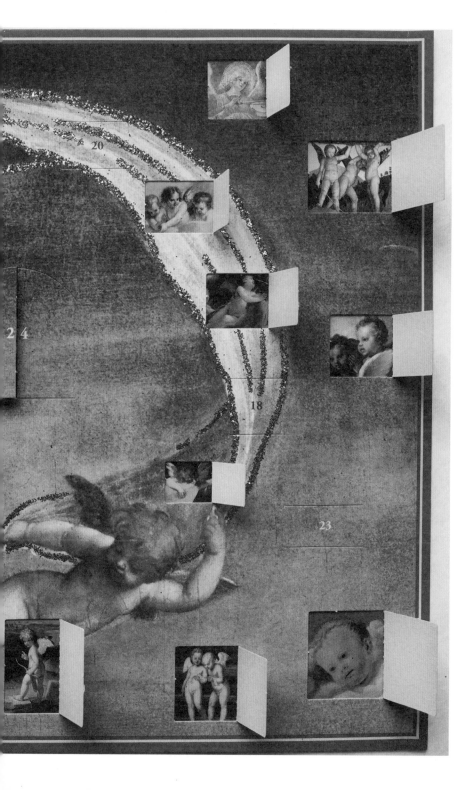

The Advent calendar

You may have left it rather late to buy an Advent calendar. The good ones go early. By good, I mean the traditional ones made to time-honoured designs and devoid of chocolate, miniature bottles of liqueurs or other silliness.

The Advent calendar is another seasonal import from Germany, having been part of the Lutheran winter celebrations since the nineteenth century. Usually made from card, it generally depicts a Christmas tree or scene from the Nativity, and is made up of twenty-five tiny numbered windows that are opened daily to reveal a picture or gift. The point is surely more than a Christmas countdown, but a moment each day to stop and think of the more spiritual essence of the season. Maybe even to say a little prayer.

I get the same excitement from them now as I did as a kid, though nowadays I tend to open the windows day by day rather than peeping ahead as I did as an eleven-year-old. Gone are the days when your calendar contained a message from the Bible. Now we have anything from little bottles of beer to chocolate truffles tucked away in the cardboard hidey-holes.

Hidden gifts behind the windows of the Advent calendar aren't new. Sweets were being used as far back as 1850. They were first mass-produced, according to Mark Forsyth, writing in *A Christmas Cornucopia*, by a Mrs Lang in Germany – clearly Frau Lang – who had originally made them to amuse her son Gerhard. I despair at some of the modern designs that contain everything from make-up to malt whisky and long to find old-fashioned ones with angels, candle-lit fir trees and scenes from the Nativity.

Cue Austria and Germany, where, at the Christmas markets and old-fashioned stationers, you can still find calendars made to the original format. Last year I picked up a beauty in Vienna, a pale blue sky with white clouds, cherubs and garlanded with ribbons, and will go back for another this year too. The hidden child in everyone comes out at different times (as you can witness for yourself each year in any major city on the Thursday before Christmas), but for me it is at the start of December, when I pull back the tiny, hinged windows of my Advent calendar to find a candle, a cherub or a glowing lantern hidden within.

I turn to another test run for Christmas Day. This time a dish that would do either as a main course, salad or side dish. Sweet pumpkin with spiced seeds and the sour kick of pomegranate.

Roast pumpkin with dukkha and pomegranate

Serves 4 as a side dish, 2 as a main course
pumpkin or butternut squash – 700g
olive oil – 4 tablespoons
coriander seeds – 1 tablespoon
cumin seeds – 1 tablespoon
hemp seeds – 1 tablespoon
pumpkin seeds – 2 tablespoons
sunflower seeds – 2 tablespoons
dried thyme – 2 tablespoons
sea salt – 1 tablespoon
nigella seeds – 1 tablespoon
shredded pistachios – 4 tablespoons
a small pomegranate

Set the oven at 200°C/Gas 6. Scoop out the seeds and fibres from the middle of the pumpkin or butternut squash. Slice the flesh into thin segments, each about 1cm thick. Lay the pieces out in a single layer on a baking sheet. Trickle over the olive oil and season with black pepper, then bake for about thirty minutes, until soft and translucent.

In a dry frying pan, mix the coriander and cumin and toast over a low to moderate heat for a few minutes, until fragrant. Add the hemp, pumpkin and sunflower seeds and continue toasting for about five minutes, stirring regularly until all is golden.

Stir in the thyme and salt, then grind the mixture using a pestle and mortar, cracking the seeds roughly. Keep the mixture rough and knobbly. Fold in the nigella seeds and shredded pistachios. Break open the pomegranate and remove the seeds.

When the pumpkin comes from the oven, scatter over the pomegranate seeds, about half the spice and seed mixture and serve. Store the remaining mixture in a jar until needed.

27 NOVEMBER

Vienna, a city of sugar and whipped cream

Vienna sparkles. A city like a christening cake. Horse-drawn carriages, as polished as a Chelsea Pensioner's boots, go clippity-clop on cobbled streets. Fir trees with golden baubles guard the doorways of the jewellery shops. Icing-sugar cakes hang in gilded cages in bakeries and strings of white fairy lights dangle between the houses like diamonds. I have only ever seen this city during Advent, when the streets bustle with Italians and the British, the carriage lanterns shine and there is the smell of Glühwein in the markets.

The weather is often crisp as an apple, with the feeling it has snowed even when it hasn't. The roads are a soft ivory white rather than dark grey, giving the impression of a city glistening with morning frost. The wind can nip your nose and bite your ears. You'll need gloves and a woolly hat.

I am here for just three nights this time, but it is enough. There are more Christmas markets than I have fingers. I go at night, when they have a punch-induced jollity. Much of the offerings can be ignored, but there are gems. A wooden stall decked with the sort of Advent calendars I haven't seen since I was in short trousers. Cherubim and seraphim under a canopy of stars; Christmas trees lit by candles; a row of cosy shops, their windows glowing with hygge. There are traditional cardboard decorations too. A series of Christmas familiars – an angel with a halo, a Santa with a sack, a tree dripping with baubles printed on heavy card to tie on to the branches with golden thread. There are folding books and snow-globes, Christmas cards with glitter, and well-thumbed fairy tales. None of these is available in mainstream shops. Few are online. These are the decorations of long ago, when printed card angels hanging from the branches were enough. Before flashing lights came on board. I buy a thick wad of them, mostly Santas and trees.

Opposite, snowflakes and stars hang from the pointed roof of a stall. Made from horn in shades of caramel and honey, they would adorn a simple white branch with understated festivity. They whisper of Lapland and snow, of moss and twigs, a log hut in the forest. Their apparent simplicity belies the fact that they are carved by hand and will last forever without shattering. I would happily hang them from a lichen-encrusted branch in the kitchen.

Locally churned butter and cheese, a stall of sausages in shades of rust, peat and garnet, another of roasted chestnuts and hot potato cakes, all catch my attention. But much here is not for me, either because of the rather lax attitude to wares' associations to Yule or because they smack of provincial craft fairs where glass pixies rub shoulders with incense sticks and macramé pot-holders. I move on with my bag of Advent calendars.

I wind my way to the village of stalls in front of the Naturhistorisches Museum, pushing through a smiling scrum of scarlet-faced Glühwein drinkers. The chalets are laid out as neatly as a suburban cul-de-sac of lace-netted bungalows. There is a buzz around red-clad ladies selling pasta from a bright red stall. Tyrolean Kasnocken turns out to be as warming as a Toby jug of Glühwein or apple-scented, alcohol-free Kinderpunsch. Paper dishes of Spätzle, the tiny morsels of boiled pasta with caramelised onions and Gruyère, are as stringy as good pizza, and come with a snowfall of crisped onions. We eat standing up at a table, fur coats against sheepskins, our cheeks getting redder by the plastic forkful.

Flushed and charmed by the buzz and bonhomie, I find amusement in clusters of dried fruits and herbs to hang in the house. Whole dried oranges, their peel scored like stripes on a Christmas bauble, or cut into slices and threaded with crisp red chillies, sticks of bark and nutmeg. The air is full of aniseed and dried fruits and curls of cassia. Less brittle, less fragrant, less subtle, cassia is something of a cinnamon wannabe, but the ribbons of bark are more suited to being tied to a wreath of dried clementines and Douglas fir.

I quicken my pace past the stalls of pixie hats and fairies on strings, suede-bound jotters and scented candles, in a bid to reach to the Kunsthistorisches Museum before a phalanx of tourists and its flag-waving guide can get to the door. Mother Goose and her goslings. The scent of gingerbread halts me. A mountain of iced cookies, butterscotch-coloured biscuits that smell of aniseed and ginger. Crisp, iced stars, plum puddings and snowflakes. Each has a hole for ribbon, the occasional silver ball and the temptation that goes

with anything home-baked and hand-iced. For a second I see them, cute as kittens, on my tree at home. Then I see them as crumbs and shattered dreams in my suitcase.

The museum is handsome, with ceilings that demand as much attention as the art on the walls. Two textbook-perfect Christmas trees flank the white marble staircase. There is much to see here, three Rembrandts, including, in room 17, his *Self Portrait with Fur* (1655), hung on a sugar-paper blue wall. But I am treading these creaking wooden floors for the Bruegels. *Die Jäger im Schnee* (1565) and the picture I have come to see, *Winter Landscape with Skaters and a Bird Trap* (1565). A scene of tobacco-coloured trees and ochre houses with snow on their roofs. A scene bathed in soft winter light, late afternoon, those last few minutes before you know you have to come in from the snow. You could spend a shorter time here and move on to another room, but this picture holds my attention for longer than I expect. There is much to see on this canvas and I could gaze at its skaters, bare branches and snow-dusted roofs every day of my life, but I don't want a copy on my kitchen wall. In the flesh it means as much to me as *The Goldfinch* does to others, or perhaps one of Turner's skies. I like snow.

There is black pudding to be eaten with mashed potato and a pool of apple sauce; thin schnitzel the size of a tablecloth, and Tafelspitz, the calming dish of sliced boiled beef, matchstick root vegetables and a dome of potato hash. I settle on coffee at Demel, a jewel-box of a café on the Kohlmarkt and regrettably on everyone's Grand Tour. If I had to pick a single shop anywhere in the world to visit at Christmas, it would be Demel in Vienna. Once you have climbed the wooden stairs (I don't like the room downstairs, with its view of the pastry chefs in the open kitchen) and done battle with those territorial fur-coated locals who attempt to push in (I would briefly love to know the German for 'Oi, love, there's a back to this queue'), the atmosphere calms, the waitresses' legendary frosted stares melt and you can pick up your paper and read the news of the day.

There will be cheesecake and dobos torte, coffee-iced Esterházy and Sachertorte. Cakes with apple and poppyseed, chestnut purée or coffee buttercream. There will be glasses of ice-cold orange juice freshly squeezed,

Anna Demel's coffee with orange liqueur and pots of lapsang tea. Most of all there will be cream. It sits in mounds on glasses of coffee, in china dishes and nudging their famous Sachertorte. Downstairs in the shop there are marzipan apples and crystallised violets, sugared almonds and bundles of jewel-coloured chocolates to hang from the tree. There are icing Santa Claus and pale blue stars, foil-wrapped hearts and glistening jars of jam in boxes. The lucky will find Christstollen in a pale wooden box like the babe in his manger, Potizenstollen, freckled with poppy seeds, and, for those who shudder at cream and sugar (and are clearly in the wrong place), there are plainly elegant ridge-sided Sandguglhupfe to eat within sight of the Dom.

Christstollen, Dresden and the Butter Letter

The flavour is of distilled Christmas. Candied orange, cinnamon, raisins, rum and cardamom. The texture is poor man's fruit cake. Fruit bread. Many have a sweet ribbon of marzipan running through the middle – a layer of buried almondy treasure, and a deep coating of icing sugar covering their craggy surface.

Each year, on the Saturday before Advent, a giant stollen makes its way slowly down the Schloßplatz in Dresden, accompanied by the pomp of soldiers dressed in pristine white trousers, tricorn hats, scarlet capes and much gold braid. Most of Dresden seems to turn out to watch the carthorses, hooves polished, feathers brushed, pulling a cake the size of small car buried in snow, through the Old Town towards the Striezelmarkt. The fruit loaf, weighing several tonnes, is then sliced into thousands of pieces by a pastry cook wielding a copy of the ancient Dresden Stollen Knife. Silver-plated and weighing in at 12kg, it is an impressive 1.6 metres long. Replicas are available. There is a crush and much white powder on bobble hats as the pieces of cake are handed out into the crowd in aid of a charity that helps encourage young bakers.

In its present form, the festival has only been going for a couple of decades, which could smack of a public relations event did its history not go as deep as it does. The Stollenfest can trace its roots to 1730. It was then that Frederick August I, a man whose love of art, festivals and apparently women showed no bounds, invited two thousand, four hundred dignitaries from all over Europe to a magnificent baroque celebration, the Zeitheiner Lustlager. Designed to showcase his military might – it was held at the Zeithein Encampment – the climax of the event involved the presentation of a vast stollen weighing almost 2000kg and drawn by eight horses. Imagine it, a horse-drawn stollen.

Made with 3,600 eggs, 326 churns of milk and 20 hundredweight of flour, the cake was baked by the celebrated master baker Johann Andreas

Zacharius and his sixty assistants. A specially built oven had to be heated eight days in advance, and the loaf was shared among the assembled guests and soldiers. The annual Stollenfest lasted until 1918, when it took a rest until the event was rekindled in 1994, and is now a firm part of the city's Christmas celebrations.

But the Christstollen itself has an altogether older story, and one our own cake would kill for. Originally a simple, hard bread eaten at Advent, a time of fasting and strict frugality, stollen was made with oil rather than butter, which was banned by the Catholic Church. Midway through the fifteenth century, Prince Elector Ernst and his brother, the Duke, wrote to the Pope seeking permission to use butter in the stollen rather than the locally made vegetable oil. Their pleas fell on deaf ears until 1490, several Popes later, when Pope Innocent VIII sent a letter to the prince and his brother granting their wish. The Butter Letter, as it came to be known, set out the conditions on which the fat could be used. Namely, payments, for everyone other than the royal family, towards the upkeep of Freiberg Minster and its magnificent gothic spire.

Once Saxony became protestant, fruit and almonds were introduced, lemon zest and candied orange, and then spices and rum were added to bring the puritanical bread nearer to the sweet treat it is today. The Prince, by the way, was kidnapped in the famous Prinzenraub – the Stealing of the Princes – and later died falling off a horse.

The cake

A good stollen is, at least for this Christophile, the pinnacle of the range of festive cakes. The yeasted, fruit-speckled bread is like a firmer panettone, and with its moist almond-paste heart is the essence of festive celebration but without the sickly extravagance of a French bûche de Noël. The cake and marzipan are entwined in the oven rather than stuck together like our own Christmas cake, which is really just a Dundee cake in fancy dress.

Its mantel of icing sugar aside, the bread is less sweet than its European cousins, and keeps well. The original recipes show cakes weighing in at two kilograms, but small ones are becoming popular now. The raisins and candied fruits are often macerated in rum or brandy before being kneaded into the dough. Eggs are creeping into modern recipes, giving a more brioche-like crumb, but are not considered traditional. As too are cherries and chocolate, apricots and poppy seeds. On being taken from the oven the warm loaf is rolled in generous amounts of unsalted butter and sugar, and if carefully packed can keep as long as Easter. As if.

Orange and poppy seed stollen

It is with some relief, as I look down at the untidy bundle that is my home-made Christmas stollen, that I remember the cake is meant to resemble the baby Jesus in swaddling clothes. There's nothing like the word 'swaddling' to give an amateur baker a comforting amount of artistic licence.

This recipe looks more daunting than it actually is. You basically make a bread dough with a bit of butter and egg in it, knead it for a while, then leave it alone to do its thing. Later, you knead it with fruit and spice, tuck in the marzipan and let it rest before baking. Despite its length, the recipe really couldn't be simpler, but because of its unavoidable double rising, may I suggest giving yourself plenty of time.

Makes one large stollen/enough for 8
butter – 100g
plain flour – 500g
fresh yeast – 40g or 7g dried
warm milk – 225ml
sugar – 30g
salt – $\frac{1}{2}$ teaspoon
an egg

For the filling:
golden sultanas – 125g
candied citrus peel – 125g
a medium-sized orange
rum or brandy – 4 tablespoons
vanilla extract – 1 teaspoon
green cardamoms – 8
poppy seeds – 2 teaspoons
ground cinnamon – ½ teaspoon
flaked almonds – 50g
marzipan – 200g
a little beaten egg

For the glaze:
butter – 50g
icing sugar

You will also need a large baking sheet, lined with baking parchment.

Put the sultanas into a mixing bowl. Chop the candied citrus peel into small dice and add to the sultanas. Finely grate the zest from the orange and add to the bowl. Squeeze in the juice of the orange, pour in the rum or brandy and vanilla, then toss together and leave for an hour.

Melt the butter in a small pan, then leave to cool down. Put the flour into a large mixing bowl. No need to sieve it. If using fresh yeast, warm the milk to body temperature (it should feel comfortable rather than cold or scalding when you insert your finger), then crumble in the yeast and stir to dissolve. Add the sugar and salt to the flour and mix well. Beat the egg. Stir in the egg, and the warm milk and butter. (If you are using dried yeast, add the yeast straight to the flour, then stir in the other ingredients followed by the warm milk, egg and butter.)

Mix thoroughly – the dough should be soft, shiny and rather sticky. In all honesty it may be very sticky. Turn out on to a generously floured board and knead for a good eight minutes. As you knead, the dough will become less and less sticky and more like a bread dough – though it will be heavier because of the butter and egg. When the dough is soft, elastic and no longer sticking to the board, scoop it up and put it into a floured bowl. Set aside, covered with a clean tea towel, somewhere warm and draught-free for a good hour or until it is well risen. (It won't be quite twice the size of the original dough but well on the way.) Alternatively, mix and knead using a food mixer fitted with a dough hook until the dough comes cleanly away from the sides of the bowl.

Break the cardamom pods open and remove their seeds. Crush the seeds to a coarse powder using a pestle and mortar or a spice mill, then mix in a small bowl with the poppy seeds, cinnamon and almonds. Dust the work surface with flour and tip your risen dough on to it. Knead the spice and seed mixture and the soaked fruits, leaving behind most of the liquid, into the dough.

Roll into a long loaf about 22cm × 16cm and flatten it slightly. Roll the marzipan into a cylinder nearly the length of the dough, then place it in the centre. Brush the edges with a little beaten egg and press together. Turn the dough over and place it on a lined baking sheet, cover with a towel and return it to a warm place to prove for a further hour and a half.

Heat the oven to 180°C/Gas 4. Place the loaf in the hot oven and bake for about thirty-five to forty minutes, until pale gold. Melt the butter for the glaze and brush over the loaf. Cool on a wire rack, then dust with icing sugar. I think you can be quite generous here.

To keep: when the loaf is thoroughly cool, wrap loosely in waxed paper or clingfilm and keep in a biscuit tin.

Ring the changes with chopped dried apricots, dried cranberries or chopped and stoned prunes. You can freeze a baked stollen quite successfully.

Tinsel, cheesecake and a windy night

There is tinsel and there is tinsel. The original silver strands – lametta – were single, fine, and possessed some of the shimmering character of the precious metal from which they were made. First produced in Nuremberg in the early 1600s, they reflected and amplified the light given by candles on the tree, giving the impression of icicles caught by moonlight under a clear winter sky. The name is derived from the old French word *estincele*, meaning to sparkle.

Tinsel was first made from silver, then aluminium, then lead foil. This latter incarnation was phased out because of the assumed risk of lead poisoning to children decorating the tree. Not that there was ever any evidence. The aluminium foil version, mastered by the French in the early twentieth century, was a cheap alternative to the original silver and had the advantage of not tarnishing. It kept its shimmer year after year.

Modern forms of tinsel consist of bushy fringe around a wire, perhaps inevitably, made from metallic-coated polyvinyl. They are exceptionally light and can lack the ability to hang as well as the original heavier silver. Chunky and often sold in colours such as purple and turquoise, they have lost their icicle-like, fairy-tale magic, and often look cheap and gaudy. If modern tinsel is your thing, then you might like to look for that with fine rather than wide strands – Wales produces most of the tinsel sold in this country. It shimmers in the lightest breeze and manages to retain something of the delicate qualities of the original.

You can still buy the delightful lametta. Much is produced in the Tyrol. It comes in the form of genuine silver plate or gold-coloured brass, and each strand is barely thicker than a hair. The 130-cm-long slivers catch the light when the tree is illuminated and sparkle like a touch of frost. It is, however, the very devil to store and ends up forming an impregnable nest, like fettuccine, so it is perhaps best to buy new each year. Rather late in the day, I order some new packets online.

The wind is getting up. I have loved it since childhood, especially at the coast or in a wood. That is when the wind talks to you. Its effect is at its most visible here with the branches of the robinia, whose spindly twigs are apt to snap in a gale. The canopy of the tree crashes around, thrashing dramatically from side to side as if trying to toss a wasp out of its hair.

On a winter's night the wind howls down the chimneys in this house. Occasionally there is a low bang, like a train emerging suddenly from a tunnel. Mostly, though, it is a long, low and ghostly moan. I find it strangely reassuring in the way you might find an old black and white horror film comforting.

As someone who falls asleep within minutes of his head touching the pillow, I am perplexed why anyone should want a 'sleep tape' of the winter wind, but they exist. YouTube is full of them, as are those sorts of gift shops that sell scented candles, massage oils and self-help books. Some are accompanied by the sounds of thunder and torrential rain. They don't make me want to sleep. They do make me feel cold though, and maybe that's the idea; listening to them, you cannot help but snuggle up tightly, like a startled hedgehog. Perhaps that's the trick.

This is a noisy house. Not noisy with the sound of traffic but as in creaks and bumps. Mysterious noises that are part and parcel of an old house that has had a life or two. (In its time, this has been an art gallery, a Catholic hospice and a slum.) Tread on one stair and another ahead of you will move. Doors open for no reason, a floorboard in an empty room will let out an unexpected creak. You might hear a footfall on the stairs. Some are quite spooked by the sounds here on a windy night. Friends have said they have felt someone brush past them on more than one occasion. But to me the unexplained sounds simply signal a change of air pressure or one of the many draughts opening an ill-fitting door.

When the wind is buffeting the house, as it is tonight, I want soup. Broth, chowder, creamy bisque or soup-stew. Something to eat from the sort of deep bowl I can cradle in my hands. We have little or nothing in the house for soup, but there are artichokes that I bought to roast then forgot about. I decide, on

a whim, to make artichoke soup but to add some frozen peas in the hope of bringing a freshness to an otherwise earthy soup. It works a treat, and I wish I had thought of it before. The inclusion of peas also seems to stop the wind, the other sort, not the one that rattles the chimneys. We follow it with a light ricotta cheesecake wrapped in flaky filo which I am so happy with it may turn up again on the table at Christmas.

Artichoke and pea soup

The chestnut and cranberry finish is entirely optional, but fun for those who might like to offer it at Christmas.

Serves 6
Jerusalem artichokes – 500g
half a lemon
chicken stock – 1 litre
frozen peas – 400g
tarragon – 15g
parsley – 20g

To finish (optional):
redcurrant jelly – 3 tablespoons
water – 3 tablespoons
cranberries – 4 tablespoons
chestnuts, jarred or vacuum-packed – 12
butter – 2 tablespoons
olive oil – 2 tablespoons

Peel the artichokes and keep them from browning in a bowl of cold water with a squeeze of lemon juice in it. Warm the stock in a large saucepan, add the drained artichokes and bring the stock to the boil. Lower the heat and let them cook for about twenty-five minutes, or until very soft.

Cook the peas from frozen in boiling water for four or five minutes, then drain and tip them into a bowl of iced water to stop them cooking and keep their bright colour.

When the artichokes are soft enough to crush, process them and their cooking liquid in a blender together with the tarragon, parsley, some salt and black pepper and the drained peas. Do this is in batches so as not to overflow the blender jug or, better I think, use a stick blender in the saucepan. Keep the soup warm.

Melt the redcurrant jelly with the water in a small pan, then add the cranberries and let them soften and burst. Fry the chestnuts in the butter and oil until the nuts are sweet and fragrant.

Pour the soup into bowls, then spoon some of the cranberries, jelly and warm chestnuts over the top.

Ricotta filo cake

Ravishing, like a fairy in a vast taffeta ball gown. Give the cheesecake time to cool down before you slice it. The pastry will shatter, which is rather lovely, offering wisps of crispness with the soft, creamy cheesecake. This is lighter and less rich than most.

Serves 6
butter – 90g
filo pastry sheets – 200g
ricotta – 500g
eggs – 3
egg yolks – 3
honey – 2 tablespoons
ground cinnamon – a pinch
caster sugar – 50g
candied peel – 75g
golden sultanas – 75g
finely grated zest of a lemon

finely grated zest of an orange
plain flour – 2 level tablespoons
vanilla extract
ground almonds – 70g

To finish:
honey – 3 tablespoons
chopped candied peel – 3 tablespoons
icing sugar

You will also need a 20cm tart tin with a removable base.

Set the oven at 180°C/Gas 4. Melt the butter in a small pan. Place a baking sheet in the oven. Line the tart tin with a double sheet of filo, letting it fall over the edges. Brush with some of the butter, then continue with all the sheets of filo, letting the pastry overhang the tin where necessary and generously brushing them with butter as you go.

Put the ricotta, eggs, extra egg yolks, honey, cinnamon and caster sugar into the bowl of a food mixer and combine to a smooth cream. Fold in the candied peel, sultanas, finely grated citrus zest, flour, a capful of vanilla extract and, lastly, the ground almonds. Using a rubber spatula, scrape the mixture into the lined tin, smooth flat, then gently fold the overhanging pastry sheets to the middle, curling them over as you go to make loose rosettes of pastry. Bake for forty to fifty minutes, until the pastry is crisp and the filling lightly firm to the touch.

Remove the cheesecake from the oven. Melt the honey in a small saucepan, stir in the candied peel, then spoon over the pastry. Dust with icing sugar and leave to cool before slicing.

Christmas windows and a soft, sweet cake

To see Fortnum & Mason's Christmas windows is to step into the pages of a book of fairy tales. Each year they glisten and sparkle, like frost on a topiary garden, a scene of old-fashioned wonder and delight. The designs are cluttered in the loveliest sense, like looking into a kaleidoscope. The attention to detail is breathtaking.

The four windows facing the Royal Academy on London's Piccadilly, like the heavy-lidded eyes of a much-loved great aunt as she nods off to sleep, usually contain a story, a depiction of a fairy tale or nursery rhyme. They often have a touch of fantasy about them, as if the old girl had taken a few magic mushrooms. Take your time: they always deserve a long look, a good five minutes at least, so you can take in every exquisite detail of *Alice in Wonderland* or *Cinderella*. 'I'll meet you outside Fortnum's' means you will have something more interesting to look at than your phone.

Among the most memorable were those based on illustrations by Kristjana Williams and featuring three hundred paper birds, leaves and flowers in deep, wine-gum colours against a black background. Meticulously crafted, others have included an arrangement of Christmas puddings amid a candlelit snow scene, with icicles and frosted twigs, a sleigh set in deep snow with falling snowflakes caught in the lights, a resplendent Santa and his sack of beribboned gifts visiting a boy and his sister as they sleep beside the chimney. There will be glitter and snow, sparkling lights and fairies, a labyrinth of bizarre and wondrous creatures. There will be snow-covered trees laden with doll's-house mince pies, glasses of fizz and bejewelled baubles. Above all, expect painstaking detail, brilliantly assembled vignettes, crafted with an extraordinary imagination. Best seen on a winter's afternoon, just as darkness falls, before taking afternoon tea at the Wolseley or at one of the several restaurants in the store itself.

Even though it is early in the season, most shops already have their windows festively dressed. You know that the visual teams of the large stores have big budgets and huge fun but also unimaginable responsibility. As always, Liberty is spectacular. This is a store that never seems to put a foot wrong. The low rectangular windows, handsomely framed by the carved oak timbers of HMS *Hindustan*, are invariably a delight, but this time, somehow, even more so. The store is always full of surprises, and this year it has worked in collaboration with the Royal Ballet to produce windows based on *The Nutcracker*. There are toy soldiers and wooden ballerinas, the intricate turning cogs of clocks and, of course, the Sugar Plum Fairy. The result is enchanting, like stepping into the magical kingdom of Drosselmeyer itself. The unusual point about the display this year is its almost total lack of merchandise. At the moment when a store can be as commercial as it likes, Liberty has bravely chosen not to. Superb.

As I walk through the West End, briefly arrested by the sight of Selfridges' sequined Santa and Tiffany's minimal extravagance, I notice the smaller shops seem to have pulled out every stop this year too. There is a heart-warming amount of imagination being put into play behind the glass. I wish I had taken a day purely to window-shop. (Well, I have, sort of.) I am reminded of last year, walking around the Georgian streets of Bath, windows lit like pantomime sets, dazzling, intriguing, hypnotic. The country's independent shops rarely fail to get our attention, as anyone knows who has witnessed the unbridled joy with which small bookshops, toyshops and chocolate shops set about their displays. Yes, Christmas windows are commercial, of course, that is their purpose, a hook to get you over the threshold, but there is also a generosity and playfulness. A round of applause for window-dressers everywhere.

Banana cardamom cake

I have been after a true banana cake for a while now. Not a dark banana bread made with overripe fruit, good as that can be, but something lighter in both colour and texture. A cake that tastes and smells like a freshly peeled banana, without the too-sweet stickiness that comes from using overripe fruit. Today I make a more sponge-like version, deeply banana-flavoured and spiced

lightly with cardamom. I am pleased enough with the result to share it. I serve it first as pieces of cake in their own right, and then as a dessert with a tropical fruit salad.

Serves 12
bananas – 375g (peeled weight)
lemon juice – 1 tablespoon
plain flour – 200g
baking powder – 2 teaspoons
salt – a pinch
golden caster sugar – 90g
light muscovado sugar – 90g
eggs – 2
groundnut or vegetable oil – 4 tablespoons

To finish:
green cardamom pods – 10
golden caster sugar – 2 tablespoons

Set the oven at 170°C/Gas 3–4. Line a square 20cm cake tin with baking parchment.

Break the bananas into short chunks, then put them into a bowl and mash roughly with a fork. Avoid the temptation to turn them into a purée. Stir in the lemon juice.

Sift together the flour, baking powder and salt.

Break open the cardamom pods, remove the dark brown seeds, then crush them to a fine powder, using a pestle and mortar. Mix them with the 2 tablespoons of caster sugar and set aside for later.

Put the golden caster and muscovado sugar into the bowl of an electric mixer. Break the eggs into the sugar, then beat, using the whisk attachment, for three to four minutes, until light and creamy. Pour in the oil, slowly, with the mixer on a moderate speed.

Fold the flour and baking powder into the mixture with a large metal spoon or by changing the whisk attachment to a flat paddle beater. Fold in the crushed bananas, briefly, taking care to distribute them evenly but without crushing them any further.

Transfer the mixture to the prepared cake tin, using a rubber spatula. Sprinkle the surface with the sugar and cardamom mixture. Bake in the preheated oven for thirty-five minutes, or until lightly firm on top. Remove from the oven and leave to settle, in its tin, for about twenty minutes.

Lift the cake from its tin, then place on a cooling rack and leave to cool. Cut the cake into three equal rectangles, then cut those into four to give twelve small pieces. Place the cake pieces on a serving plate. Serve with the tropical salad below.

Papaya, persimmon and cardamom

I have always used lime juice to illuminate the subtle flavour of papaya. But I have found something else. The juice of passion fruits, especially the ripe, wrinkled ones, does the job better.

> *Serves 4 (9 as an accompaniment)*
> passion fruit – 6
> a small orange
> cardamom pods – 4
> persimmon – 1
> papaya – 2

Slice the passion fruits in half, then squeeze their juice and seedy flesh into a small sieve over a bowl. Press the juice and pulp through the sieve with the back of a teaspoon, then discard the seeds. Cut the orange in half and squeeze its juice into the bowl of passion fruit juice.

Crack open the cardamom pods with a heavy weight such as a mortar or rolling pin, then drop them, whole, into the juice. Cover and place in the refrigerator.

Slice the persimmon thinly, then add to the passion fruit juice.

Slice the papayas in half, scrape out the seeds with a teaspoon and discard, then remove the yellow skin from each half with a vegetable peeler. Slice the papaya in thick pieces, each about the width of a pencil. Mix the papaya with the persimmon and passion fruit juice, tossing the fruits tenderly together, then cover and leave for a couple of hours – or overnight – in the fridge.

Remove the cardamom pods – they have done their work – then divide the fruits between four small bowls or serve them with slices of the banana cake.

Mistletoe, malt loaf and a salad of cobnuts

I need to track down a supply of mistletoe. Along with bundles of holly and ivy, its soft green stems have long decorated this house at this time of year. Mistletoe is heavy with folklore. *Viscum album*, the variety of the genus that produces the white, translucent berries, is the one we need to deck our halls at Christmas. A parasitic plant that needs a host tree on which to attach itself, it is abundant in Britain but particularly so in the Midlands, Herefordshire, Worcestershire and Somerset. I could not think of Christmas without it.

The plant's olive-green leaves and currant-like berries have deep associations with Yuletide. It is considered sacred, magical and medicinal. The Druids would cut balls of mistletoe from their sacred oak trees at the start of the winter solstice, the ceremony taking place on the sixth night following the new moon following the solstice. The tradition of hanging a bunch from a doorway was not originally for kissing under, though it was certainly considered an aphrodisiac. (Early belief was that the berries contained the sperm of the gods.) The hanging bunch's first function was to protect the home against thunder and lightning.

The genus appears in Celtic rituals such as the ancient Ritual of Oak and Mistletoe, a religious ceremony in which a Druid climbs an oak tree to collect its haul, catching the ball of evergreens in his cloak. (Legend has it that mistletoe should never be allowed to touch the ground.) My long-held romantic vision of my mistletoe being gathered by white-cloaked Druids climbing ancient trees is sadly off the mark, though. Most of the stock available in London arrives in a decidedly unromantic lorry from France.

Balls of mistletoe, most easily spotted in winter when the trees are bare, grow famously on apple trees but also on blackthorn, crab apple, lime and hawthorn. I have always associated its appearance with tall trees and open countryside. It is not a woodland creature. Despite the association with dark days, *Viscum album* needs light to thrive.

I think of it as an essential part of our winter landscape, and as a child would excitedly point out the untidy globes of golden-green as we walked through the Worcestershire lanes, in the same way I did poppies in cornfields. The tangles of forked-stemmed greenery are spread from tree to tree by birds, particularly the blackcaps, which wipe the sticky, inedible seeds off their beaks on the nearest patch of bark. Particularly prolific in Germany, it is known by over thirty different names, including the magnificent Drudenfua.

According to the Mistletoe Pages, a website celebrating the phenomenon in all its forms, *Viscum album*, the original variety, is the only one that has the symmetrical leaves and white berries we look for. I have to admit to not being aware of more than one type, so this could explain why so much I see is missing its berries. I must point out that mistletoe is poisonous to both humans and household pets.

The habit of kissing under the mistletoe is curiously English. We seem to have conveniently forgotten that a berry should be picked each time a kiss is given, and once the berries are no more, then so are the kisses. Because of its pagan origins, it is occasionally still banned in some churches.

Tenbury Wells in Worcester has been associated with my favourite Christmas evergreen for centuries and is home to the annual mistletoe festival. The town was part of my childhood. As a family we went there every few weeks, not initially for mistletoe but because of my father's obsession with clematis, for which the area was also famous. I was happy enough to tag along, though mostly for the coffee and walnut cake in the local café. Each Christmas we would drive off to the mistletoe market, returning with the boot of the car full of string-tied evergreens. Held at the Tenbury Wells livestock market until 2004, the area's associations with the plant are now upheld by the Tenbury Mistletoe Association, who are campaigning for today to be officially declared Mistletoe Day. I hope they succeed. (There is a mistletoe market held on the last Tuesday of November and the first two Tuesdays of December each year, but check their website for details.)

Despite its toxicity, mistletoe has long been revered, often controversially, for its healing qualities.

It has also long been considered a plant of peace, which may be why this variety is held sacred by the Druids. Legend also has it that fighting armies in the Middle Ages would put down their weapons and call a truce once they spotted the plant growing in the trees; couples who promised to marry under its branches would have a long and happy marriage; for those who weren't, this was the place to kiss and make up. In more recent, less politically correct times, the habit of kissing under a sprig of mistletoe was reduced to copping a snog in the office. Now, a hanging bunch of *Viscum album* is returning to a place where lovers tenderly steal a kiss.

Farmers' markets are sound hunting grounds, as are garden centres and florists. I pick mine up as late as I can, so it still sports its berries on Christmas Day, but it is worth thinking about it early, especially if you plan to pick it up in quantity and locally grown. Stored outside it will last longer, though the berries, and therefore its point, will be at prey to the blackbirds.

I go shopping and find sweet crunchy figs and some cobnuts in their frilly coats. Not green and fresh as I like them (and when the nuts are particularly milky), their crunch is nevertheless one of my favourite elements of an early winter salad. I pick up a wedge of blue cheese too, returning to make an exceptional plateful of food.

Fig and blue cheese salad

Serves 2

honey – 1 teaspoon
white wine vinegar – 2 tablespoons
fennel seeds – 2 teaspoons
a small beetroot, red, white or candy
cobnuts or hazelnuts – a handful
apples, small – 2
lemon juice – a squeeze
figs – 4
blue cheese – 200g

Put the honey into a small bowl, then combine with the white wine vinegar. Lightly crush the fennel seeds using a pestle and mortar, and add them to the vinegar. Peel and thinly slice the beetroot, push the slices down into the marinade, turning them over so they are thoroughly coated, then set aside. Leave for a good hour.

If you are using fresh cobnuts, crack open the shells and extract the nuts. If you are using hazelnuts, toast them in a dry, shallow pan and rub them in a dry cloth until the skins flake off. You may need more than one attempt. Cut the nuts in half. If you are using fresh cobnuts, don't toast them, simply cut them in half.

Cut the apples into quarters and remove the cores. Slice the apples into thin wedges, toss briefly in a little lemon juice to stop them discolouring and set aside. Tear the figs in half. Toss together the apples, figs and nuts and pile on to plates. Set the beetroot slices among them.

Break the blue cheese into large pieces and tuck among the salad. Trickle over the marinade from the beetroot.

Malt loaf and me

I have no idea when I stopped eating malt loaf, I only know that I did. Perhaps it was its resolutely unfashionable character that sent me looking elsewhere. Or the fact that tracking it down was getting more difficult with each passing year. More likely, I gave up the damp, deliciously fruit-laden loaf because other, more exciting, things got in the way.

And then, out of nowhere, I got a fancy to rekindle our old friendship. I longed for a thin slice of buttered malt loaf, the slightly tacky feel on my fingers, that smell of dried fruit and tea I once held so dear. Stripped of the traditional waxed paper wrapper of the commercial brands I wasn't sure it would be quite the same, like a KitKat without the silver foil. Yet one sniff of the baked loaf – think fruit cake meets Ovaltine – and all the good stuff came floating back. Malt loaf is something of a safe harbour, a cloud of raisin- and malt-scented nostalgia – in a complicated world. It tastes of home, of ticking clocks and quality time spent with your Gran. At least it does for me.

The method is straightforward, a recipe anyone can attempt, but it is worth noting that the texture of the uncooked cake mixture is akin to that of raw ginger cake. In other words, a soft batter you can almost pour into the tin, rather than stiff and creamy like the texture of uncooked fruit cake. Sometimes you have to trust a recipe rather than follow your own intuition.

Malt loaf is something of a keeper. Wrapped in foil and stored in a cool corner of the kitchen, it will not only keep for a few days, but will be better for it. Like Christmas cake, this fruit-packed loaf matures benignly. It is a good idea to brush the outside of the freshly baked bread with some of the malt extract directly from the jar. The sweet, mahogany brown goo will be partially absorbed by the loaf, giving the characteristic tackiness that should become part and parcel of such a recipe. A recipe that takes you back to simpler, gentler times. Sometimes, you can have too much excitement.

A sound malt loaf

Malt extract is still around, but you may have to go to a large supermarket or wholefood store for it. If the surface of the loaf browns more quickly than you would like it to, cover with a piece of kitchen foil for the last few minutes of cooking.

> malt extract – 150g
> light muscovado sugar – 100g
> black treacle – 2 tablespoons
> plain flour – 250g
> baking powder – 1 teaspoon
> salt – a pinch
> prunes, stoned – 100g
> black tea – 125ml
> eggs – 2
> sultanas or raisins – 100g

To finish:
a little more malt extract

You will also need a deep, rectangular cake tin measuring 20cm × 9cm (measured on the base), lined with baking parchment.

Preheat the oven to 160°C/Gas 3. Put the malt extract, muscovado sugar and black treacle into a small saucepan and warm, without stirring, over a moderate heat until the sugar has dissolved.

Sift the flour, baking powder and salt to combine thoroughly in a large mixing bowl. Chop the prunes into small pieces. Pour the warm malt and sugar mixture into the flour, together with the tea. Break the eggs into a small bowl, beat lightly with a fork and fold into the batter with the chopped prunes and the sultanas or raisins.

Scoop the mixture – it is quite soft – into the lined cake tin and gently smooth the surface. Bake for one hour, until lightly springy, then remove from the oven and leave to cool in the tin. While the cake cools, brush the surface with a little more malt extract.

To Nuremberg and the Christkindlesmarkt

Slowly we dawdle, scarfed and toasty-hatted, into the market square. The lights illuminating the stalls are switched off. Families cluster around the two fir trees standing guard at the church, but others attempt nonchalance, pretending they are not determinedly securing the perfect vantage-point for their clicking Canons. This time, the perfect spot is actually taken by a police surveillance van. I find an excellent viewpoint outside the communal entrance to a block of flats.

By five o'clock there is an air of quiet excitement, as if a band was about to come on stage at a festival. Which in a way they are. A loud voice. A slow wave of hush. A long speech of which I understand not one solitary word. And then the angel, the golden-crowned Christkind, appears. A girl, always a girl, blonde, flanked by braided trumpeters, like those announcing the arrival of the Queen in *Alice in Wonderland*, she takes a centre spot on the balcony in the shadow of the stained-glass window. After the prologue, the Christkind blesses the market, even though it has been open all day, with a lengthy prologue that ends:

> *You men and women, who once yourselves were children,*
> *Be them again today, happy as children be,*
> *And now the Christkind to its market calls,*
> *And all who come are truly welcome.*

No problem with this man being a child today. It's hard not to be. Over the coming weeks, crowned and caped, the Christkind will attend over a hundred charitable events, mostly in children's homes, before finally appearing on Christmas Eve, with gifts at one of the city's children's hospitals.

The choir sings. Softly. Reverently. As good as anything I have at home on Deutsche Grammophon. *Stille Nacht. Heilige Nacht*. Sung in its native

German by children under a twinkling fir tree, you would have a heart of stone not to well up at 'Silent Night, Holy Night'.

As the crush reaches panic-attack level, the moment is lightened by a woman shoving her way steely-souled through the throng, pushing a double bass on wheels. It would be difficult to think of anything harder to navigate through this sea of gentle revelry than a double bass wrapped in an overcoat. I am pushed back hard against the wall. Suddenly the sound of twenty or more voices shouting, 'Allo!' Apparently I have leaned against all the entry bells of the block of flats.

The Christkindlesmarkt covers the market place but straggles along the surrounding streets, winding its Glühwein-scented path up the hill. Staggers might be a more appropriate word. I am not entirely sure where everyone gets their steaming painted pottery mugs from, but everyone, save us, seems to have one. Truth told, I don't actually love mulled wine enough to find out. Or, indeed, souvenir mugs. What I do like is the smell of mulled wine, at least, in the open air, with the prickle of frost under my nose.

Many of the stalls are those of local shops, festive pop-ups; others are here purely for the duration of the market. I spot the stollen stall in much the same way a magpie might spot a dropped wedding ring. Rows of icing-sugar-dusted, flattened logs of dough, like low alpine houses with snow on their roofs. Stollen with sultanas and orange peel. Stollen with dried mango. With peach and pistachios. The fruited scent of Rumtopf. One with advocaat and marzipan. Yet another that has something to do with Mozart, though quite what I am unsure. There is a dark-chocolate-covered stollen with a pale gingerbread-coloured crumb, the sight of which is like all my Christmases come at once.

There is a bit of a scrum at the painted-cookie stall. A crumb-scrum. Gaudy and apparently as hard as nails, the biscuits are attracting controversy. 'Can you eat them afterwards?' an American lady enquires of her friends. They look like home bakers. I want to venture that I am not sure anyone would want to eat a cookie that has been hanging in the hall all season, but I mind my own business. I can see her point. Who wouldn't have a nibble as they dismantle their tree? The angels in pink dresses blowing trumpets are cheerful, as are those biscuits painted with burning candles amid wreaths of holly and others decorated with scarlet bells and white bows. The colours are at the poster-paint end of the spectrum. The point of each star has a hole for threading your ribbon through. I can barely pull myself away from a row of cookies emblazoned with children in spotted scarves making a snowman. But they have crossed a line, perhaps because of their strong colours and varnished coating, and seem more decorative than edible. Tempting for their naivety – there is an unsuppressed jollity to them (the rocking horse has a magic all of its own) – but I pass on them, knowing I have more subtle and crumbly versions already in my bag.

A stall with painted wooden fir trees, a toy hanging from every branch. Another of porcelain angels in stiff golden net, bearing harps, that wouldn't look amiss in the back of a magazine with the limited-edition mugs of the Queen Mum. To make up for this sudden flash of angelic kitsch there is a green-decked stall of Lebkuchen, the ginger- and cinnamon-spiced confectionery that sings so sweetly of Germanic Christmases. Rounds and hearts and houses dripping with icing snow, the Lebkuchen are nothing if not fragrant.

I cannot miss the Hutzelbrot. The sister to our Christmas cake and with sultanas wedged tightly among dried pears, apricots and prunes, the southern German recipe has something of Italian panforte to it. For which, read reassuringly heavy. There is aniseed and cinnamon, honey and cloves, walnuts and sliced almonds, spiked with citrus zest and baked to a texture somewhere between Christmas cake and stollen. About the size of a house brick, the glistening brack will sit neatly in my suitcase.

Never having thought of myself as a cookie-cutter type of guy, I am nevertheless fascinated by a thousand shining templates hanging from a pinboard. Candy canes and teddy bears. Douglas firs and saws. Reindeers and a sleigh. There is a night-sky of stars in every size and shape, gingerbread people and churches with steeples. They are meant for bakers but my father was an engineer, and the quality of them intrigues. The crispness of the image, the curve of the half-moon, the solder of the soldier. I choose a couple of snowflakes and a good star or two. In cookie-cutter land the points of a star should be sharp, like an arrow, not soft and rounded like a ghost with its arms up.

The most difficult to access through the throng is that of a second generation of stallholder with the sort of tree baubles to send collectors weak at the knees. I join the scrummage, asserting myself with my elbows, like a granny at a jumble, aware that any sudden jolt could send a hand-painted globe crashing to the cobbles. I pounce on a pomegranate, its centre glistening like a jewellery box. There are figs too and wedges of watermelon. I buy pear halves in soft shades of silver and lemon, and some poisonous toadstools displayed in a nest of moss, straight from the Brothers Grimm. I'll be lucky to get such fragile treasures home in one piece, but they will be well cushioned with bubble-wrap, the modern-day answer to swaddling clothes.

What you should not miss is right above your head. Frosted fir cones and feathered birds, snow-sprinkled globes and glitter-encrusted stars, gaudy en masse but in isolation each piece as exquisite as any Fabergé egg.

3 DECEMBER

Mince pies and the shop windows of Nuremberg

The Christmas windows of Nuremberg are cluttered with the toys I never had. A tower of painted toy soldiers in hats: a bandsman's cap in green and gold; a bearskin you want to stroke; a shiny pointed Pickelhaube. A marching drummer with braided red jacket and golden chinstrap. A barman in a gingham shirt, with a bowler and frothing Pilsner. A bearded man in an Amish hat. A mouse in a crown and a mushroom with a shining red cap. It occurs to me that a mushroom probably always wears a cap.

A second window of hand-painted characters. A white-suited doctor with a stethoscope round his head. A witch. A train guard with a whistle and a blue-aproned chef. A snowman with a carrot for a nose. Another selling Schneebälle for 50 cents. The colours are as bright and solid as Father Christmas's coat. There are dolls with plaits and dead eyes. A feathered Tirolerhut. A flowered dirndl. A knitted doll in a red pixie hood. A hound in a Santa suit.

The third window, a cage of shimmering feather-tailed birds. A golden canary. A turquoise kingfisher and a pure white swan. There are scarlet birds and silver ones, a gold and blue macaw and a peacock with a saffron and royal-green train. No robin. Some are on golden threads, but most are on metal clips with a spring, the sort you can never quite get in the right position on the branch.

We move up a notch. A window of wooden set-scenes. Whole worlds at which to stare and dream. Vignettes in which to disappear. A red Ferris wheel with green seats and gilded spokes. A child-filled merry-go-round with waving parents and a naughty dog. A wooden house with a pointed roof, its windows ablaze while children build a snowman outside. A carousel of horses on poles, each with a harness in red and blue or rust and gold. Scarlet-coated riders bobbing up and down under striped awnings. At four hundred Euros you expect detail, care and craftsmanship and that is what you get. You get a story into which to climb, a snow-covered Narnia of your own.

These are the windows I never had as a child. The windows I dreamed of, to gaze at wide-eyed in awe and wonderment. The windows I knew from another life. 3D fairy stories set in snow. There are no Scalextric cars to crash or trains to derail. No screens to touch or consoles to turn. Just scenes into which to climb. Secret places in which to make up your own stories.

You could do the windows of Nuremberg by day. Start in the shops near the Christkindlesmarkt. But to do that is to miss the details. The faces, the expressions and, it must be said, the darker side. Toys, especially wooden ones with hand-painted faces, come to life only at night. When they think we are all asleep. It is then and only then, when the sky is dark and the spotlights have no competition, that you spy the tiny differences, the life that the painters have put into each one. There is nothing churned out in a Chinese factory here. Each piece is hand-painted. The characters they send out into the world to have adventures with their new young friends.

Me and the mince pie

My life is chock-a-block with rituals. The way I light a candle on the kitchen table before I sit down to write on a winter's morning. Choosing a radio programme to listen to, something from 'best of the week', while the coffee drips through the filter mid-morning. The fuss I make over the pre-dinner drink that one observer suggested was akin to a monk embarking on a Japanese tea ceremony. (I'm sorry, but there is just something perfect about that end of day drink in the right (chilled) glass, olives in a dish that quietly flatters their colour, with a second, smaller one for the stones.) And never more so than at Christmas, when my rituals come by the sack full.

Christmas Eve inevitably starts with me unfolding a paper print-out, fading, and a little dog-eared, an article Jeanette Winterson wrote for *The Times* about making mince pies. 'When you are satisfied that the pastry is cold, get out your Punch and Judy rolling pin.' I read it every year, before getting out my own rolling pin. It's not Punch and Judy, but near enough. Carols are playing, the table is dusted with flour and the pastry cutters are having their annual outing. This is the day I relish almost more than any other. And in part, because it is the day I get to make mince pies.

As sweet food goes, I would rather eat a diminutive, sugar-dusted mince pie than almost anything else. More than lemon meringue or treacle tart, plum pie or gooseberry crumble. Well, maybe not more than that last one, but certainly more than a French apple tart fine or a slice of bread and butter pudding. A mince pie carries with it everything I hold dear about this time of year; it is an edible symbol of the generosity, the kindness and the festive spirit. In that tiny morsel lies the very spirit of the season. There is no real religious significance, though one could, at a push, think of the pie as a manger, its sweet contents as the Christ child.

Lift the lid. A glossy paste of currants and raisins, brown sugar and cinnamon, mixed spice and citrus zest. There is candied peel and the comfort of Bramley apples and suet. A preserve, sweet, spicy, fruity, whose history goes back to the Middle Ages, and whose smell is redolent of the happiest moments of my childhood.

The crust

Shortcrust, sweetcrust, rough puff or puff? There is no traditional answer so it becomes a matter of choice. But let us go back a bit. The early pies were savoury, the pastry made with lard rather than butter. As someone who will take any opportunity to eat any part of the pig, I often swap some of the butter for lard.

Using a sweet paté brisée, the French sweet shortcrust, is surely pushing the sugar bag too far. Puff and rough puff doughs introduce a welcome lightness and is what I would use if my handiwork is to be eaten the day it is made. Neither keep well. Even stored in a biscuit tin the crust tends to toughen up overnight. Rolled thinly and eaten no more than an hour or two after baking, a puff pastry mince pie can be exquisite, warm and crisp and buttery and as fragile as a butterfly.

My go-to crust is made with half butter and half lard, and no sugar. I roll the dough as thinly as I dare and ensure that the bottom is always slightly thicker than the top. As good as thin pastry is, we must never forget it also has a job to do. Many a mince pie is eaten without a plate.

A jolly good mince pie

A classic, simple mince pie, devoid of bells, whistles and creative meddling. The pastry is a rich but workable shortcrust. It won't collapse in the carol singer's mittens. The pies themselves will stand or fall by the quality of mincemeat. Go for broke, Christmas is not the time for parsimony. The little darlings are at their most delicious when eaten warm. Baked a day or more before, they reheat nicely.

Makes 18 small pies
unsalted butter – 75g
lard – 75g
plain flour – 150g
an egg yolk
a little cold water
good-quality mincemeat – 375g
icing sugar, for dusting

You will also need a 12-hole tartlet tin, each hole measuring 6cm x 2cm deep. It is best to bake the pies in a batch of twelve, then a second of six.

Cut the butter and lard into small pieces and rub it into the flour with your fingertips until you have what looks like coarse, fresh breadcrumbs. If you do this in the food processor it will take a matter of seconds. Add the egg yolk, then mix briefly with just enough water to bring to a smooth dough. You will probably need only one or two tablespoons. Bring the dough together into a firm ball, then knead it gently on a floured board for a couple of minutes until it softens. Reserve half of the dough, then roll the remainder out thinly. Set the oven at 200°C/Gas 6.

Using cookie cutters or the top of an espresso cup, cut out eighteen discs of pastry. (There may be a tiny bit left over.) Place twelve discs of the pastry in the tartlet tins, reserving six for the second batch, smoothing them up the sides so the edges stand very slightly proud of the tin. Fill each one with a dollop of mincemeat. A level tablespoon is probably all you will get into them, unless you have especially deep tins. Be generous. Roll out the reserved pastry with any leftover trimmings and make a further eighteen discs of pastry, reserving six again. Slightly dampen each of these round the edge with cold water then lay them over each tart and press firmly to seal the edges.

Using the point of a small kitchen knife cut a small slit in the centre of each pie and bake for twenty minutes until golden. Let them cool for a few minutes, then slide them out of their tins with a palette knife and serve warm, dusted with icing sugar. Repeat with the remaining pastry discs and mincemeat.

Mincemeat and mascarpone tarts

Puff pastry for these. I can't pretend I make my own. There is far too much to do to revisit Miss Adam's domestic science lessons – 'roll, fold and fold again'. The bought stuff is fine if you make sure it is made with butter and you roll it out so it is thinner then brushed with melted butter or beaten egg, the way I suggest below.

Makes 12
For the pastry:
frozen puff pastry, defrosted – 500g
good-quality mincemeat – 300g
mascarpone – 120g

To finish:
an egg
caster sugar, for dusting

You will also need a 12-hole patty or muffin tin, an 8–9cm cookie cutter and a 7.5cm cutter for the tops.

Cut the pastry in half and roll out one half thinly on a floured board. Using pastry cutters or the top of an espresso cup, cut out twelve discs of pastry that will fit your patty tins. Place them in the tartlet tins, smoothing them up the sides so the edges stand very slightly proud of the tin. Fill each one with a dollop of mincemeat then a spoonful of the mascarpone.

Roll out the remaining pastry on a floured board and cut out a further twelve discs. Slightly dampen each of these round the edge with cold water then lay them over each tart and press firmly to seal the edges.

In a small mixing bowl, beat the egg lightly then brush over the top of the tarts, and sprinkle generously with sugar. Using the point of a small kitchen knife, cut a small slit in the centre of each pie. Bake for twenty minutes until golden. Let them calm down for a few minutes, then slide them out of their tins with a palette knife and serve warm and if you wish, dusted with icing sugar.

A family mince pie

A large, round mince pie will need some sort of top if it is not to look suspiciously like a cow pat. An entire pastry crust might be too much, so a bundle of shortcrust pastry strips, woven into a lattice, is often called into place. This works well, and looks best if each ribbon of pastry is twisted slightly as you lay it on the filling. My fondness for pastry means I sometimes cover the entire surface with the stuff, as if I were making an apple pie.

Open-top tarts

The top crust of a mince pie is there to keep the filling moist, but you can bake them without, like a jam tart. Unprotected by a crust, the mincemeat will caramelise round the edge, which is a good thing. The filling lacks the gloss of a dark jam such as blackcurrant or raspberry, so a dusting of icing sugar will spare their blushes.

Star-topped tarts

Get out your star-shaped cookie cutters. Roll out the pastry and cut out a large star for each tart. More beautiful, to my mind are stars of various sizes, laid over the filling, with their points slightly overlapping. Before baking, brush them with lightly beaten egg and sprinkle with caster sugar. A constellation of pastry stars, set against the night sky of dark, fruit-laden filling.

A crumble top

A rough pebble-dash of crumble makes a delightful alternative to a pastry lid, and looks attractive with a dusting of icing sugar. Like gravel under a fall of snow. The recipe here will cover a tray of twelve small tarts.

For the crumble:
plain flour – 220g
butter – 100g
light muscovado sugar – 3 tablespoons

Rub the butter into the flour until it resembles breadcrumbs. Stir in the sugar.

Marzipan and a suggestion of orange zest

The traditional shortcrust pastry lid can be replaced with a piece of almond marzipan; 100g of marzipan is enough for twelve tarts. Roll out the marzipan to a thickness of 5mm on a very lightly floured board, cut star shapes with a cookie cutter, then lay them on the filling in place of pastry tops. Bake for fifteen minutes at 190°C/Gas 5. You may like to knead a tablespoon of finely grated orange zest into your marzipan before you roll it out.

Christmas tarts

It seems unfair that those who have an aversion to mincemeat don't get a little tart to eat when they come back from Midnight Mass. These open-topped versions smell like mince pies but have a filling that is chewier and sweeter and somehow even more fragile. A modern version, and one I think is worth trying.

Makes 24
unsalted butter – 150g
plain flour – 295g
salt – a pinch (optional)
a little cold water

For the filling:
golden syrup – 200g
sultanas – 75g
candied peel – 50g
mixed spice – a pinch
butter – 25g
soft amaretti Disaronno – 4, or
4 tablespoons plain, soft cake crumbs
a large egg

You will also need 2 × 12-hole tart sheets or 24 small tart tins with a width of 4cm and a depth of 1cm.

To make the pastry, cut the butter into small chunks and rub it into the flour with your fingertips. It should resemble coarse, fresh breadcrumbs.

I sometimes add a pinch of salt, but it is up to you. Sprinkle a little cold water over the crumbs and bring them together with your hands to form a soft, but not sticky, ball. Pat the dough into a sausage the same diameter as the holes in your tart tins, wrap in clingfilm and chill in the fridge for half an hour.

Preheat the oven to 190°C/Gas 5. To make the filling, warm the syrup in a saucepan with the dried fruit, mixed spice and butter, then stir in the amaretti or cake crumbs. Remove the pan from the heat, then stir the beaten egg into the mixture. Cut the roll of pastry into twenty-four thin slices, then use one to line each hole in the tart tin. Trim the edges with a small knife. Divide the filling between the tarts, but don't overfill them, then bake until golden and bubbling – about fifteen to twenty minutes.

As the pastry is very rich, the finished tarts are very fragile so let them cool in their tins for eight to ten minutes before removing them.

Fig and orange shortbreads

Another alternative to the traditional mince pie.

Makes approximately 12–16
For the fig paste:
dried figs – 150g
golden sultanas – 100g

For the shortbread:
butter – 200g
golden icing sugar – 90g
vanilla extract – a few drops
ground almonds – 140g
plain flour – 190g
shelled pistachio nuts – 80g
the zest of an orange

To finish:
icing sugar
dried rose petals

Set the oven at 180°C/Gas 4. Line a baking sheet.

Remove and discard the hard stems from the figs, then put the figs into a food processor, add the golden sultanas and process to a coarse paste. Set aside.

Put the butter, cut into small pieces, into the bowl of a food mixer, add the icing sugar and beat, with a flat paddle beater, to a pale, soft cream. Pour in the vanilla extract, blend in the ground almonds and flour. Roughly chop the pistachios and fold them in, together with the orange zest.

Lightly flour a chopping board. Take a level tablespoon of the fig paste and roll it into a ball. Scoop up two tablespoons of the almond shortbread dough, roll it into a ball then press a deep hollow in the centre. Place the ball of fig paste in the hollow and draw the almond shortbread around it to completely enclose it. Flatten the balls lightly, then place on the lined baking sheet, with a little space between them.

Bake for twenty to twenty-five minutes until pale biscuit-coloured, then remove from the oven and allow to cool. Sift icing sugar over the biscuits and, if you wish, scatter with dried rose petals.

5 DECEMBER

Krampusnacht, and a cake that smells of sugar and spice

The fallen leaves remain in crisp piles under the chestnut trees outside the house. No one sweeps them up. Instead, we leave them to break down into a chocolate-brown loam. I planted narcissi under them once, but the bulbs mysteriously moved house to further down the road, where they bloom, laughing at me, each spring. A branch has broken off in the wind and I pick it up and bring it into the house.

I like the bare branches of winter, their brittle twigs and lichen-covered bark. They are more sculptural once the leaves are off, and look handsome in a large, heavy-based vase. (You sometimes need a rock in the bottom to stop the weight of the branch pulling the container over.) In a week or two, the tips of the branches will be hung with wooden decorations on fine cotton, laser-cut stars mostly, the colour of driftwood. An idea I spotted in a candlelit window in Gothenburg last winter.

There are other foraged woods in the house too. A mossy stick from the robinia in the back garden; two or three long branches of spruce; the odd lump of wood with peeling bark the colour of a cinnamon stick, picked up from the park. I value these as much as any bunch of flowers, all the more in frosty morning light when their shapes have a haunting beauty against the white lime render of the kitchen walls.

I settle the branch into its new home in the hall, where it will stay until I accidentally snap the finer twigs off and it shifts from elegant relic to sad stump. I bake, a second version of a cake I have been attempting for some time. A chocolate cake with the same spicing that appears in Lebkuchen.

My plan is to ice the finished cake with dark chocolate, and perhaps a few cubes of sticky preserved ginger. I rarely cook with chocolate, preferring crisp dark squares to a slice of cake, but the idea appeals when it meets praline or spices. This time the cake is a success, less gooey than before (I have rather had enough of gooey chocolate cakes), with mysterious back-notes of cinnamon and mace, ginger and spice. I am really rather pleased with it. A chocolate spice cake that smells of fairy tales.

Dark chocolate spice cake

Makes 12 little cakes
ground cinnamon – 2 teaspoons
ground ginger – 2 teaspoons
ground mace – $\frac{1}{2}$ teaspoon
self-raising flour – 250g
dark chocolate – 100g
marzipan – 80g
dates, stoned – 200g
golden syrup – 200g
butter – 125g
dark muscovado sugar – 125g
crystallised ginger – 3 balls
candied orange peel – 70g
large eggs – 2
milk – 240ml

To finish:
dark chocolate – 150g
preserved ginger in syrup – 3 lumps

You will also need a 24cm square baking tin.

Mix together the cinnamon, ground ginger and mace, stir into the flour and set aside. Roughly chop the chocolate. Cut the marzipan into small pieces. Roughly chop the dates. Set the oven at 180°C/Gas 4. Line the baking tin with a piece of baking parchment.

Put the golden syrup, butter and sugar into a small pan and place over a moderate heat to melt. Cut the ginger into small dice and add it, with the candied peel, to the melted butter and sugar. Let the mixture bubble for one minute, then remove from the heat.

Break the eggs into a bowl, beat lightly with a fork, then mix in the milk. Remove the butter and sugar mixture from the heat and pour into the flour, stirring smoothly and firmly with a large metal spoon. Mix in the milk and eggs, chopped chocolate, dates and marzipan. Then pour into the lined tin, scraping the bowl clean with a rubber spatula. The mixture should be runny, not cake-like.

Bake for forty minutes, or until a metal skewer comes out without any raw mixture attached. Take out of the oven and leave to settle and cool before removing from its tin and on to a cooling rack.

Melt the chocolate in a bowl over simmering water. Cut the cake into twelve equal squares, pull them slightly away from each other, then spoon the melted chocolate over the individual cakes, letting it trickle down the sides. Cut the ginger into small dice and place some on top of each of the twelve little cakes. Let the chocolate set crisp before eating. They will keep in an airtight tin or plastic container for several days.

Krampusnacht

After dinner, I curl up in a chair in front of the fire, reading. The wind settles into a haunting moan. Shadows flicker. Candles gutter in the draught. I pull a blanket over me and read about Krampus.

Tonight is Krampusnacht, the feast of the legendary Krampus. A Santa Claus for naughty children, he is thoroughly menacing, part goat, part demon, hairy with huge curling horns, a long tail and a terrifying tongue. Long a figure of folklore in many parts of Europe, rather than bringing gifts to good children he punishes those who have misbehaved during the previous year.

The legend of Krampus has been celebrated for centuries in many Alpine towns and villages, particularly in Bavaria. He is known throughout Germany, Austria, Hungary, Croatia and the Czech Republic. Much less so here and in the United States.

On this night, folk who dress up as the mythological horned creature will come lumbering through town, waving flaming torches to a cacophony of bells and crashing of chains. In reality it is an event probably more suitable for adults than kids. Krampus often carries Ruten, a bunch of birch twigs with which to swat children. Occasionally he will appear with a basket on his back (for carrying away the particularly naughty ones).

Krampus scares the pants off me. Not the silly American film of the same name, but the rituals that come to life in Alpine villages on this night every year. But then I have always enjoyed being slightly scared. As a child, spooky fairy tales, ghost stories and horror films were always high on my list. It is easy to enjoy being scared when you are tucked up in the safety of your own home. Probably less so when you meet Krampus in real life.

Should Krampus turn up at your home tonight, and I sincerely hope he doesn't, for he is very, very scary, it is best to offer him some schnapps and perhaps a piece of cake. The one on page 205 will do nicely.

A tale of two polentas

Our family tree contains centuries of blacksmiths, gunsmiths, silversmiths and metalworkers, in what sometimes reads like an episode of *Peaky Blinders*. My grandmother worked in a dairy, delivering milk by horse and cart. A single mum, she brought up a daughter and four sons alone. (My grandfather died aged thirty-two.) I knew her only towards the end of her life, when she was bad-tempered, contrary and exhausted. Visits to her house were memorable, if only for the tin bath hanging by the coal-fired kitchen range and my puzzlement at being in a house without an indoor bathroom.

I have no idea how she made ends meet or how she gained a reputation for her lavish Christmas entertaining. My aunt, who died aged one hundred, would tell stories about how she would look after the dairy while my grandmother would put her apron on and bake for Britain. (Come to think of it, I never actually saw my gran without her apron, faded and worn thin from years of washing.) She baked mostly sweet things – fruit cakes, pies and enough lemon curd tarts to feed half the street. My aunt told of the smoking black kitchen range being covered in trays of little tarts and pastries. (My guess is, short of money, she made them to sell to her neighbours.)

My grandmother insisted that Father Christmas existed, even during one winter visit when we sat by the fire and I whispered to her that I knew otherwise. She wanted me to go on believing. Fifty years on, I can see it was she who wanted to believe in him.

Santa Claus is possibly the most complicated character in history. He is, by turns, Greek or Turkish, American, Dutch and British. He is pictured as a bishop, a goat and a fat guy in a red coat. The only thing we know for sure is that he is benevolent, the bringer of gifts to good children. And yes, of course he exists.

The figure we know as Father Christmas, a jolly, bearded gentleman in red who distributes gifts to children on Christmas Eve, is derived from St Nicholas, a fourth-century Middle Eastern bishop, and later saint, who gave gifts to the poor, in particular children. But the picture of a large bearded character in a long cloak who rides across the night sky far more resembles Odin (Woden in old English), the Norse god worshipped in pre-Christian times.

Saint Nicholas, the patron saint of children and pawnbrokers, was a Greek Christian bishop who resided in Myra, once part of the Byzantine empire, now in Turkey. In the Middle Ages he was celebrated on December 6, when gifts would be given in his honour, an observance which was later moved to Christmas Eve.

Today is the Feast of St Nicholas, a day barely recognised in Britain but celebrated elsewhere and nowhere more enthusiastically than in Holland. There is a painting of the feast in the Rijksmuseum – one of my favourite art galleries of all – by Jan Steen. Finished in 1668, it depicts a large family, the happiness of the children evident in their faces (few paintings of the period depict anyone smiling) as they hold their presents – an orange, a gingerbread man, a doll dressed in white. The magnificent, burnished bread resting against a table laden with fruit, coins and sweetmeats caught my eye.

The traditional food of the feast is indeed mostly sweet: rich brioche-style yeast breads in the form of St Nicholas decorated with almonds and currants. Depending on where you are celebrating, you may be offered biskupský chlebíček, a Slovak bread in the form of a bishop; slavski kolach, a Serbian bread decorated with a cross and flowers, or cream cheese-filled bread purses, a delicious reminder of the coin purses St Nicholas would toss through the window. There may be coffee cake or perhaps Nikolausstiefel, where the dough is shaped as a sweet-laden boot, decorated with poppy seeds, powdered sugar and liquorice. American St Nicholas buns are decorated with candy canes and sprigs of pine.

It should be noted that whether you know him as Santa Claus, Saint Nicholas, Saint Nick, Kris Kringle or Father Christmas, he will only deliver gifts to good children. By which he probably means kind, polite and well-behaved. It is worth remembering too that Krampus may also visit.

Santa resides at the North Pole. The Royal Mail deals each year with thousands of letters to Father Christmas. Children who write to him need to get their letters in by December 9 and must remember to include their name and address on a stamped envelope. (Apparently, many forget to include their address.) Most will get a reply from the Royal Mail Chief Elf, which must surely be the best job title on Earth. His address, by the way, is:

Santa/Father Christmas
Santa's Grotto
Reindeerland, XM4 5HQ

We don't really celebrate this day here, although we do find ourselves raising our glasses to the saintly Nicholas, bringer of gifts and all round good guy, as we tuck into grilled pork chops and deep, warming pools of cheese and spinach polenta.

I should tell you about the polenta, because it has gone from being something I now feel I ate somewhat grudgingly, to something whose silken comforts I cannot get enough of. Polenta is now a winter staple chez Nige, but it took me a long time to find its joy. A lunch cooked by Florence Knight in Soho opened my eyes to what I had been missing. I had simply been making my polenta too thick. Too much grain, too little liquid. I had been too sparing on the cream and butter and cheese.

The more slovenly the texture, oozing lazily on to the plate, the more I like it. I now make two versions, one with the texture of potato purée, the other a little softer and more soupy. The choice, as always, is yours. Be prepared to have a little extra cream and butter to hand, as grains vary and you may wish to add more.

Pork chops, spinach polenta

Serves 4
pork chops – 4 × 300g
oil

For the polenta:
spinach – 250g (weight with stalks)
water – 500ml, plus a few tablespoons for the spinach
milk – 500ml
fine polenta – 125g
double cream – 100ml
butter – 50g
Parmesan – 50g, finely grated

You should probably get the spinach on before you start the polenta, as it is virtually impossible to juggle both tasks. Wash the spinach well, then put it into a large pan set over a moderate heat and pour in a few tablespoons of water. Cover tightly with a lid and bring to the boil. As soon as the leaves start to wilt – a matter of two or three minutes – turn the leaves over with kitchen tongs and cover once more. Continue cooking for a minute or two, until the leaves are soft and bright green. Remove them from the heat and drain in a colander. Refresh them in cold, running water, then squeeze firmly in your hands to remove as much water as you can. Place the spinach on a chopping board and roughly chop.

Pour the water and milk into a large, deep pan and place over a moderate heat. Bring the mixture to the boil, then salt generously. Rain the polenta into the liquid in a steady stream, stirring continuously. Take great care that the mixture doesn't bubble and spit at you. Lower the heat as necessary.

Keep stirring over the heat for a good twenty minutes, until the mixture is smooth and creamy. It should be quite wet. Meanwhile, oil, season and grill the chops. Warm the cream in a small pan. When the chops are ready, beat the butter and cream into the polenta. Stir in the grated Parmesan, then fold in the chopped spinach. Check the seasoning, adding salt and black pepper to taste.

Spoon the polenta on to plates and serve with the grilled chops.

We also make a meatless version, with slightly softer, soupier polenta, piling it with roasted onions in place of the pork.

Soft cheese polenta with roast onions

A soft, almost soupy polenta to eat with roasted onions. I sometimes add 100ml of double cream, warmed in a small saucepan, to the polenta. I use Tunworth or another soft cheese to finish. Camembert will do.

Serves 4
For the onions:
onions, medium – 4
olive oil – 50ml
butter – 50g, a thick slice
thyme sprigs – 10

For the polenta:
water – 500ml
full cream milk – 500ml
fine polenta – 150g
butter – 50g
Parmesan – 100g, finely grated
soft cheese to finish – 200g

Set the oven at 200°C/Gas 6. Peel the onions, halve them, then cut each half in two. Put them into a roasting tin, trickle the oil over them, dot with butter and a few sprigs of thyme, then bake for twenty to thirty minutes, until golden and soft, basting from time to time.

Make the polenta: pour the water and milk into a large, deep pan and place over a moderate heat. Bring the mixture to the boil, then salt generously. Rain the polenta into the liquid in a steady stream, stirring continuously. Take great care that the mixture doesn't bubble and spit at you (it can be like a volcano). Lower the heat as necessary.

Keep stirring over the heat for a good twenty minutes, until the mixture is smooth and creamy. It shouldn't be too thick. Beat the butter into the polenta, then stir in the grated Parmesan. (At this point you could add a little warmed cream if you wish.) Check the seasoning, adding salt and black pepper to taste.

Spoon the polenta into warm dishes and top with the baked onions. Place the cheese on top of the onions and let it soften.

A cracker, a quacker and a Danish charm

Roast duck, and the invariable ensuing fug of smoke, is just the thing for a winter's night. In fact, there is no other time of year I eat it. The juices and fat that come from the bird are too full of promise to sit in the bottom of a roasting tin. By stuffing the bird with potatoes, breadcrumbs or grains you can sponge up and exploit much of that goodness.

Pearl barley, not the nuttier brown 'pot' barley, makes a toothsome stuffing when seasoned with thyme and mushrooms and a dash of sherry (I often use mirin). The pale grains soak up much of the fat from the duck, swelling with flavour and goodness.

It occurs to me, as I spoon the moist stuffing out on to the plates, that this might make a splendid Christmas dinner for two (with enough left over for duck and watercress sandwiches).

While the bird is crisping nicely in the oven, I take another look at my Christmas list and wonder whether or not we actually need crackers.

The atmosphere at a family Christmas dinner was once almost ruined because of my throwing a tantrum over being forced to wear a paper hat ('a stupid, STUPID, paper hat') throughout the meal. I don't know quite why I made such a fuss, but I did. Crackers, those foil-decorated cardboard tubes filled with corny jokes, useless toys and paper hats, are pretty naff really. They serve no real purpose and if anything sum up the sheer waste of Christmas. And yes, the paper hats within are embarrassing. And yet, I now secretly rather enjoy pulling a cracker. The daft mottos, the mild snap as if a cap has been fired from a toy gun, the pointless gift being fired across the room, are all daft things that used to annoy me about the season but no longer do.

The cracker has been with us since the 1840s. There is a reason it resembles a bon-bon, a sweet wrapped in foil. The first commercial cracker was made by Tom Smith, the owner of a sweet company whose sugared almonds were sold in a twist of coloured paper. To increase sales at Christmas he invented the idea of a giant version, and in 1860 introduced a device that snapped when pulled, resembling the crack of twigs burning in the hearth. The idea was a success. The mottos and trinkets were added by his son, Walter, to distinguish Smith's crackers from any others. The company continues to this day, and crackers have become as much a part of the Christmas Day table as the flaming pudding.

The snap, incidentally, is made by the involvement of a layer of silver fulminate, a mild explosive so fragile it can be set off by the smallest movement. It may be useful to know that Tom Smith's website has a minute by minute countdown to Christmas, so you know, at any time of year, how much longer you must wait to pull your cracker.

And the paper hats? The idea dates back to Saturnalia, the Roman celebration held on December 17, when slaves were allowed to wear conical felt hats to the feast at which they were waited on by their masters. But here's the real point. You can't pull your own cracker. You have to pick an aunt, a grandparent, anyone, to pull it with you. It's a bonding thing. Which is why the Christmas table seems to come to life once the crackers come out. Though to this day, I still won't wear my paper hat.

Roast duck with pearl barley and red cabbage

Serves 4
pearl barley – 200g
chestnut mushrooms – 300g
olive oil – 4 tablespoons
garlic – 3 cloves
chopped rosemary – 2 tablespoons
thyme leaves – 3 tablespoons
mirin or dry sherry – 4 tablespoons
finely grated zest of a lemon
a duck, oven-ready – 2.5kg
red cabbage – 400g
greens such as cabbage or Brussels sprouts – 200g
red wine vinegar – 2 tablespoons
redcurrant jelly – 2 tablespoons

Rinse the pearl barley briefly, then cook in lightly salted boiling water for thirty minutes. Drain and set aside. Set the oven at 220°C/Gas 7.

Cut the mushrooms into quarters. Warm the olive oil in a pan, then add the mushrooms and let them fry for ten minutes or so, until golden. Peel and thinly slice the garlic, add to the pan and let it colour, then stir in the chopped rosemary leaves and the thyme. When everything has continued cooking for a couple of minutes, mix in the mirin or sherry and the lemon zest. Season lightly with salt and black pepper, then stir in the cooked pearl barley and remove from the heat.

Place the duck in a roasting tin. Fill the chest cavity of the bird with the pearl barley stuffing. If there is too much, add it to the roasting tin. Roast in the preheated oven for twenty minutes, then lower the heat to 160°C/Gas 3 and cook for eighty to ninety minutes. If the skin appears to be browning too quickly, cover loosely with a piece of kitchen foil.

Shred the red cabbage and the greens into strips about the width of a pencil, keeping any shredded tough stalks separate. Spoon about 4 tablespoons of

fat from the duck roasting tin into a deep saucepan, place over a moderate heat, then add the shredded red and green cabbage stalks. Let them fry for five minutes, then add the shredded red cabbage leaves. When they are tender, stir in a little salt and the red wine vinegar, then, when the vinegar has finished spitting and sizzling, add the shredded green leaves and the redcurrant jelly. Turn the cabbage over until it is glossy and coated with jelly.

Carve the duck, spoon out the pearl barley stuffing and serve with the red cabbage.

Rice with cream, almonds and scarlet fruits

Pudding today is also grain-based, not that you would know it. It is also a dish I have been practising for Christmas, my take on the velvety ris a la mande, the Danish pudding of rice, chopped almonds and cherry sauce. Despite its Dansk origins I first met it one dark winter's afternoon at the Litteraturhuset in Oslo. The creamy rice and scarlet fruits eaten by the light of a single candle, a simple scarlet votive, after a dish of pale and serene cauliflower soup. Thoroughly toasty, I ventured out into the deliciously frosty Norwegian air.

The Danish have a charming ritual. When they make the traditional version of this dish, with chopped almonds rather than flaked, they reserve a whole nut, which they then bury deep in the pudding. The finder wins a prize. Nowadays this is usually confined to coins, but Danish friends tell me that it was often a marzipan pig.

I should also add that this is an essential part of my weekday winter breakfast, for which I usually add blueberries or frozen blackcurrants to the compote.

Serves 4
pudding or Arborio rice – 95g
water – 320ml
full cream milk – 320ml
half a lemon
a star anise
a vanilla pod

caster sugar – 4 tablespoons
flaked almonds – 50g
double cream – 150ml

For the compote:
frozen cherries, lingonberries or cranberries – 250g
caster sugar – 50g
a star anise

Put the rice into a saucepan with the water and milk and bring to the boil. Using a vegetable peeler, remove four strips of zest from the lemon. Add them to the rice with the star anise, the seeds from inside the vanilla pod, scraped from the pod with the point of a knife, then turn the heat down so the rice simmers, gently, for about fifteen minutes, until tender. Watch it carefully, stirring regularly.

Stir in the sugar and set aside in a dish to cool. (It will be quite liquid at this point.) When the rice is cool, refrigerate for a good two hours until cold and thick. Toast the almonds in a dry pan.

Put the frozen fruits into a saucepan with the caster sugar, 6 tablespoons of water and the star anise. Bring to the boil. Lower the heat and let the fruit simmer until the berries are starting to burst and release their juice, and the sugar has dissolved. Keep warm.

Lightly whip the cream, then fold into the rice pudding together with the toasted almonds (reserving a few for the top). Spoon into bowls and trickle the fruit compote over.

Note to self: order crackers.

8 DECEMBER

Spice, crumbs and cream

There has been a golden tin by the coffee machine for some time now. Each year I fill it with round Lebkuchen that I bring back from late-autumn trips to Cologne, Oslo, Gothenburg or Vienna. The best I have ever had hail from Nuremberg. You can buy them in Britain, of course, but I like to hunt them out nearer their spiritual home. Soft, open-textured and spiced with mace and ginger, they are mercifully unsweet. Even those with an almost transparent crust of icing. The small, dark-chocolate-covered ones are my favourite, despite their pesky layer of rice paper, like a macaroon.

Texturally, Lebkuchen hangs between biscuit, cookie and cake. Some might argue that the disc of honey and spice is technically a cookie (because of its soft texture) or a cake (but only in so much as a Jaffa cake is legally a cake). It is, though, categorically a form of gingerbread, soft and chewy with nibs of almonds and often a thin disc of rice paper on its base. Often known as Pfefferkuchen because of its spicy character, it also has notes of honey, marzipan, cinnamon and mace. The name is most probably derived from honey cake.

Honey has for centuries been considered to have healing qualities (despite the fact it is just sugar with good PR), and honey cakes were once worn as a talisman to ward off evil spirits. Lebkuchen have been made since the thirteenth century and are something we must thank Franconian monks for. There is a record of them being made in 1395 in Nuremberg, and a legend that Emperor Friedrich III gave four thousand of the gingerbreads away to children at a party in 1487, each bearing his portrait.

The ingredients are honey, hazelnuts, almonds or walnuts, candied peel, aniseed, ground cloves, ginger, coriander, allspice and cardamom. The breads are decorated with whole skinned almonds, then baked until softly firm with a light, crisp outer crust. I buy them from Christmas markets, where they are sold as rounds, rectangles or even heart shapes. Decorated with coloured icing, messages ('a souvenir from Nürnberger Christkindlesmarkt'), whole nuts, or dipped in chocolate. They are at their most charming when decorated as gingerbread houses, with snow icing dripping from the roof, but also come in discs the size of an old record, as logs covered with dark chocolate and as scarlet-iced Christmas stockings, complete with a ribbon to hang from the tree.

You can locate the site of a Pfefferkuchen stall in one of the Nuremberg Christmas markets just by sniffing the air. Little Hansel and Gretel houses scented with cardamom and honey, they are as irresistible to me as a packet of sugared almonds.

At least once a year I make a pudding with Lebkuchen by crumbling the biscuits into softly whipped cream and leaving the spiced crumbs to soften and bleed into the cream. It is the easiest, most useful dessert in the world. I contrast the general creaminess with a layer of dark chocolate that sets as crisply as ice on a pond.

Lebkuchen chocolate cream

A pudding based on one of my mum's that she made with cream and ginger-nuts. The texture of the cream is crucial. As it starts to thicken, slow down the speed of your whisking so that you can stop as soon as the cream will just hold its shape on the whisk. It should still be able to slide, albeit slowly, off a spoon. The cream and biscuits need a good four or five hours in the fridge for the biscuits to soften and flavour the cream.

Serves 4
double cream – 250g
Lebkuchen or other spiced ginger biscuits – 200g
dark chocolate – 90g

In a chilled bowl, slowly whip the cream until it is just starting to sit in waves. It should barely keep its shape. By no means must it be stiffly whipped. Crumble

the Lebkuchen into the cream and gently fold together. Do this slowly and tenderly so that the cream doesn't thicken any further. Divide between four glasses or small bowls. Set in the fridge for a good four or five hours.

Break the chocolate into pieces and melt in a heatproof bowl resting over a small pan of simmering water. Once the chocolate is liquid, spoon it over the whipped cream and biscuit mixture, then return to the fridge to set crisp.

Note to self: buy stamps.

The Christmas card

The e-card, the modern version of Henry Cole's 1843 invention, lacks everything that the traditional paper card embodies. The shuffle of envelopes as they fall on the doormat; the quizzical analysis of the handwriting; the tugging of the tightly wedged card from its envelope – and the delight on finding a greeting from someone you haven't seen for a while or whose writing you didn't recognise. The idea that the card has been chosen specially for you and has been handwritten by the sender brings with it a warmth of friendship that no electronic greeting could even aspire to. *'That has been handwritten'*: in the days of texts, emails and tweets, that reads like something out of Dickens.

If we are to send cards at all, they require more involvement than smugly pressing 'send'. Or worse, 'send all'. The handwritten card says you care. The e-card says you don't. Cold, efficient and a wee bit too business-like. If you are going to send an electronic Christmas greeting, I'd rather you didn't, thank you. If you can't be arsed to put pen to paper, then don't bother.

The first Christmas card was commissioned by Sir Henry Cole, civil servant and inventor (he had a hand in the design of the Penny Black) from the illustrator John Callcott Horsley (a prude, who protested against the introduction of nude life models). The illustration featured a group of people raising their glasses to the recipient, surrounded by two vignettes of folk giving food and clothing to the poor. The batch of two thousand cards was the beginning of the phenomenon that is only now starting to wane.

The first cards went into mass production in the late 1800s, and within the next twenty years, now-famous firms, such as Hallmark and Raphael Tuck, started producing cards in their millions. The idea of a handwritten card really took off during the First World War, when people wanted to send greetings to soldiers stationed away from home. The Christmas card has not stood still. The illustrations have gone through various stages, from glitter-

coated village scenes, with churches and snow, to reproductions of paintings of the Nativity. But the religious element was never the original intention, only toasting your friends and loved ones, the early cards depicting fairies, flowers and paintings of children rather than the babe in the manger.

The habit of sending cards to all and sundry has for the most part disappeared. During my teens I would be commandeered in early December into writing all the family's cards and addressing the envelopes. I well remember the horror on my father's face the year I wrote them all with a biro instead of my usual fountain pen. I can only imagine what he would make of the e-card. We would send upwards of two hundred, to everyone from the grocer to every neighbour in the village.

The charity card first became a phenomenon thirty years ago, when a proportion of the profit from the sale of each card helped to fund a well-known charity. The now famous UNICEF card, ahead of its time, was introduced in 1949, Oxfam's a few years later, and now almost every card that lands on my doormat is charity-based. I like guessing which charity each sender has chosen before I turn the card over.

Then the occasional envelope arrives embellished with foil stickers. I have to admit to rather liking these. I rather wish I had been in Germany in 2004, when the German post office gave away twenty million scented stickers to make your cards smell of everything from fir trees to gingerbread. Presumably, you could smell the post arriving as well as hear it.

The handwritten card's days are numbered. The writing is not so much on the card as on the wall. Most of us receive fewer cards than we did the previous year, and the habit is leaning towards sending fewer but more expensive cards. Those I give tend to be bought individually rather than in packs, each one carefully considered as to whether it is right for its intended recipient. Cards now come decorated with everything from embroidery to jewels, bits of fabric and even twigs and bits of lace. There are a few that I especially look forward to receiving, greetings from friends who clearly enjoy choosing elaborately produced examples, literally works of art, and many of which I use throughout the year as bookmarks.

My first Christmas card arrived yesterday. A trifle too early, I feel. It has spurred me into writing the few I actually send. There is no one day when I buy them all. I tend to know whom I am buying for and pick them up gradually over a few weeks, as and when I see something special. I have been known to buy them as early as September. Though if I am honest, I usually end up losing them, only to have to buy a replacement. The original, perfect card usually turns up shortly after the event, when I am having the post-festive tidy.

I should add that my father's hurt, steely glower has stayed with me and I write all my cards in fountain pen.

A few notes

How you send your cards is your business, and I add the following notes as observations rather than as a guilt trip. It is a personal aide-memoire rather than a decree.

- If you are unsure whether you should send someone a card, then may I suggest you don't? They will only be as puzzled as you are.
- Don't surprise people you haven't communicated with for ages. They will only think you had some cards left over.
- 'Funny' cards are rarely as amusing to the recipient as they are to the buyer.
- Refuse to buy any card covered with glitter. Unless, of course, it is your intention to actually annoy your friends.
- If there is a verse, read it carefully to make sure it is appropriate.
- Never send a card with a verse.
- There are two formats of card: portrait and landscape. The latter rarely stays up for more than a day or two, then slowly flattens, pushing the other cards over.
- Remember that much recycled paper doesn't like fountain pen, acting more like blotting paper. Use a fibre tip.
- Never send your cards too early. It looks like you're 'getting them out of the way'. (Which, of course, you are.)
- It is better not to send a card than to send one that arrives in the flat days after Christmas. A lone card on the doormat on December 28 tends to look somewhat forlorn.

- Check the last posting dates. They seem to get earlier every year, and some are rather surprising. The last date for economy surface mail to all non-European destinations, the Middle and Far East is around September 28, which is something of a shock. For South Africa, Hong Kong and Singapore, the USA and Canada, the date is around October 13. For Western Europe it is around November 17. If you are sending air mail, now known as International Standard, you will need to send cards to Africa and the Middle East by the first week of December. Greetings to Greece, Australia, New Zealand, the Czech Republic, Japan, the Caribbean and Italy can wait until the following week, but best get them in by the 10th. The last posting dates for local cards to mainland Britain varies a little from year to year, depending on the day on which Christmas falls, but generally get second class cards in by the 18th, first class by the 20th.
- Never use the office franking machine. At best it makes you look cheap. At worst, dishonest.
- It is worth remembering that cards can mean a lot to the elderly and those living alone. They are worth every moment of your time.

Addressing cards is not a penance – I am fond of the sound of pen nib on paper – but I still feel a treat is called for.

Passion fruit cream buns with lemon thyme

Makes 8
For the buns:
water – 125ml
butter – 50g
strong flour – 75g
salt – a pinch
eggs, beaten – 2

For the filling:
double cream – 250ml
passion fruit or lemon curd – 75g

To finish:
caster sugar – 2 tablespoons
lemon thyme leaves – 1 tablespoon
white chocolate – 200g

Set the oven at 200°C/Gas 6. Line a baking sheet with baking parchment.

Pour the water into a small saucepan, add the butter and let it melt, then add the flour and salt. Stir with a wooden spoon until you have a thick paste, then remove from the heat. Transfer the paste to the bowl of a food mixer and add the beaten eggs, a little at a time, beating at a fast pace with a flat paddle attachment. When you have a thick, creamy dough, place 8 generously heaped tablespoons of the mixture on the baking sheet.

Bake for approximately twenty-five minutes, until crisp and well risen, then remove and lift on to a cooling rack.

Make the filling: whip the cream until approaching stiffness – it should just hold its shape on a spoon. Stir the passion fruit or lemon curd gently into the cream. It isn't necessary to completely combine it, which might result in over-mixing; just a thread of lemon through the whipped cream is enough.

Pierce a hole in the side or base of each puff, and fill with the lemon cream.

Put the sugar and lemon thyme into a food processor and process until the sugar turns green and smells deeply of lemon. Break the chocolate into a small heatproof bowl, balanced over a pan of simmering water, and leave it to melt. It will melt more smoothly if you leave it to become liquid without stirring. White chocolate tends to 'seize' when stirred.

Dip each bun into the chocolate or spoon a little over the top of each. While the chocolate is still wet, scatter the lemon thyme sugar over the top. Wait until the chocolate is crisp before serving.

Choosing the tree

Today, the tip of a fir tree waving over the top of the shutters, carried past the house on broad shoulders. Its branches are tied tightly to its trunk with netting, and there is the sound of an excited child or two in tow. I feel they are a little premature, but in truth I can't wait to join in. Forget making mincemeat and baking the cake – it is only when the tree is finally up, shimmering with lights, that it is officially Christmas.

The space outside the greengrocer's, the scene of Charles Greene's 1854 balloon ascent, was once the entrance to a notorious music hall, complete with high-wire acts, masked balls and pantomime. The hall was closed in 1871, due to bawdy behaviour and prostitutes working in the bushes. Nowadays it is far less fun, but it is where each December the local greengrocer sets up a little forest of Christmas trees, and one of several places I go rummaging for the perfect tree.

Believe me when I say I have always wanted to join in the last-minute search for the spindliest little runt, the lonesome tree that no one else wants, and give it a home. I never do. Instead I embark on a steely, determined hunt for the most symmetrical specimen, complete with evenly spaced branches, the right-coloured needles, the most monumentally thick trunk. Not to mention its need to be deeply aromatic, freshly cut and generally in fine fettle. It takes two of us to carry the thing into the house and an extra pair of hands to get it standing straight in its stand.

The tree is important. In many ways it is the pivotal point of the festivities. The heart of the Christmas home, the place where the presents are tucked, it scents and lights the room and is the focus of much seasonal merriment. And it is, of course, what you are going to stand around and sing carols on Christmas Eve. The tree is the modern-day answer to the fire we used to dance around in more pagan times.

One of my favourite bits of the season is seeing other people's trees on social media. (I always look forward to Kirstie Allsopp retweeting photographs of her followers' trees on Twitter, a delightful spreading of Christmas joy and a reminder of how social media can be used in a positive way.) I am grateful, too, to those who generously leave their blinds and shutters open for others to spot their tree. An act of sharing rather than showing off.

I have had people at my door twice this week, asking if they can take my order for a tree, which they will deliver directly to the house. Some even offer to put it up, for which we should all be grateful. The delivery service is brilliant for the time-short or those unable to haul a heavy tree home. The downside is that you miss the opportunity of choosing one for yourself.

I know choosing a tree sounds as easy as buying a chicken, but in the past I have made life difficult for myself by not thinking ahead. Here are a few pointers that a first-time tree-hunter may find useful. Think of it as your gift, a thank-you, to the house.

· Measure your ceiling height before you set off. It is surprisingly difficult to gauge whether your tree will fit your room once you are out in the open. (Those scratches on my ceiling? Well, that's how they got there.) Allow an extra 15–20cm or so for the tree-stand, and don't forget to include the height of your angel, fairy or star.

· Clear a space in the room where the tree will live before you go. It will make life much easier. Ideally, somewhere where the branches won't be constantly knocked every time someone walks past.

· Avoid the risk of your tree drying out, or even catching alight, by siting it away from radiators and fires. (Obvious, I know, but I once had a neighbour who gutted his drawing room through a thoughtlessly placed tree.)

· Measure your tree-stand. You will probably have to trim the trunk anyway. But you don't want one whose trunk is way too wide for the stand. Ideally, it should have a reservoir for water.

· Wear gloves: some species of tree are surprisingly prickly.

· Take a friend, if only to help you turn over the umpteenth candidate for inspection and to share the weight on the trek home. The nearer it gets to Christmas Day, the more likely the sellers are to be busy and not have time to help you get it into the car.

- A straight trunk is essential. A wonky tree is the very devil to put up and its lop-sidedness will bug you all Christmas.
- Look out for official signs and tree-tags from a recognised tree association and avoid those roadside pop-up merchants. The tree may have been illegally cut (yes, it goes on at the dead of night), elderly or just a bit crap.
- Look for one that has been freshly cut, with no sign of drying to the needles. Shiny, perky needles are an encouraging sign.
- Shake the tree firmly – there will inevitably be some falling needles, but more than a few is not a good omen.
- Crush a few needles in the palm of your hand – they should smell deeply fragrant.
- Go for a tree that feels heavy; a light tree may be drying out.
- A firm knock on the ground before packing should remove any loose needles. Get the tree netted to keep it compact during the journey and don't be tempted to remove the wrapping until you are indoors. Once the net is removed, the branches will splay out and may be wider than the front door.
- The tree can only take up water from a fresh cut, so saw a centimetre or two from the base as soon as you get it home. It is probably best to do this outside.
- Don't strip the bark from the base of the trunk. The bark is needed to absorb the water.
- Leave the tree overnight before decorating, giving the branches time to relax back into their natural shape.
- We all like a drink at Christmas. So does your tree. Water it daily, especially during the first couple of weeks. They need a good 1–2 litres a day. Like us. Ignore any advice about feeding your tree aspirin and the like to keep it fresh. Believe me, popping a Nurofen won't make the slightest bit of difference to your tree.
- Water the tree at night, with the lights switched off at the mains.
- If you have bought a potted tree, keep it moist but not soaking wet. In order for a tree to emerge from Christmas in a fit state to survive being planted out, it needs to be kept cool for the entire time. Central heating is the death of most firs.

Varieties of Christmas tree

There is no more a single variety of Christmas tree than there is a single variety of apple. The choice will depend on whether you prefer your tree slim or fat, greeny-blue or emerald, with round or pointed needles, tightly packed branches or wide-spaced for low-hanging baubles. There are majestic, highly priced trees at garden centres, budget-priced, uniformly sized examples on the supermarket aisles and sweet potted versions at local florists. You can buy them ready-cut or growing in soil, conveniently wedged into a wooden stand or, somewhat sadly in my opinion, ready-decorated. In other words, there is a tree for every home and every purse.

Norway spruce, Picea abies
The tree of Victorian Christmas cards, glittering with tinsel and real candles, and the one that most of us think of as the Christmas Tree. The Norway spruce has fine, sharp needles of a mid to dark green, and its bark is often a deep red-brown. If it comes with cones, which is unlikely, they will hang down like long, elegant baubles.

One of the most aromatic of trees, it was the one chosen by Prince Albert for Victoria in 1841, thus introducing the German habit of decorating a tree at Christmas. The upward-pointing branches are particularly good for hanging decorations and displaying tinsel.

It dislikes overheating and is the ideal variety for those who like to put up a tree outside, simply decorated with white lights, and who can remember to water it. Rather prickly, it is sadly a needle-dropper, with a short lifespan once cut. It can look rather sad and moth-eaten by Twelfth Night.

The Norway spruce is the one Norway gives us each year, mainly as a thank-you for our help during the Second World War. It is the splendid tree that lights up Trafalgar Square, a focus for carol singers. (I take slight issue with those responsible for decorating it: the lights used are often too big.) If you want an old-fashioned Christmas, have a cool room or outdoor space and a water-retaining tree-stand, then this is the one for you. Your vacuum cleaner will be horrified, though.

Nordmann fir, Abies nordmanniana

Introduced into Britain in the mid-nineteenth century, the Nordmann is named after Finnish zoologist Alexander von Nordmann. A professor of botany at Odessa, he also has a butterfly named after him. A ghostly white, black and grey one, with deep amber spots. I have chosen a Nordmann for the house for quite a few years now, appreciating its symmetry and highly aromatic scent. Originally from Russia, the Nordmann is one of Denmark's most popular trees, wide and generously bushy, although, being a slow grower, it is understandably on the expensive side.

Barely a needle drops from mine while it is indoors, even though I often forget to water it. The one I used outside last year was still bright and bushy-tailed in March. What works for me are the wide, layered branches that allow the decorations to hang unimpeded, and the flat, soft, silvery-green needles. It is one that children can decorate without fear of being spiked.

A handsome tree with a great lower girth, it gives the impression of a whirling dervish at full tilt.

Blue spruce, Picea pungens

Germany's most popular tree, a striking silvery blue-green, with robust branches as prickly as a bottle brush. Native to the Rocky Mountains of America but now widely grown, this variety is delightfully fragrant, with good needle retention as long as it is kept fairly cool. A bold and visually stunning tree. Many of the branches end in several short, stubby fingers, giving plenty of hanging space for your treasures.

Fraser fir, Abies fraseri

The Fraser fir, named after John Fraser, a Scots botanist, has a fine pyramid shape, compact with tightly packed branches. Having a narrower base than the Nordmann, it suits a limited space. This is America's most favoured tree, and is traditionally the one in the White House.

The Fraser is a highly scented variety with a delicate citrus note. The non-drop glossy needles have a green-blue sheen to them with a silvery underneath. This one often has a bit of a lean to the growing tip, which might make your fairy feel a bit pissed but adds a certain charm.

A slow-growing, gorgeous tree, it is a good one to buy pot-grown, for planting outside once its moment in the candlelight is over.

Scots pine, Pinus sylvestris

A fragrant, soft-needled tree with a blue-green colour, this is our only native timber-producing conifer. In the wild it sports long, down-pointing cones. Handsome, even stately, when left to grow, this is a lovely tree to have in your house at Christmas, though not as easy to find as you might expect.

Serbian spruce, Picea omorika

Central Europe's favourite tree, tall and slim with down-hanging, medium-length cones. Native to eastern Bosnia and Herzegovina, it sports particularly long and delicate branches, perfectly suited to simple, elegant decorations. Sometimes labelled Omora, it has a sweet fragrance, though its needle-retention is not the best.

Noble fir, Abies procera

Introduced to Britain in the 1830s, this can grow to a great height in the forests of Oregon and Washington. Non-drop, aromatic, softly spiked leaves of a gorgeous bluey green. This variety has a long tap root, so is unlikely to be found pot-grown.

Lodgepole pine, Pinus contorta

A faintly spiced-orange-meets-pine scent and its superb ability to keep its needles are reasons enough to choose this variety. Its name, by the way, comes from its strong, straight trunk, capable of holding up tepees and lodges. The minor downside is its slightly open, unconventional shape and vivid green colour.

I must mention the existence of the British Christmas Tree Association and its 320 members. Each tree will carry a log kite mark, an assurance that the tree has been grown and sold to the highest standards. They have a contest for Grower of the Year. Some companies within the association work with charitable trusts such as Tree Aid, which helps with planting trees in Africa.

Spotting someone carrying a Christmas tree is rather like watching a person with a bag of crisps. I need one, immediately. This year, as usual, I ask my friend Katie, who does so much work in my garden, to help. She can spot a sound, freshly cut tree from twenty feet away. I end up with a beauty, a handsome, symmetrical tree, a Nordmann, that looks and smells everything I could have hoped for. We drag it into the house, manoeuvring it through the obstacle course of the hall and its fireplace, and manage to fit it into its pot, for once without any damage to the walls.

I have given up with tree-stands. They work perfectly well for most trees, but I have had difficulty in the past finding one strong enough to hold a large tree securely. Instead I use a leakproof tin (for water) inside an enormous terracotta pot full of rocks, which I then cover with hessian. The tree is lowered into the tin, then the rocks are wedged in around it. You need three people, one to hold the tree upright, another to stand a few feet away checking that the trunk is perpendicular, and a third to wedge in the rocks around the base. We actually use old 'sets', the square grey cobbles used for pathways, which we bought from a building-supply store. Such preparation may seem over the top, but having had a tree collapse, I feel safe is better than sorry. Braces and belts and all that.

I water our splendid new addition to the house generously, and leave it overnight before decorating. The branches have been tied up in netting for a while and need several hours to relax back into their natural position. And if by any chance you come downstairs during the night, you will be met with the citrus-pine note of freshly cut Christmas tree. A smell that is both ancient and fresh, clean and homely. The scent of forests and snow.

Decorating the tree and a lamb roast

The winter I was nine seemed no different to any other. I had taken a day off school to make decorations for the house. A paper chain or two and some foil garlands. Mum, who had no time for pushy parenting, had happily given me a sick note for the day, and we sat together at the kitchen table, needles of icy rain pattering against the leaded windows, cutting, folding and gluing. I made a string of leaves from red and green foil and paper chains from wrapping paper.

That evening my father turned up from work with an eight-foot tree. I stood there, jigging up and down with excitement while he cursed as he attempted to secure the trunk in its stand, my mother doubled up with laughter. I had no idea it would turn out to be our last Christmas together.

We kept the decorations in the attic, a long tunnel of a room that ran the length of the house and was known as the bogey-hole. The trip up the wobbly ladder to get there terrified me. Low-ceilinged, with dark beams, a single light bulb and a floor that creaked like a coffin lid in a horror film, the attic was filled with temptation and terror. Each dusty cardboard box was home to gaudy baubles wrapped in old newspaper, curled strands of tinsel and a tangle of fairy lights. There was a brass candle-holder with angels that spun round once the candles were lit; dusty globes decorated with grim, fading faces; a box of wooden marionettes with a nest of strings; Pelham Puppet frogs and a discarded wooden Pinky and Perky that regularly featured in my childhood nightmares.

The boxes were passed down one by one, and I rustled my way through each piece of crumpled newspaper to find my favourite decorations. A glass Santa, a string of plastic cups each with a bulb inside and decorated with a scene from a nursery rhyme; a box of small, slightly tarnished globes each with an indentation on one side whose striations caught the light, and a squashed foil star that stood in for an angel to top the tree. It was the one night of the year

I was allowed to stay up beyond nine o'clock and I relished it. Each decoration had a special place, with certain favoured bulbs coming to the front. My father's coloured birds got a look in too, but only to appease him. I liked decorations that reflected the light and made the hall glisten and shine.

I take as much trouble in cladding the branches now as I did then. To this day I take time unwrapping the tree decorations, greeting each one like an old friend. I put carols on, open a bottle of something nice and decorate the tree, commandeering the help of anyone else in the house at the time. (And yes, I move any less than thoughtfully considered additions after they have left.)

This year there are a few new jewels with which to festoon the branches. Antique painted balls I picked up in Cologne, sugar cookies from Nuremberg and single strands of tinsel from the Tyrol. If I hadn't collected decorations for years, I would use nothing more than white lights, no balls, no lanterns, no ribbons. It is hard to imagine a tree more lovely than one threaded with nothing but a single tiny strand of white lights. But I secretly hanker after Queen Victoria's 1850s overladen tree, its candles flickering against the crimson walls.

A few notes on decorating the tree

- Test the lights before you start. LED lights are kinder to the needles, remaining cool for longer.
- Unpack all your decorations before you start, laying them out on the floor, table or sofa.
- Put the lights on first. It is virtually impossible to thread strings of lights on the tree once the hanging decorations are in place, so wrap the lights round first. Hopefully the bulbs are held on a green or black wire rather than white. There are two methods. You can either start at the base of the trunk working upwards, wrapping the lights around the trunk then working along the branches, until you get to the top. Alternatively, divide the tree into four and wrap the lights around the branches on each of the four sides from bottom to top. I prefer the first method, but each to their own.
- The branches are strongest at the trunk end, so hang the heaviest ornaments there, rather than at the tip, where they may slide off as the season progresses and the branches become more brittle.

- Hang particularly reflective decorations close to the bulbs, so they shine in the light. Those with an indentation on one side are designed for this.
- Hang the largest globes and heaviest decorations first, evenly dispersed throughout the branches, then fill the gaps with smaller pieces. Lastly, add ribbons, tinsel and garlands.
- The tree will be at its most splendid if the rest of the lights in the room are kept dimmed.

Decorating the tree is one of those activities, like baking bread, that allows us to do other jobs at the same time, and I often take a day or two to complete the job. This year is no different, and I make a spiced lamb roast with a creamy accompaniment of beans and spinach in between hanging the decorations. (Today feels something of a celebration, so we open a bottle of Champagne, making Christmas somehow official.)

Rare lamb and creamed beans

I like that moment when meat and its roasting juices meet a creamy accompaniment on the plate. When mac 'n' cheese melts into the gravy of the Sunday beef, for instance, or when roast chicken nudges a pool of nutmeg-scented bread sauce. Or, as happened this week, when I made a dish of creamed spinach to nestle with slices of roast shoulder of lamb.

Actually, the accompaniment was more than creamed spinach. It was a classic white sauce flecked green with chopped spinach and bolstered with fat, slippery butter beans. The beans should have rendered the idea of potatoes redundant, but we put a few in around the meat anyway. I doubt I'm alone in thinking Sunday just isn't Sunday without a roast potato. I grated a little nutmeg in too. Not much, just a brief grating from a halved nutmeg rubbed eight or nine times on a fine grater. It's enough. I sometimes like to drop the rest of it into the sauce as it cooks – the effect is subtle but worth

doing, like adding a bay leaf. I have to admit it's the devil to find among the spinach afterwards.

I bought a shoulder of lamb rather than a leg. I've been doing this a lot lately. Trickier to carve (I end up hacking at it), but its fat seems to cook more crisply. Crisp roast lamb fat being high on my list of reasons for living. The accompanying sauce was cooked old school. Long and slow. With a proper white sauce, not just double cream, so the spinach and beans oozed slowly in pursuit of the lamb's vermouth-and-rosemary-scented juices.

Roast lamb with coriander seeds and rosemary

The timing here is for medium-rare, quite pink, meat. Alter the cooking time to your taste. If the crust hasn't browned as much as you would like, turn up the heat to 200°C/Gas 6 for the last fifteen to twenty minutes of cooking. I regard the resting time as essential.

Serves 6
shoulder of lamb, bone in – 2kg
garlic – 3 cloves
rosemary – 3 bushy sprigs
coriander seeds – 1 tablespoon
olive oil – 80ml
stock or dry white vermouth – 200ml

Using a very sharp kitchen knife, score the fat of the lamb at 1cm intervals, cutting just below the fat, first one way then the other to give a lattice effect. Place the lamb in a roasting tin and set the oven at 180°C/Gas 4.

Peel the garlic and drop it into a food processor or blender. Add a generous grinding of salt and pepper. Pull the needles from the rosemary sprigs and add to the garlic together with the coriander seeds. Pour in the olive oil and blend to a coarse, slightly runny paste.

Spread the paste over the surface of the lamb, pushing it right down inside the score marks. Roast in the preheated oven for about an hour and fifteen minutes. That will give a medium-rare result.

Remove the lamb from the oven and leave it to rest, covered, in a warm place, while you complete the beans and spinach.

Just before you serve, lift the lamb on to a carving board, pour most of the fat from the roasting tin, then place the tin over a moderate heat. Pour the stock or wine into the pan and bring to the boil, stirring and scraping at any tasty bits in the pan. Season thoughtfully.

Creamed butter beans and spinach

I start the sauce shortly before the lamb comes out of the oven.

Serves 6 as a side dish, 4 as a main course
spinach - 750g
butter beans - 2 × 400g tins

For the sauce:
milk - 500ml
half an onion
cloves - 3
bay leaves - 2
black peppercorns - 6
butter - 40g
plain flour - 40g
a nutmeg, for grating

Pour the milk into a saucepan, add the onion, cloves, bay leaves and black peppercorns and bring almost to the boil. Immediately remove from the heat and set aside.

Remove and discard the thickest stems from the spinach, then wash the leaves very thoroughly in deep, cold water. Place a large, deep saucepan over a moderate heat, pile in the spinach with 4 tablespoons of water, then cover tightly with a lid and steam for three or four minutes until bright and wilted. It is a good idea to turn the leaves over once or twice as they cook. I use kitchen tongs.

Remove the spinach from the pan, cool quickly in a colander under running cold water, then drain. Squeeze the leaves in the palm of your hand to remove as much water as possible. Roughly chop the spinach and set aside.

Melt the butter in a saucepan, add the flour and cook over a moderate heat for a couple of minutes, stirring, then pour in the infused milk through a sieve. Season with salt, ground black pepper and just a little grated nutmeg. Leave to simmer for a good fifteen to twenty minutes, stirring regularly, until you have a thick and creamy sauce.

Drain the beans of their canning liquor, then stir them into the sauce, followed by the chopped spinach. If you need to keep the sauce warm while you slice the lamb, place a buttered sheet of paper over the top and leave in a warm place or over a very low heat.

Slice the lamb thinly and serve with any roasting juices and the creamed beans and spinach.

A fine and fruity chutney

Chutney, the ever-useful sour-sweet splodge for sharpening up slices of cold roast lamb or a wedge of pork pie, is one of those recipes that changes over time. What appears a little acidic as it simmers in the pot will often as not calm down after a few weeks in a jar on the shelf. Even a week trapped in a glass storage jar allows the fruit, vinegar, spices and aromatics a chance to mellow. Sour, sweet and spicy become one harmonious mixture rather than opposites fighting for supremacy. Best make it now, then.

Some form of vinegar-based pickle is a fine thing to have to hand in the winter. It can balance the slightly soporific character of casseroles, pies and stews. A spot of chutney can perk up a shepherd's pie no end. The essential quality of a chutney, and the main reason it is worth making our own, is that it should dazzle. It should be alive and kicking. The punch of chillies and red wine vinegar, of lemon juice and sour apple, with a soft, mysterious depth provided by soft brown sugars and fruit.

I need a couple of jars that I can make any time, their recipe not being tied to the fruit of any particular season. A tracklement that will be as happy nudging up to a lump of Cheddar as it will to a slice of cold roast turkey. James decides to make inroads into the vast amount of dried apricots I seem to have accumulated. (Sod's law my larder has either a dearth or a surfeit of something, rather than the right amount.) What emerges from his afternoon of quiet bubbling is a preserve the colour of a winter sunset. Tart little apricots becalmed in a sea of soft, sweet onion, cider vinegar and Bramley apple.

Apricot and tomato chutney

Makes 2 large jars
a red onion
a yellow onion
olive oil – 4 tablespoons
dried apricots – 450g
root ginger – 25g, a thumb-sized lump
a lemon
golden caster sugar – 200g
cider vinegar – 250ml
Bramley or other sharp apples – 2 large
yellow or orange cherry tomatoes – 200g
a pomegranate

Peel the onions, then halve and cut each half into quarters. Separate the layers of onion. Warm the olive oil in a deep, heavy-based pan. Add the onions and let them cook for ten to fifteen minutes, or until soft and translucent.

Cut the dried apricots in half and add to the onions, then peel and finely grate in the ginger and the lemon zest. Stir in the caster sugar, then, as the mixture starts to bubble, introduce the cider vinegar. Partially cover with a lid and leave over a low heat.

Peel the apples, quarter and core them, then roughly chop. Add the apples to the pan, then the juice of the lemon. Once the apples start to collapse, halve the cherry tomatoes and stir them in. Add salt and, if you wish, some coarsely ground black pepper, then bottle and seal. You should get a couple of decent-sized jars out of it.

You could easily eat this the next day, but it will keep, depending on the trouble you go to seal it (sterilised jars, please) for a good few weeks in a cool place. Sometimes I crack a pomegranate and add its ruby seeds to the chutney at the table.

Note to self: wrapping paper, sticky tape.

Broth and bones. Coming in from the cold

I have been working in the garden, digging mostly, planting scented white narcissi into soil the colour of wet tobacco. White tulips too, in old terracotta pots for the spring. My hands are scratched. The ground is heavy and sodden and every step is like wading through treacle. The sun, a watery orange-pink seen through witchy black trees, is sliding down towards the earth much like my wet socks have ruckled down my boots. It takes an age to get them off, standing first on one leg then the other outside the kitchen door, determined not to traipse any more mud into the house than absolutely necessary.

The light from the kitchen windows has been beckoning (pleading almost) for me to come in. The kitchen door gets stiff on cold days, as if it doesn't want to let the cold air in, and who can blame it. The smell of dinner is coming from the oven. Calm waves of meat-scented juices that have cooked for hours. Mellow, savoury and nannying, the smell of my grandmother's kitchen, where she cooked on a blackened range that she fed hourly with coal. My dad said he was brought up on brown broth and potatoes.

Through the glass oven door, I can just about recognise the casserole dish, portly, like St Nicholas, with its cargo of meat and bones. I have cooked many a good thing in that dish. A heavy lid to lift. A big spoon to lower into dark broth. Sweet onions and spoon-soft meat to lift into the hollows of deep plates. We pull the meat from the bones, most of which falls away with ease; the rest we pick up and gnaw. There is gravy on our plates, deep walnut brown scented with woody herbs and shallots. We gnaw and slurp, the juice warms us and defrosts my frozen fingers. Our cheeks rush with colour – though maybe that's the red wine.

This is the winter food I love. Patient food, recipes that wait for us, untroubled by the ticking of the clock or a gardener wanting to do 'just one more job'. Dishes that are done when they're done and refuse to be hurried into readiness.

Benign, good-natured recipes whose smells calm us like an extra blanket on a stone-cold night, and warm us slowly, thawing out our frozen souls. Meat that melts from its bones, broths that restore, flavours that reassure.

Oxtail with butter beans and sherry

There is a calming quality to oxtail, as we might expect from something that spent its life at the other end of an animal peacefully munching grass. A tumble of heavy bones, stewing with stock, sherry and thyme. There are the traditional aromatics in there too: onions, carrot and bay, soon to be joined by flat, mealy butter beans to soak up the beefy juices.

Where this cut wins me over is the high ratio of bone to beef, a guarantee of flavoursome, good-for-you stock to keep out a winter's night. The tail is usually hacked into user-friendly lumps by the butcher – don't try to do it yourself – and asks little more from us than patience. No bit of the carcass requires longer cooking to come to tenderness, though most of that is entirely untroublesome to the cook.

The liquid of an oxtail stew is too flavoursome to waste, enriched as it is with the goodness from the meat, bones and connective tissue. I like to soak it up with mashed potato or swede. This time, I used butter beans, warming them through in the gravy before serving, then mashing them into the thyme-flecked juices with our forks. Other beans would do the job, but what appeals about the butter bean is its particularly generous size and its especially starchy quality. The perfect thing for mopping up gravy from your plate.

Serves 4
olive oil – 3 tablespoons
oxtail, prepared – 1.5kg
onions – 4 medium
celery – 2 ribs
bay leaves – 3
dry sherry – 300ml
beef stock – 500ml
thyme sprigs – 8
butter beans, jarred or tinned– 2 × 400g tins

To serve:
chard, spinach or cabbage, steamed

Warm the olive oil in a deep-sided casserole, then place the oxtail pieces into the hot oil and let the meat brown, turning each piece with kitchen tongs, lightly colouring as many of the sides as you can.

Peel and thickly slice the onions. Remove the oxtail from the casserole, then add the sliced onions and let them soften and turn gold, stirring them from time to time. Cut the celery into thin pieces, then stir into the onions and continue cooking. Add the bay leaves, then return the oxtail to the pan, followed by the sherry and then the beef stock.

Season with black pepper and a little salt, then tuck the thyme sprigs around the meat and bring the liquid to the boil. Cover with a lid and place in the oven, letting it bake for two hours. About halfway through the cooking time, turn each piece of oxtail over.

Lift the lid and introduce the butter beans, drained of their bottling or canning liquor, distributing them amongst the meat. Replace the lid and continue cooking, covered, for a further thirty minutes. Check the seasoning and serve with steamed greens, spooning over the cooking juices and beans as you go.

Pickled quinces and a Christmas stocking

Do you know why there is often an orange in the bottom of a Christmas stocking? No? Well then, let me tell you. The story starts with a poor man who had three daughters. He worried about their future once he was dead. When Saint Nicholas was passing through their village, he heard the story and secretly threw three golden balls into the family's house. The balls landed in the girls' stockings, which were hanging up in front of the fireplace to dry. The daughters' future was assured. And that is why to this day it is traditional to hide an orange in the foot of a Christmas stocking. A golden ball for good luck.

The tradition of hanging a stocking out for gifts on Christmas Eve may well have started another way altogether. According to German legend, Odin, the god of Norse mythology, husband of the goddess Frigg, had a flying horse called Sleipnir. At Christmas, children would stuff their boots with hay and sugar and place them near the chimney for Sleipnir, who might be passing overhead. Odin returned the kindness by leaving gifts in their shoes to be found on Christmas morning.

Either way, it is the rule that a large stocking should be hung on the mantelpiece on Christmas Eve. The next morning it will be filled with small gifts, sweets and treats. An orange is barely considered a treat nowadays, but was once a rare and special find. So much so that they were always sold wrapped in tissue paper and foil.

I gave up hanging my stocking aged seven. After that it became a pillowcase at the foot of my bed. Such are the expectations of modern children. You can buy fancy stockings trimmed with cotton wool or embroidery or make them yourself. Some parents like to have their children's names emblazoned on them. Nowadays they come filled with mobile phones and electronic games, books and chocolates, but I still think they should, in memory of the poor old man and his daughters, contain a foil-wrapped orange.

I would rather like my own stocking be filled with good things to eat. A jar of rose petal jam, a tin of jasmine tea and a packet of sugared almonds in pastel colours. A greaseproof paper packet of thinly sliced jamón Ibérico, a perfect orange complete with its leaves, a jar of home-made marmalade or pickle and a foil-wrapped chocolate orange. There could be a fruit cake in a tin, some dark chocolate-covered ginger biscuits and a pomegranate. You would make my day by including some sugar-dusted Turkish delight and a foil-wrapped tin of marrons glacés. I would dearly love you to sneak in a packet of Japanese matcha-flavoured Kit Kats. Oh and there could, of course, be a jar of pickled quinces.

Pickled quinces

I regard the quince as the high point of winter fruit. More so than the pineapple, the pomegranate or even the Comice pear. It is, though, a cook's fruit and its mysterious scent and soft creamy pink flesh are only released after considerable work in the kitchen. That said, a bowl of the raw fruit will scent an entire room on a winter's day. The fruit is charitably unsweet, and as well as a fine pie or crumble the quince makes perhaps an even more delicious pickle. Something to keep for a few weeks and bring out with cold meat and cheeses.

> *Makes 2 large jars*
> red wine vinegar – 500ml
> granulated sugar – 350g
> juniper berries – 2 teaspoons
> coriander seeds – 1 teaspoon
> bay leaves – 3
> black peppercorns – 12
> quinces – 3
> a lemon

Pour the vinegar into a saucepan, then add the sugar, juniper berries, coriander seeds, bay leaves and peppercorns and bring to the boil.

Peel the quinces, rubbing the cut area with a halved lemon to prevent browning, halve them from stem to core, remove their cores, then lower them into the pickling liquor. Turn the heat to a simmer and leave them to cook for a good hour, occasionally turning them over to encourage even cooking. Test the fruit regularly by piercing the flesh with a skewer, to check their progress until they are butter-soft.

Remove from the heat, lift the fruit carefully into sterilised jars, then pour over the hot pickling liquid. Seal tightly and eat the next day or store until Christmas.

Enough preserving. I need dinner. Something hot, simple, sweet and quick.

Sweet potato and kale bubble and squeak

Serves 2
sweet potatoes – 1kg
cumin seeds – ½ teaspoon
dried chilli flakes – a pinch
sweet, mild paprika – ½ teaspoon
butter – 50g
kale – 150g

To finish:
a little extra butter

Heat the oven to 200°C/Gas 6. Peel the sweet potatoes and cut them into large chunks. Place them in a steamer basket or colander and cook over boiling water, covered with a lid, for about thirty to forty minutes, until tender to the point of a knife.

In a dry frying pan, toast the cumin seeds and the chilli flakes. Remove and mix them with the ground paprika.

Lift the sweet potatoes out, tip them into a bowl (or the saucepan emptied of its water) and mash them thoroughly with the butter, some salt and a grinding of black pepper, then the toasted cumin, chilli and paprika.

Remove the tough stalks from the kale (you need 100g trimmed weight). Cook the kale for a minute or two in a saucepan with about 1cm of water, covered by a lid. Drain and roughly chop.

Fold the kale into the sweet potato. Pile into an ovenproof dish, top with a few knobs of butter and bake for about twenty-five minutes, until lightly crisped on the top.

Note to self: order the bird.

Pickles, pruning and a baked apple

I crave sharp, piquant flavours. That snap of acidity, that spike of lemon or vinegar. A spoonful of fruit chutney, a curl of soused fish or a little pile of pickles on my plate. It is these bright, clean acidic side notes that keep me interested in what I'm eating.

This morning I saw the first of the forced rhubarb, a box of delicate pink stalks sold by the long, straight stem, like amaryllis. (By forced, I mean grown under lights in warm, dark sheds rather than out of doors.) They were too expensive for a crumble or a cake, so I bought a couple only, and will wait a week or two for the price to come down. Rhubarb like this, early, tender, as pretty as apple blossom, is something I wait for each year, as I do gooseberries and damsons. This is the earliest I have ever seen.

I came late to pickles. It's the price I paid for having first tried the dark, sugary, sour 'pickle' of commerce, hating it and deciding that all pickles must be the same. If only that initial taste had been a crisp dill-pickled gherkin or a rollmop. If those first mouthfuls had been village fête chutney or a forkful of home-made pickled cabbage, I wouldn't have wasted so much time thinking pickles weren't for me.

Sitting watching television it is not a sweet I crave, or a biscuit, but a stinging hit of pickled fig or cucumber, a teaspoon of fruit vinegar or the crunch of a few wisps of sauerkraut. And never more so than now, in the depths of winter.

Only the last few leaves remain on the trees. There are still a few on the horse chestnuts, the medlar and the cornus, but mostly they lie in deep, crisp piles, ripe for kicking.

Winter trees have a stark beauty. Shorn of their fluff of green leaves, their bones are slowly revealed, their architecture is apparent. It is only now that we see the full beauty of their bark, their lichen and moss and their handsome shape. It is an unsullied beauty, simple and strong. It is also now that you can

see which branches need to go, the tangles of twigs that need thinning, the branches the trees would be better without.

Vines and most free-standing fruit trees are best pruned in the winter, when they are dormant and before the sap rises once more. In the garden, I sort out the muddle of medlar branches, cutting out with a small yellow saw the branches that cross one another. When I swapped lawn for trees and bushes all those years ago it never occurred to me that even in a compact urban garden, I would ever find use for a saw. The shape of the removed wood is elegant, a forked branch whose grey bark is encrusted with dots of yellow lichen. It gets to live another day in a huge glass vase on the dining table.

Pickled rhubarb and salmon

A good starter this, something to sharpen the appetite, as so few first courses do.

Serves 2
white wine vinegar – 150ml
golden caster sugar – 1 tablespoon
black peppercorns – 10
white peppercorns – 6
coriander seeds – 1 teaspoon
fennel seeds – $\frac{1}{2}$ teaspoon
rhubarb – 100g
peashoots – 2 handfuls
samphire, watercress or other shoots – 50g
salmon – 300g

Combine the vinegar, sugar, peppercorns, coriander and fennel seeds in a stainless steel saucepan and bring to the boil. Remove from the heat.

Slice the rhubarb into small pieces no thicker than 1cm and put them into a bowl, then pour over the pickling liquid, cover and set aside to cool. Leave in a cool place for three hours. The rhubarb should still retain something of its crispness, but will be deliciously sweet-sour.

Wash and dry the salad leaves. Remove the skin from the salmon and slice the fish into small cubes, about 1cm. Divide the salad leaves between two plates or shallow bowls. Toss the salmon and pickled rhubarb together and serve on the salad leaves, together with a trickle of oil and a little of the pickling liquor.

And a pudding

Fallen leaves make me think 'baked apples'. The two go hand in hand just like beaches and ice cream or lawns and strawberries. It's a snow and soup kind of link, like movies and popcorn, one of the food associations that make up so many of our eating habits. And so, I bake apples, big fat Bramleys from the greengrocers, but on this occasion I turn them into a fool.

Baked apple mascarpone fool

The point of baking the apples here rather than stewing them is the caramelised honey sweetness you get from their time in the oven. A rather nice touch is to finish this soft and creamy dessert with a couple of slices of apple, something sweet and firm like a Cox, that you have fried for two minutes in a little butter and sugar until they start to caramelise.

Serves 4
sharp apples, such as Bramley – 850g
caster sugar – 100g
double cream – 250ml
sweet Marsala – 4 tablespoons
mascarpone – 125g

Heat the oven to 200°C/Gas 6. Core the sharp apples and score a line around the circumference of each fruit, piercing just below the skin, then place them snugly in a roasting tin. The scoring will stop the fruit exploding as they cook. Bake the apples for about twenty to twenty-five minutes, taking an occasional peep to check their progress. They are ready when they are risen and the top has fluffed up like a soufflé. If they have collapsed into a puddle of froth, no matter.

Remove the fruit from the oven and scrape the flesh into a bowl, using a small spoon, discarding the skins as you go. If there are any caramelised juices in the tin, combine them with the apple, then set aside.

Put the sugar, cream and Marsala into the bowl of an electric mixer and beat until thick and creamy, but not so stiff the mixture can stand in peaks. Fold in the mascarpone and combine with the crushed apple, taking care not to over-mix.

17 DECEMBER

Panettone, a love story

A dome of pale yellow cake wrapped in brown and gold waxed paper. Here and there a nib of candied peel, crisp sugar crystals embedded in its walnut-coloured crown. Light, sweet, soft, fluffy even. A fairy cake made by angels.

What I remember most clearly is not the taste, but the scent of vanilla. It hung in the air, trapped between the polished marble floors and the high glass ceiling of the Galleria. It floated beside the deeper smell of coffee coming from the café where we were seated, blowing our student budgets on dolls'-house portions of hot chocolate.

I knew vanilla as the posh word for 'tastes of nothing'. Like plain crisps. A vanilla ice meant a swirl of soft, creamy-white ice cream that tasted neither of strawberry nor chocolate. I hadn't then met the real vanilla, with its roots in the orchid family, the vanilla that comes in long slim pods blackened by curing, whose seeds are sticky and are scraped from their jacket like black jam and used to scent custard or cream or folded into chocolate or cake mixture. I hadn't yet met my favourite sweet spice.

The tall, paper-clad confection is a member of the family of airily light baked goods, dithering between bread and cake, that are sliced and eaten in fat wedges or toasted and served with thick cream or soft, sweet cheese. A distant cousin of both the Russian Kulich (serve with creamy, almond-scented Pashka) or the Sally Lunn of Bath (toast and spread with clotted cream), panettone often shares a plate with mascarpone, and occasionally a glass of zabaglione.

Panettone is the lightest of all breads, an effect achieved by a long, slow rising process. That first meeting, at a café in Milan forty years ago, close to the spires of the Duomo, changed how I felt about it. Until then, bread was for toast and cakes were about buttercream and glacé icing, whipped cream and crème pâtissière. That single wedge of panettone, light as duck down, almost spartan, devoid of cream or icing or chocolate, nudged me in a new direction. I suddenly

265

understood the quiet, almost monastic joy of plain cake. The soft, buttery crumbs of seed cake, Madeira cake and gingerbread, a world away from the triple-layered horror of gâteaux and anything with a swirl of Italian meringue on top. To this day I'd rather have a slice of panettone than any of them.

'Panetto' means small loaf. I'm glad to have met my first panettone in Milan, for that is reputedly its home. Which is rather like first meeting a fat rascal in Harrogate. Milan was where the money was. A city of merchants and noblemen who could afford bread studded with citron peel and sultanas. The cake appears in *The Peasant Wedding* (1567), a painting by Pieter Bruegel the Elder, currently housed in the Kunsthistorisches Museum in Vienna.

The name derives from whichever story you choose to believe. There is, of course, a love story. Always tempting. Ughetto degli Atellani, a young man of noble birth, fell in love with Toni, the daughter of a poor baker. Disguising himself, he charmed his way into the job of apprentice purely to be near her. He invented the fruit-speckled bread and named it after her. Pan de Toni. They married and lived happily ever after. The story will do for an old softy like me, though the colder-hearted may prefer the less romantic version. In the Milanese dialect, Pan di Tono simply means luxury cake.

The cakes are boxed to protect their tender crumb from damage. The boxes often come with a ribbon attached, perfect for hanging from the ceiling of an Italian delicatessen, and with it the subtle suggestion that they are meant as a gift, something to be handed over. I often say my favourite smell is that of snow or woodsmoke, but the rush of vanilla and candied citrus as you take a fresh panettone from its crinkly cellophane on a winter's morning comes close.

Few Italians would consider making their own panettone. There is little point. Fine, artisan-made versions, scented with real vanilla extract and studded with hand-chopped crystallised peel, are not difficult to find for those who care. Keep watch for the ones possessing a decidedly open texture, generous nuggets of peel and charmingly wobbly contours. They need nothing more than to be torn and eaten mid-morning, with coffee. There are also reliably identical, mass-produced cakes flavoured with chemical vanillin, piled high in supermarkets and sold at a reasonable price.

Eat them as wedges, or, less traditionally, in thick, flat slices cut across the cake. Either can be torn and dipped into a small glass of vin santo or Marsala or coffee. As you tire of the simple cakes, cook with them, baking them with a cream and Marsala custard – a sort of Italian bread and butter pudding – or sandwiched with flavoured mascarpone, cream and berries to make a layer-cake. Once the excitement and vanilla-scented fug of a freshly open box has passed, I slice mine, toast it and serve the golden discs with a spread made from whipped mascarpone, cream and sweet Marsala.

Panettone ice cream

The custard must not reach boiling point. If you overheat it, it will curdle (I guarantee). Make certain that the spoon gets right into the corners of the pan. Your most helpful utensil will be a sink of iced water. If there is even the remotest sign of curdling, quickly pour the custard into a clean bowl, sit the bowl in the ice, and whisk like you mean it.

Serves 6
panettone – 250g
milk – 300ml
single cream – 300ml
a fat vanilla pod
egg yolks – 6
caster sugar – 150g

To finish:
a thick slice of panettone, toasted

Reduce the panettone to coarse crumbs in a food processor, then spread them out in a single layer on a baking sheet. Keeping a watchful eye on proceedings, lightly brown the crumbs under a hot oven grill, then set aside. Alternatively, brown them in a frying pan.

Pour the milk and cream into a saucepan. Split the vanilla pod, scrape out the seeds and stir them into the milk, then bring almost to the boil. Tip the crumbs into the milk and cream, then remove from the heat, cover and set aside.

Beat the egg yolks and caster sugar until light and fluffy. Pour the warm cream and crumbs on to the beaten eggs and sugar, mix, then pour back into the saucepan. Place over a low to moderate heat, stirring almost continuously with a wooden spoon for five to ten minutes until you get a smooth custard.

Once the custard is thick enough to thinly coat the back of the spoon, remove it from the heat, pour it into a cold basin and leave it to cool. Once cool, refrigerate it for a good half-hour before pouring into an ice cream machine and churning until almost frozen.

Serve in rough scoops, with a little of the toasted panettone crumbled on top.

Panettone passion fruit cake

A gift of cellophane-wrapped Italian cake comes my way. (Panettone tends to arrive in the style of buses. Nothing, then four in a row.) I have eaten it straight from the box, sliced and dunked into coffee, toasted, or toasted and buttered, and have eaten it for breakfast with chocolate hazelnut spread.

It occurs to me that the more utilitarian of them could appear as dessert, spread with cream and layered, like a birthday cake. I slice the bread, remove its crusts, then brush the layers with a bright, sharp cocktail of passionfruit and orange juice. I forgo any form of buttercream (of which I am not that fond) in favour of a passion fruit curd folded through mascarpone. Lemon curd will do. The result, after an hour's rest in the fridge, is sort of trifle-meets-cake. Soft, scented, creamy, refreshing. A Christmas cake for those with no wish to bake.

Serves 6
passion fruit (lightly wrinkled and heavy for their size) – 6
oranges – 3
caster sugar – 4 tablespoons
panettone – 500g

For the filling:
mascarpone – 500g
passion fruit or lemon curd – 250g
passion fruit – 2

To decorate:
sugared rose petals – 8
golden sugar – 2 tablespoons

Cut the six passion fruit in half, then scoop the pulp out into a small sieve over a small saucepan and push through as much of the pulp as you can. Discard the dry seeds left in the sieve. Finely grate the zest from one of the oranges and stir into the passion fruit juice. Cut the three oranges in half and squeeze their juice into the pan. Place the saucepan briefly over a low heat, add the sugar and stir until the sugar has dissolved. It shouldn't take more than a minute or two; don't let it get too hot, as the juice will lose its fresh flavour.

Put the mascarpone into a bowl and stir in the passion fruit or lemon curd. Cut the two passion fruit in half and stir the seeds and pulp into the mascarpone.

Slice the top and bottom from the panettone and discard (good with coffee, or crumble them up for the birds). Cut the cake into five thick rounds. Using a large cutter or a plate as a template, cut away the outer crust from each slice.

Place the base disc of panettone on a plate or board and spoon some of the passion fruit and orange juice over. Spread over a thin layer of the mascarpone cream. Place a second disc on top and spoon a little more of the juice over, followed by a thin layer of the mascarpone. Continue until you have used all the layers of cake and all the juice.

Finish with the remaining mascarpone cream, smoothing it over the top and sides of the cake with a palette knife. Decorate with the sugared rose petals, finely crushed, and the golden sugar. Set aside for an hour or so in the fridge before serving.

Carols

Carols hold a boxful of magic for me. Each verse full of innocence and wonder. The first few lines of 'While Shepherds Watched Their Flocks by Night' or 'Oh Little Town of Bethlehem' carry with them every memory of the happiest days of my childhood. Everything that is good about those early Christmases is held within those first few lines. I start playing carols the day I start planning Christmas, and there is barely a day of December when 'The Holly and the Ivy' isn't heard in this house.

Carols, at least my most loved ones, are chock-a-block full of memories. The winters I remember as clearly as yesterday. The days I would be allowed to stay home from school to make paper chains; the day I made the Christmas cake with my mother, or the entire evening I spent cross-legged on the hall floor quietly untangling the Christmas lights. They take me back to standing in prayers at school, singing 'I Saw Three Ships' in a tone as rumbustious as a sea shanty, and an art lesson where we painstakingly painted the massive classroom windows in the style of stained glass only to return in the morning to find our work had been cleaned off by the (furious) cleaners.

The origin of the carol ('choraula' is the Latin for choral song) probably lies in the wassail, the rather enthusiastic singing by villagers on Twelfth Night to bring good health to the local orchards. Certainly 'The Holly and the Ivy' has that feel to it. Both evergreens have been deeply associated with winter since pagan times, though the religious explanation is rather different. The white flowers of the holly are a symbol of purity, the red berries represent Christ's blood, the prickles are a reminder of the crown of thorns. Either way, it is a rip-roaring carol best sung with gusto. The *Oxford Book of Carols* suggests that the melody and lyrics come from a Mrs Clayton of Chipping Campden, supplemented with words from Mrs Wyatt of East Harptree, neither of whom may have had 'gusto' in mind.

There is a moment in church when a congregation stands, there is a rustle of hymnbooks and coats, the thud of an organ stop and a deep intake of many breaths. It is a sound that never leaves us, no matter how long it has been since our last visit to church. While carols such as 'Hark the Herald Angels Sing' and 'While Shepherds Watched' sound perfectly fine when being sung by any small assembly of people, there are a few that really need a whole choir. At least to my ear. I would argue that 'Silent Night' and 'Once in Royal David's City' require the solo perfection of a trained chorister. Beautifully sung, either is capable of bringing me to tears. I have never understood why I, possibly the least religious person you could imagine, find those two carols so emotional. There is an ever-present innocence and vulnerability to them.

A word about Wesley. The eighteenth child of Samuel and Suzanna, Charles Wesley was born in December 1707 and became one of our most prolific of hymn writers. Living just down the road, I rather like the idea that 'Hark the Herald Angels Sing' came to him as he walked past St Mary's Church in Islington on Christmas Day 1738. Whether that is true doesn't really matter to me, only that he left a legacy of some of my favourite hymns. He was, of course, one of that jolly bunch, the Methodists, and the Reverend Mark Lawson-Jones, in his delightful book *The History of Christmas Carols*, points out that Wesley preferred 'slow and reflective' renditions of his hymns. 'Hark the Herald' would have been sung to a completely different tune.

Not all carols have such clear ancestry. The story behind 'O Come, All Ye Faithful' is a mystery complicated enough to pique the interest of any admirer of who-dun-its. And despite claims that it was written by the King of Portugal, the hymn seems to have been a one-off by Catholic layman John Francis Wade. Certainly the earliest copies of the manuscript, written in Latin, bear his signature.

My favourite carol, however, has since childhood been 'Silent Night'. Those lines, 'All is calm, All is bright', are what I want to hear once the lights are twinkling on the Christmas tree. The melody was composed in 1818, by schoolmaster Franz Xaver Gruber, in the village of Oberndorf bei Salzburg. The words were written in 1816 by Joseph Mohr, a young priest. The first performance of 'Stille Nacht!' was at midnight mass in the village of Arnsdorf, Austria, where Gruber was church organist, shortly after he and Mohr put the words and music together. This year I heard 'Stille Nacht' sung at the

The words of this beautiful song were written in German by Father Joseph Francis Mohr, who was Curate at the Church of St. Nicholas at Oberndorf, near Salzburg.

On the 24th December, 1818, he composed the verses of this song, and his friend Franz Gruber, set it to music the same day, studied it quickly with the Church Choir, and performed it for the first time at the Midnight Mass (in German: Christmette), so that less than twenty-four hours had been sufficient time to write, compose, rehearse and perform this jewel of a song, which has made its way from Oberndorf to almost every corner of the globe. The words of this edition are as near a translation of Father Mohr's as possible, and the harmonisation maintains Franz Gruber's style with regard to simplicity.

𝕾𝖎𝖑𝖊𝖓𝖙 𝕹𝖎𝖌𝖍𝖙

Music by FRANZ GRUBER

Lyric by FR. JOSEPH FRANCIS MOHR

English Translation and

Musical Arrangement by C. SAUERZWEIG

appearance of the Christkind in Nuremberg. I have put in a request for it to be played at my funeral.

Just as there was a golden age of chocolate bars (when Mars, Bounty, Milky Way and Topic were invented), and some would say of comic books and television advertising, there was also a golden age of carols. I have several versions of the same ones. My favourites being, somewhat inevitably, the various collections by King's College Choir, Cambridge. They are the soundtrack to my Christmas cooking.

The almond paste

The origins of the ancient paste made from ground almonds and sugar are complex but it almost certainly came to us from the Middle East. The earliest mentions attribute its invention to the Persians, whom we should also thank for formal gardens, cheques, etiquette, polo and postage stamps. The paste was originally eaten not as a sweetmeat but for its medicinal qualities. A product of the apothecary rather than of the confectioner. Rhazes, a Persian doctor, wrote about the curative qualities of what we now know as marzipan as far back as the ninth century AD.

In the late twelfth century the paste made its way, via Turkey, to Europe, where it soon became something of a speciality in both Sicily (where it was known as panis martius or marzapane) and Lübeck in northern Germany. It is hard to say who loved it more, the Germans who made it into thick bars, sometimes coated in chocolate, or the Italians who to this day fashion it into miniature cauliflowers, bunches of grapes and even Brussels sprouts. The results glisten, like an edible fairy story, in the windows of the Pasticceria Fratelli Freni in the via Chiossetto in Milan. Believe me when I say your eyes will fill with tears at the exquisite creations of almond paste and crystallised fruits under the lights.

The word itself – mazapane (Italian), massepain (French), marzipan (German) – has many possible origins. Venetians traded precious sweetmeats, crystallised fruits and almond paste in small boxes known as matabans from the Far East. Mataban is still the Arabic word for box or jar. Some believe the word, tweaked to mazapane, was then used to describe the box's precious cargo. Early English references use the word marchepan, literally, March bread. Pan, of course, means bread, so the Spanish mazepán and Portuguese maçapão fit neatly into this theory too. My bet is on the Latin term 'martius panis', which means bread of March. Marzipan was traditionally made at Easter.

NIGEL SLATER

Whatever its etymology, we have it now. Blocks of marzipan covered in chocolate, hidden in sugar-coated stollen and in a thick layer under the icing of our most festive cake. A mixture of ground almonds, sugar, occasionally eggs, almond extract and honey, has always been a luxury. The nuts are the reason we are asked to pay so much for it. I have visited nut traders in the bazaars in Tehran that have every imaginable grade of almonds, sold fresh and green, dried in their shells, cracked, skinned, flaked, shredded or ground, and all were sold with a reverence and care we reserve for a ripe mango. I refuse, however, to keep this confection for wrapping the cake. Marzipan will always be precious to me, like Turkish delight, marrons glacés and crystallised fruit jellies. Sweet jewels for special occasions.

Making the paste

I make my own almond paste in a deep, wide mixing bowl, my biggest, in fact. This is because no matter how careful I am, the icing sugar, when sifted, tends to fly everywhere, coating the entire work surface with fine, saccharine dust. I do sift the sugar too, because the lumps are nigh on impossible to remove afterwards.

To cover a 20-22cm cake generously
icing sugar - 250g
ground almonds - 500g
a large egg
lemon juice - 2-3 tablespoons

Sift the icing sugar into a bowl and stir in the ground almonds. Break the egg into a small bowl and beat lightly for just long enough to mix the white and yolk. I find the mixing easiest using a food processor with a flat paddle. Add the egg to the almonds and sugar, then introduce enough lemon juice, little by little, to bring the mixture to a stiff, smooth paste firm enough to roll. Bring together into a ball, then turn out on to a wooden board dusted lightly with icing sugar. Roll into a fat cylinder or cake and wrap in baking parchment or clingfilm.

If you are covering your cake with marzipan only and you use golden icing sugar, your paste will have a soft, honey-coloured hue, like that of antique linen.

Even the most hardened minimalist will agree such a cake needs something in the way of decoration. Marzipan stars of differing sizes pressed on to the smooth almond paste can look suitably festive, especially if their edges are blowtorched here and there, or perhaps a sprinkling of edible glitter will banish any thoughts of Cromwell.

It may be wise to buy your almond paste ready-made, the results being both easier to roll and available in a variety of colours, some of which are actually appropriate. (No one wants a blue Christmas cake.) The trick when making your own is to get the proportions of almond, egg and sugar in perfect harmony, otherwise it will be either too sticky to roll or too crumbly to lift on to the cake. You know where the recipe is.

Mary Berry says you need 675g of paste to cover the top and sides of the cake. My love of marzipan requires a slightly more generous layer. It takes 300g of almond paste to ice the top of a 20cm round cake. Less if you want a thin layer. The sides take a further 500g. Only you know how much you like almond paste.

You will need jam too, not much, less than half a jar of apricot. The jam is essential for sticking the almond paste to the cake, but it is also a tiny bit of sharpness among the general sweetness. In other words, apricot, gooseberry or plum. Not the oversweet strawberry or raspberry.

Covering the sides

I find it easier to put the almond paste in place on the sides of the cake using two shorter lengths of paste rather than doing battle with one ridiculously long one. Those more dextrous than I will probably do it in one go. I use a light dusting of icing sugar to stop it sticking to the work surface.

Measure the circumference of the cake with a piece of cotton or string. Roll a strip of almond paste the same length as the string, and the same width as the height of the cake. (For a 20cm cake this will be about 66cm long and 9cm high.) Brush the sides of the cake with apricot jam, then lift the cake on to its

edge and first roll, then press the strips into place, trimming as necessary. Join the strips by pressing lightly with your thumbs, bearing in mind that the sides will be covered with icing.

Covering the top

Roll out the remaining almond paste with a rolling pin on a work surface lightly dusted with icing sugar. Using the base of the cake tin as a template, cut a disc of paste that fits the top of the cake. Brush the surface of the cake with apricot or gooseberry jam (you need a tart fruit to contrast with the sweet icing), then lower the almond paste into place. Smooth flat with the palm of your hand or, using very light pressure, with a rolling pin.

Leave the paste to dry overnight in a cool place before lowering carefully into a biscuit tin and covering with a lid. Should you not have a spare cake tin, you can wrap the cake loosely in baking parchment, then in foil. It is rather important that the cake is stored somewhere cool and dry, otherwise the covering will turn sticky. Four days is about the right time to allow the covering to dry out. If you ice it too soon the marzipan will show through.

A shimmering marzipan cake

A deep snowdrift of icing is a gorgeous decoration for the cake but I rather like the idea of a cake covered purely with marzipan. To make sure no one confuses it with a Simnel cake, I suggest a few stars cut from a little extra paste, stuck on with jam. The paste can then either be coloured under a hot oven grill (watched like a hawk), or blowtorched, whichever you prefer. A ribbon, perhaps gold, would finish the cake appropriately.

You could go further still and brush the edges of the stars with gold food colouring, giving the impression of a shimmering crown. Silver, bronze and gold edible cake paint is available online and from cake-decorating shops. It sounds rather tacky, but if used sparingly can be quite delightful.

Sour pickles. Sweet comfort

It isn't cold enough. We are almost at midwinter and you would barely know it here in London. The occasional frosty morning, some fog delaying flights at the airports, but I find myself envying the north of the country, with its early morning frosts and 'persistent' fog. Scotland has had much snow and a temperature of –11°C has been recorded in Cromdale, Moray. Generally, though, the weather has been milder than in recent years. Today there is some sign of proper cold weather, frost stays on the hedges all day and there is word of a storm on its way.

Pickling figs in the kitchen, I start looking at colder destinations. Places where I will get a white-out, where I can walk through virgin snow early in the morning and where the scent of woodsmoke lingers almost permanently in the air. Each year in February and March I head for Japan. Today, I decide to move the dates forward to catch some snow.

Pickled figs with fennel seeds and allspice

We need some pickles to go with plates of cheese and prosciutto. The greengrocer has trays of small purple figs that are cheap enough to preserve either as jam (wonderful on water biscuits with soft fresh caprini or sheep's milk cheese) or in vinegar. I figure the latter will be more useful.

Makes 1 medium Kilner jar
white wine vinegar – 500ml
white sugar – 300g
fennel seeds – 1 teaspoon
allspice berries – 6

white peppercorns – 8
black peppercorns – 6
bay leaves – 3
small figs – 400g

Pour the vinegar into a small saucepan, add the sugar and bring to the boil, then add the fennel seeds, allspice berries, white peppercorns, black peppercorns and bay leaves. Cut the figs in half and place them in a sterilised preserving jar. Pour over the boiling pickling liquor, seal and allow to cool. They will keep for several weeks, but you can eat them within a day or two.

Roast cauliflower, carrot hummus

Tonight is the anniversary of Mum's death. I am not an especially sentimental person, but I rarely forget this day – who would – and often wonder what she would make of things if she were here today. Tonight, a dinner of quiet comfort, soft sweet flavours uplifted by Middle Eastern notes of mint, green olives and pomegranate. (I can only imagine what Mum would have thought of anyone roasting a cauliflower.)

There is sweetness here, softness too, and then in contrast the piercing garnet pomegranates and cool/hot hit of mint. I am extraordinarily fond of hummus, the smooth, whipped paste of chickpeas and olive oil, and have recently taken to eating it hot, the chickpeas mashed with suitable vegetables such as beetroots and, today, carrots. I sometimes think I might prefer it hot to cold.

If you can bear to, I think it worth skinning the chickpeas for hummus that is to be served cold. You get a smoother result, like soft-serve ice cream. It doesn't matter for hummus to be served hot. Or perhaps I should say warm, because that is how I like it best, when it is at its most comforting.

I like roasting cauliflower. It sounded ridiculous until I tried it. But you need to remember to baste it with olive oil or butter as it cooks, to stop it drying out. I often serve it raw, dipping the florets into bowls of camel-coloured hummus, so it seems worth trying it hot. The result has a there-there quality, soothing as much as satisfying.

Although I probably wouldn't make this a principal vegetable dish for guests at Christmas, it will turn up in at least one of the many festive meals.

Serves 4 as a main dish
a small cauliflower
olive oil – 4 tablespoons

For the hummus:
onions – 3, medium
carrots – 300g
olive oil – 125ml, plus 4 tablespoons
half a pomegranate
chickpeas – 2 × 400g tins
mint leaves – 8
green olives, stoned – 150g

Set the oven at 200°C/Gas 6. Peel the onions and roughly chop them. Roughly chop the carrots. Put the onions and carrots into a roasting tin with the 4 tablespoons of olive oil, season, and bake for forty to fifty minutes, until the carrots are tender and the onions are golden. Cut the pomegranate in half again and remove the seeds.

Once the vegetables have been roasting for thirty minutes, break the cauliflower into florets and place them in a single layer, not too far apart, in a second roasting tin. Pour 4 tablespoons of olive oil over the florets and roast for twenty-five minutes, turning them over in the tin once during cooking. Test them for tenderness with a metal skewer.

Once the carrots and onions have been cooking for thirty minutes, add the drained chickpeas (keep a spoonful of whole chickpeas to finish) and return to the oven.

When the carrots and onions are ready, remove from the heat and blend in a food processor or blender, adding the 125ml of olive oil until you have a smooth paste. Tear up the mint leaves and roughly chop the olives. Spoon the carrot hummus on to a serving plate, add the roasted cauliflower, then scatter with the pomegranate seeds, mint, olives and reserved whole chickpeas.

A wreath for the front door

The wreath is a symbol of welcome. America and Scandinavia have a long tradition of tying a ring of evergreens to the door, but the habit has only recently become popular here. Indeed, I walk down streets in London where there is barely a front door unadorned. Wreaths of holly and red ribbons; wreaths of mistletoe, wreaths of Douglas fir and rosemary. Some are clearly the handiwork of professionals, others rely on the charm of amateurism. I spot one finished with beech leaves and copper and green pheasant feathers in a way that lets everyone know the owners have a second home.

I am uncomfortable with the idea of buying a ready-made wreath, but have been less than happy with my own attempts. Even bending the wire coat-hanger, the sort that comes with the dry cleaning, into a perfect circle was beyond me. I have come to a deal with myself. I buy a simple ring of holly, Douglas fir or fir cones, then put my own signature on it. A cop-out, but the sort I can live with. The ring stays solid on its woven willow base, and it is a delight, rather than a chore, to personalise it.

My base came from the greengrocer. A plain ring of Nordmann fir. I pick browning hydrangea heads from the garden (leaving plenty in place for the birds, who like swinging on them) and tuck them into the thicket of woven willow. Then in go bay leaves and sprigs of rosemary, dried beech leaves and some lichen-covered twigs and florist's moss. My fir cones came attached to their own twiggy branches, but had they not, I might have resorted to a spot of garden wire to secure them. I'm not sure I would trust myself let loose with a glue gun. Black berries – rather than blackberries – the sort you find on laurel bushes and viburnums, usually work well here, but I can't always find them.

We can get extravagant. Dried oranges spiked with cloves; cinnamon sticks and curls of cassia bark. Sprigs of dried herbs and poppy heads look splendidly archaic. (I find the smell of dried oranges and cloves a bit musty

in an auntie's-wardrobe kind of a way, but it appeals to others.) The garland could include rosehips, deep-red hawthorn berries and white snowberries. Avoid shiny laurels.

The most charming wreath, the one that I was happiest with, was the one I bought from Fern Verrow, when they had their now much-missed Bermondsey market stall. It gave the impression of having been made by elves. Jane Scotter's tangle of twigs, honesty, old man's beard, moss and berries was everything I wanted my wreath to be. It was admired by many. Others, whose taste probably ran to purple baubles, seemed less than impressed by its elfin magic.

I have a simpler version on the kitchen door. A circle of woven hazel twigs, with cobnuts in their shell. I insist it has a pagan charm.

The early examples of wreaths were for the most part made up of evergreens, ivy and laurel but often wheat too. They were worn by Etruscan rulers as symbols of strength, the green leaves surviving through the bitter cold of winter. They symbolise the harvest, and winners are often seen to wear them, but they are best known as a sign of welcome to Christmas visitors. Traditionalists will nail their wreath to the door on the first Sunday in Advent. Most of us would declare that too early. They might look a bit moth-eaten by Christmas Eve.

In domestic terms, we can thank the Lutheran church for the Advent wreath, from its first appearance in Germany, in the sixteenth century. True Advent wreaths contain four candles, with another, the Christ Candle, at the centre. This last one being lit on Christmas Day. The Christian meaning is to celebrate the coming of Christ, and the idea of using evergreens is to represent everlasting life.

My personal rule is to imagine the wreath as a hat. If it would look fine on the head of a Morris dancer, a mummer or a Druid, then I'm happy. More suited to the head of a racegoer at Ascot or a reveller at an office party, it's a definite no.

Favourite ingredients of mine for a wreath include:
For the base: Nordmann or Douglas fir, moss, holly, lichen and heather.
To decorate: fir cones, beech leaves, bay leaves, honesty, rosemary, feathers.
To finish: cassia bark, dried poppy heads, stars of anise, birch bark, moss, old man's beard, white or blue-black berries, hawthorn berries, crab apples, holly berries. The occasional slice of dried orange can look good, as can whole dried fruits, but they do bring a rather commercial look to the occasion. One of the most charming ideas of recent years was that of Petersham Nurseries, who used tiny red apples against a ring of glaucous leaves.

By the way, I am not sure what sort of person nicks a Christmas wreath from someone's door, but in my experience they do. I like to leave a very sharp piece of wire well hidden, so at least I have the comfort of knowing there is a chance of the thief drawing blood as they yank my handmade treasure from its hook. This is not, of course, a recommendation.

The bonhomie of sharing a pie

We have several people for dinner tonight and I fancy bringing a pie to the table. I could do my usual quick chicken and leek version, the one in *Kitchen Diaries*, Volume II, but I feel something more festive is called for. A bit of 'rolled-up sleeves cooking'. The butcher has a mass of little birds, oven-ready and not too expensive, on display. I decide to push the boat out and make the mother of all Christmas pies, a sort of festive sausage roll, served as a generously filled, circular pie with pieces of partridge breast tucked among the well-seasoned stuffing. It is simpler than I have made it sound. There is a bit of work to be done here, but not as much as it at first appears. It takes me just over an hour to get this beauty in the oven.

To get a crisp bottom, make the pie on the removable base of a steel tart tin and bake on a preheated baking sheet. The bones from the little birds can be browned and simmered with bay leaves and onion, then used as a stock with their leg meat and some pearl barley or small pasta such as orzo, to make a light but sustaining broth. The pie is jolly good eaten cold too, like a pork pie. In which case I would unscrew the lids on the pickles.

Pork and partridge pie

Serves 6
partridges – 3
bay leaves – 3
a small yellow onion
red onions – 2
carrots – 3 medium
celery – 2 ribs
olive oil – 6 tablespoons
butter – 20g
smoked streaky bacon – 8 rashers
thyme – 8 sprigs
rosemary – 2 bushy sprigs
garlic – 2 cloves
herby butchers' sausages – 8
ground allspice – $\frac{1}{2}$ teaspoon
ground cinnamon – $\frac{1}{2}$ teaspoon
ground mace – $\frac{1}{2}$ teaspoon
puff pastry – 500g
eggs – 2

You will also need a loose 24cm round tart tin base on which to cook the pie.

Put the partridges into a deep saucepan and pour over enough cold water to cover the birds. Bring to the boil with the bay leaves and the yellow onion. Lower the heat to a simmer, cover with a lid, and let the partridges cook for thirty minutes.

Meanwhile, peel and finely dice the red onions, finely chop the carrots and cut the celery into small slices. Warm the olive oil and butter in a large, deep pan, stir in the onion, carrot and celery and cook for five minutes, until the

onion is translucent. Roughly chop the bacon and stir into the vegetables. Pull the leaves from the thyme sprigs and the needles from the rosemary. Chop the rosemary finely. Peel and finely crush the garlic and stir, together with the herbs, into the onions and aromatics.

Remove the skins from the sausages and put the sausage meat into a large mixing bowl. Add the ground allspice, cinnamon and mace and season with salt and black pepper.

Remove the birds from their cooking liquor, let them cool briefly, then remove the breast meat from the bones. It should come away easily; if not, slice it off the bones with a kitchen knife. Retain the remaining meat, bones and cooking liquor for stock.

Stir the softened onion and bacon mixture into the sausage meat, mixing thoroughly. I tend to use my hands here.

Cut off one-third of the pastry and roll it to fit the tart tin base, with a little extra overlapping the edge. You can trim this later. Pile half the sausage and herb stuffing on top of the pastry, leaving 2cm or so of bare pastry round the rim. Smooth the surface level, then place the six partridge breasts on top and add the remaining mixture, smoothing the top into a dome.

Roll out a second piece of pastry from the remaining pastry piece to fit generously over the meat. Beat the eggs in a small bowl and brush the edge of the bottom layer of pastry generously. Lower the second piece over the top, then trim any overhanging pastry with a knife. Press firmly and pinch the edges to seal. Brush with beaten egg.

Use any pastry trimmings to make leaves or holly berries with which to decorate your pie, and press them into place. Brush with more of the beaten egg and rest the pie in the fridge for twenty minutes. Set the oven at 200°C/Gas 6, placing a baking sheet in the oven to get hot. Carefully put the pie, on its tart-tin base, on top of the hot baking sheet and bake for about fifty minutes, until golden. Let the pie rest for ten minutes before serving.

Sauce for the pie:
a clementine or small orange
dried cranberries – 50g
dry Marsala – 150ml
redcurrant jelly – 4 tablespoons

Cut the clementine or orange in half and squeeze the juice into a saucepan. Remove and discard the flesh, then cut the peel into very fine strips, as thin as you can. Add these to the juice, then stir in the cranberries, Marsala and fruit jelly. Bring the sauce to the boil, immediately lower the heat, and serve with the pie.

Note to self: buy ingredients for gravy.

Decorating the cake

You could taste the icing even before you came downstairs. The powdered sugar hung in the air, wafting ghost-like into every room, settling in a sweet veil on every piece of furniture. Even the dog tasted like a bon bon.

I sat, head on hands, for hours, watching my mother decorate the cake. She struggled to get the texture thick enough to make the necessary waves. Too thin and the peaks collapsed, too stiff and the curls of snow break, looking as if Santa's sleigh had flown too low and flattened the lot.

The snowdrift effect is made by dabbing at the surface of the iced cake with a blunt-ended knife. One of the knives with yellowing bone handles we inherited from my gran does the job perfectly, having the correct width and soft edges. Mum made the snowscene with the flourish of someone who has done it all her married life. I watched intently, looking out for the best wave, by which I mean the highest and most perfectly formed. To a nine-year-old this means the Matterhorn rather than the Malverns.

Our cake was always wrapped in a wide red and white ribbon, made from thick paper with heavily frilled edges which cuddled the cake like a roll-necked sweater. It came with a bit of last year's icing stuck to the fringe. The extravagance of the ribbon comes as a blessing, instantly disguising the less-than-perfect sides. The top, with its pure white drifts of Tate & Lyle loveliness, had, for years, been adorned with a trio of pointed bottle-brush trees, their green spines dusted with paint; a short fat gnome, a curious-looking creature, neither Santa nor elf with a lump of icing impacted on the base. Finally, the job is signed off with a piece of gold plastic, shaped like one side of a sleigh, bearing the legend Merry Christma. The 's' having been snapped off one year in a moment of over-excitement as the cake was sliced.

There may have been a red and white spotted mushroom too, though I'm not quite sure what the highly poisonous fly agaric has to do with Christmas.

I was eight, and with a deep sigh Mum was handing the cake decorating over to me. It came after years of whining 'please can I have a go.'

Finally, weary from the whole kerfuffle of Christmas, Mum wiped her hands on the thin flowery apron she always wore in the kitchen. 'I've had enough of this, dear. You do it.'

That was to be our last Christmas doing the cake together. The final time we peeled off the brown paper that protected the cake from burning as it baked; the last time I sat impatiently waiting to press the little plaster Santa into the snow; the final time we would taste the icing sugar air on our tongues. 'Mum, the air tastes like sherbert.' Come to think of it, that would be our last Christmas.

A Christmas cake should have a touch of fairytale magic to it. Unlike the dark-brown pudding or the pale pastry case of the mince pie, the cake can be as much Hans Christian Andersen as you like. The cake is a thing of wonder, a little piece of fantasy, whose decorations bring the same sort of childlike delight as a shaken snowglobe. I rally against tasteful cakes, designer cakes, and will have no truck with any type of healthy cake.

The decoration of my own cake, the one I make every year, has always been my take on Mum's snowdrift style, although some years it more resembles a choppy sea. I make the icing with golden icing sugar, giving it the colour of old parchment and a flavour of butterscotch rather than a simple hit of sugar. No one eats the icing, of course. Its sole purpose being to prevent the cake from drying out and I suppose to take me back to one of the happiest moments of my childhood.

Embellishing the cake

I rather like the idea of a cake tastefully draped in a layer of perfectly smooth marzipan, unsullied by plastic reindeer and resting like a pristine white duvet over a dense, dark cake. In reality, the paste is never quite smooth enough and the cake looks at best unfinished, at worst mean-spirited. Decoration of some sort is, I'm afraid, non-negotiable. There are as many possibilities as there are cooks, but I offer a few thoughts here.

The minimalist

Use coloured almond pastes in shades of walnut, caramel or hazelnut. Brush off any loose icing sugar with a dry brush otherwise your cake will look like it needs dusting. Tie a light, wide ribbon over the cake with a generous bow on top. Stick to gold, bronze and deep reds. The fabric will need to be crisp enough to stay put for a few days without sagging. Velvet is out of the question. Stiffly starched netting will work, as will some of the wider lace ribbons if you spray them with starch. A deep burgundy ribbon would look gorgeous on a caramel-coloured cake. Could I recommend VV Rouleaux, the ribbon shop in London's Marylebone? A veritable cornucopia of ribbon and braids for the well-dressed cake.

The almond cobble cake

There is much delight to be had in the simplicity of a naked fruit cake, stripped of its almond paste or icing vêtements, its dark, gently domed surface encrusted with lovingly placed almonds. A toothsome and tempting cake, homely and old fashioned, which carries with it the enduring happiness of holidays, picnics and long railway journeys. For all its nakedness, tied with a wide, simple red ribbon, such a cake is festive enough. Just make sure your almonds are placed with generosity and utter precision.

Make sure all the nuts are perfect. Broken ones will look like a squirrel has been at work. Use ready skinned nuts, it makes the job infinitely more straightforward. If not, soak the nuts for ten minutes in boiling water then remove the skins by pressing them individually between your thumb and forefinger. The white nut will pop out of its skin easily. If it doesn't, leave it to soak a little longer. Dry the nuts on a tea towel.

Toast the skinned almonds in a shallow pan over a moderate heat until evenly golden brown. The nuts will, somewhat annoyingly, brown only in one place, so you must move them almost continually around the pan to avoid little black patches. It's a bore, though the homely smell of toasting almonds on a winter's night makes up for the time taken and the gentle swishing sound of nuts on Teflon is faintly soporific.

You then push the golden nuts into the marzipan to form a crunchy coat. A random arrangement, however time-efficient, is likely to disappoint, resembling the one house on the terrace that someone has decided to pebble-dash. If the effect is to work at all, the nuts should be placed in soldierly rows, snugly abutting one another, going in ever-decreasing, tightly packed circles. It's a good look, providing protection for the marzipan and offering the crunch needed to balance the soft almond icing.

P.S. Don't be tempted to mix your nuts, otherwise the effect will, despite your best efforts, look as if you were clearing out last year's festive fruit bowl.

The toasted hazelnut cake

A layer of shelled, evenly toasted hazelnuts – pointed ends uppermost – is actually rather stunning, especially if somewhere you can find space for a lone Christmas tree, either bottle-brush or a real twig. I rather like icing the cake then freckling it with whole, roasted hazelnuts and crystallised pears.

The crystallised fruit cake

Crystallised fruits, thoughtfully arranged on the surface, give a fairytale effect to your cake and look enchanting in candlelight. They also have the advantage of being the quick alternative so you can finish the cake on Christmas Eve. The downside is the overdose of fruit, the cake itself being already chock-a-block with raisins and cherries. I suggest you do the job properly and take a trip out to the red-carpeted halls of Messrs Fortnum & Mason, whose selection of glacé fruits is akin to a stage set from *The Nutcracker*. (The Royal Academy opposite has lovely Christmas cards. You could treat yourself to a day out.) Consider the tiny sugared pears, Carlsbad plums and clementines. Whole orange slices are the very devil to arrange and even worse to cut. If your creation is to look magical, go for any fruits that are white, gold or palest pink. Avoid the green and red unless you are going for a Blackpool Illuminations look. The fact that each piece of the sticky fruit will stick to your knife as you slice the cake is something you must live with, but dipping it into hot water between slices will help.

The praline cake

Stand jagged pieces of praline into deep peaks of snow-white icing. The colour needs careful attention, try to remove the caramel from the heat once it is the shade of maple syrup. Add the toasted almonds and pour onto a lightly oiled baking sheet or piece of baking parchment and leave to set. Snap into large shards and stick them into the icing. A few edible gold stars can be fun here too.

The icing

What are we to do about icing? Clearing the plates after slices of cake have been passed around leads to the inevitable pile of unwanted icing. Thick white strips of the stuff, like a pile of gum shields they wear in boxing matches.

Icing the cake has become a token, a sort of inedible wrapping for the cake within. The truth is that no one save the odd sugar addict would go near your precious frosting. Perhaps we need to make other arrangements.

The snowscene

The icing must be thick. By which I mean so thick a spoon can stand up in it. A consistency that involves mountain upon mountain of icing sugar. If the texture is not suitably stiff your snowdrifts and peaks will slowly flatten until you have something resembling bodies buried in snow. The trick is to add the lemon juice and egg white a very little at a time. Once you have added too much, it will take boxes of the white powdered sugar to right the wrong. Believe me, I've been there. And at midnight.

The snowy peak effect is achieved by dipping a round-bladed knife into the deep surface of the icing and flipping it up into a little peak. You can go on for hours perfecting your style, replacing one peak with another, until the icing starts to set. A word of icing wisdom, don't be tempted to cover the cake with a tea towel until the peaks have set. The weight of even your lightest piece of spotless Irish linen is enough to flatten your perfect peaks.

White icing for the Christmas cake

egg whites – 4
icing sugar, golden or white – 850g
lemon juice – 4 teaspoons

In a large, clean bowl beat the egg whites with a fork until you can see a few bubbles appear, then sift in the icing sugar. Mix to a thick icing, folding in the lemon juice as you go, a very little at a time. You need the consistency to be stiff enough to spread without it sliding off the cake, so add more lemon juice only as necessary.

When the icing is stiff, pile it on to the sides and top of the cake and smooth it over with a palette knife. Using the handle of a fork or the tip of a round-ended knife, pull the icing up into peaks then leave to set. Once set, this is the point at which you can add any decorations you may wish, such as fir cones or plaster decorations. You can add a sprig of holly at a later date. The cake should be ready in 48 hours.

Store the cake in a tin or in a cool, dry place covered with a clean tea towel.

Greeting old friends

The sight of a cluster of dark green bottle-brush Christmas trees in differing sizes still brings a lump to my throat. They decorated every Christmas cake of my childhood.

The most welcome decorations, the ones that bring joy to everyone's heart, are surely those that come out year after year. The feeling of familiarity, of Christmas cakes past and a certain continuity, is comforting. Even the most chipped Santa receives a welcome like an old friend. (The fact that your snowman has had the same brick of yellowing frosting attached since 1984 only seems to add to the fondness the family has for it.) The cake decorations are the nearest some of us get to family heirlooms.

There are, of course, those who insist on moulding their own decorations out of marzipan or modelling icing, painting them with edible colouring with a certain fastidiousness. All thoroughly admirable yet somehow strangely wrong. As if someone is trying a bit too hard. While we are marvelling at the latest masterwork of creativity what we really want is that chipped Santa and cheap, bottle-brush tree. That little piece of family history. It's a Christmas cake, not the Sistine Chapel.

A word in praise of mulled wine

It is fashionable to trash the very notion of mulled wine. The dissenters have a point. Most mulled wine is indeed quite horrid, bargain-basement red, a squeeze of acidic, watery orange, more spices than a bowl of cheap pot pourri. Most unforgivable of all are those recipes that involve clearing out the drinks cupboard or made in a desperate determined attempt to get everyone pissed as quickly as possible.

Maybe we just have to admit that mulled wine is simply about having a good time. A drink with which to celebrate a jolly, frivolous occasion. Let's think of it as end-of-term for grown-ups. Nothing more sophisticated than that. Hot spiced wine comes into its own as something that will smell suitably festive, get everyone in a rumbustious mood and generally knock the edge off things.

A nice, simple spiced wine for serving hot

It's 6.30pm, you are weaving your way through the crowd with their earmuffs and scarves, reindeer hats and woollen mittens, trying to get to the south end of the market, where women in white aprons are baking flatbreads with onions and ham. You manoeuvre your way past huddles of office workers and students, shoppers and tourists clutching their steaming mugs. (We are not talking paper cups here, but decorated china mugs, often dated and to be kept as souvenirs.)

The air is all ice and spice. Chilly enough to need your scarf, yet warm with cinnamon and aniseed and the deep grapey notes of red wine that has been simmering in cauldrons with spirits and cloves. I have drunk glögg in Stockholm, Glühwein in Cologne, gløg in Oslo and glögi in Helsinki and all have the ability to turn a frozen tourist into the happiest man alive within five sips. It comes as no surprise that Glühwein translates as 'glow wine'. The mixture of steaming red wine, warm cloves, cinnamon, allspice and star anise is the very essence of Christmas. I know of few other drinks that so accurately tell you the time of year in one sip.

Recipes for mulled wine vary with country, city and tradition but have much in common. We have been warming wine and spices since Roman times. There is a recipe from 1390 in *The Form of Cury*, one of the earliest printed recipe books, which suggests grinding together cinnamon, ginger, galangal, cloves, long pepper, marjoram, cardamom and grains of paradise with red wine and sugar. Most modern recipes seem to include nutmeg, orange, lemon and an aniseed spice such as the suitably festive star anise or fennel seeds. Some gild the lily with a shot of whisky, vodka or rum. In theory, the mugs or glasses of warming punch are served with some form of biscuit or bun, usually spiced with ginger or cardamom, but I have only ever seen them accompanied by heartier fare such as creamy Spätzle. Nothing short of a plate of tartiflette will warm the soul quite so effectively.

My recipe for mulled wine owes more to glögg than our own mulled wine. I do think a shot of spirit helps, but it must be a small one otherwise you will end up adding too much sugar to take the rawness out.

Mulled wine

Serves 6
vodka – 200ml
cloves – 6
cinnamon stick
star anise – 3
cardamom pods – 10
an orange
a lemon
fruity red wine – a 750ml bottle
flaked almonds – a handful

Pour the vodka into a jug, add the cloves, cinnamon and star anise. Crack open the cardamom pods and add them, pods and all. Remove the peel from the orange in long strips (use a vegetable peeler) and add to the vodka together with the strips of peel from half the lemon. Set the mixture aside overnight.

The following day, strain the aromatics. (I tend to keep the star anise and return them to the wine as I serve.) Pour into a large stainless steel pan and add the wine, then warm slowly over a moderate heat. Don't, whatever you do, let it boil. Toast the almonds in a dry frying pan and scatter them over the surface of each cup as you serve the wine.

A terrine or two

I make lists. Shopping lists, to-do lists, Christmas card and present lists. Lists long and short, urgent lists and pipe dreams. And never more so than in the days that bookend Christmas. The one I write today is unusually long and detailed. A stream of consciousness that may or may not be followed. Either way it is an aide-memoire I feel I cannot live without. There is no point in reproducing it here, because a list is your own and pretty much useless to anyone else.

As well as waste my time with handwritten lists I do two brilliantly useful things today – a couple of cut-and-come-again terrines to last over the bank holiday and a practice run for the pumpkin custards I am doing for the non-meat eaters' lunch the day after tomorrow. Which from now on I shall know as national bain-marie day.

A terrine has saved my life more than once at this time of year. A coarse pâté tucked away in the fridge is a host's life raft. A squirrel store. Money in the bank. You cut a slice or two, make some toast, open a bottle of wine. Everyone's happy.

Making a terrine, something rough-textured, crumbly and studded with nuts or fruits, is not a stone's throw away from making plum pudding. A capacious mixing bowl, some minced stuff, a few spices and nuts. A terrine feels festive, generous, congenial. The result is endlessly useful and can be brought out for lunch, as a starter or for a light evening meal when everyone says they don't want much to eat. They're lying, of course.

A home-made terrine will also make you look clever, in a 'secret recipe' sort of a way, especially if you put your masterpiece on a wooden board with a dish of vinegar-sharp pickles and toast from a decent loaf. Your guests will think you are Elizabeth David.

Pig's cheek and prune terrine

I know what you're thinking. No one likes prunes. Well, they do. People only don't like prunes when they know they are eating them. So don't tell them.

Serves 8–10
stoned, dried prunes – 200g
Marsala – 100ml
the juice of an orange
a medium onion
butter – 30g
garlic – 2 cloves
minced pork – 500g
smoked streaky bacon – 200g
pork cheeks – 300g
tarragon leaves – 3 tablespoons, chopped
juniper berries – a handful

You will need a 1-litre capacity high-sided baking dish or terrine.

Cut the prunes into four, then leave them to soak in the Marsala and orange juice for an hour. Peel the onion and roughly chop it. Melt the butter in a small pan, add the chopped onion and cook for five or six minutes, until translucent. Peel and crush the garlic, stir into the onion and continue cooking for one or two minutes. Remove the onion from the heat.

Put the pork mince in a large mixing bowl. Roughly chop three-quarters of the bacon, and add to the pork. Remove any white sinew from the pork cheeks with a knife, then cut each cheek into four thin strips (if the pieces are too large they will be tough), then add to the other meats.

Chop the tarragon. Season the meat with salt and black pepper, then combine it with the tarragon and the prunes and onion mixture. Put the meat into the terrine or baking dish, packing it into the corners and lightly smoothing the surface. Set the oven at 180°C/Gas 4.

Arrange the reserved rashers of smoked streaky bacon over the surface, tucking them down the side of the meat, leaving gaps of meat showing on top. Add the juniper berries, pressing them into the meat. Cover the dish tightly with clingfilm, then with kitchen foil.

Put the terrine into a roasting tin and pour enough hot (not boiling) water into the tin to come halfway up the sides of the dish. Transfer the tin to the oven and bake for ninety minutes. Remove from the oven and place a heavy weight on top of the terrine to press it down. As soon as it is cool, transfer it to the fridge, still topped with its weight, and chill overnight.

Terrine of pork, smoked bacon and cranberries

A coarse, fruit-speckled pork pâté to serve over the holidays. I like to keep the texture moist by using minced pork that is generously marbled with fat. Stored in the terrine or glass jar in which it was cooked, well refrigerated, it should keep for a week. I like a loose texture, but if you prefer a more dense consistency that cuts neatly, press the terrine when it comes out of the oven by putting a heavy weight on top. Knobbly cornichons provide an accompanying snap of acidity, and I also like to serve mine with hot toast and green olives, the saltier the better.

Serves 8
a medium onion
butter – 30g
thyme leaves – 2 teaspoons
rosemary leaves – 1 teaspoon
smoked bacon – 250g
minced pork – 400g
ground mace – $\frac{1}{2}$ teaspoon
juniper berries – 12
dried apricots – 80g
fresh cranberries – 60g
Marsala or brandy – 2 tablespoons

To finish:
bacon – 2 rashers
bay leaves – 4
juniper berries – 12
fresh cranberries – 6

You will also need 2 small (500ml) ovenproof preserving jars or a suitable earthenware terrine.

Preheat the oven to 180°C/Gas 4. Peel and finely chop the onion. Melt the butter in a deep pan over a low to moderate heat, then add the chopped onion and leave to soften, stirring from time to time. Chop the thyme and rosemary and stir into the softening onion.

Remove the rind from the bacon, then chop the rashers finely. Put the pork mince into a mixing bowl and add the bacon. Remove the pan from the heat, then add the cooked onion to the minced pork. Season with the ground mace, $\frac{1}{2}$ teaspoon of salt and plenty of black pepper. Crush the juniper berries using a pestle and mortar. Chop the dried apricots and mix them into the pork together with the crushed juniper berries, the fresh cranberries and the Marsala or brandy. Check all is mixed well, then push the mixture into the jars or terrine.

Cover the surface with the bacon rashers, tucking them down the side of the jars, then press the bay leaves, juniper berries and cranberries into the surface. Cover loosely with the lid (do not seal with the metal clip) or cover the top with baking parchment, and secure with string or a rubber band, then with tin foil.

Place the jars or terrine into a roasting tin, then pour in enough water to come halfway up the sides. Bake for eighty minutes. Leave to cool in the switched-off oven, then remove and refrigerate overnight.

Herb-flecked, sprout-studded custards

The pumpkin feels as much a part of Christmas as it does of the harvest festival. The flesh glows like flames from an open fire. The shape – portly, heavy round the middle – has a touch of Santa Claus about it. The sweetness fits like a glove with the season's eating, and the spices we use with it, cinnamon, nutmeg and mace, are those of the Christmas pudding or mincemeat. It fits.

Crown Prince, Turk's Head and other tough-skinned squashes last conveniently through to the New Year. They may be sitting patiently in the vegetable rack or possibly as a door-stop. Either way there is brilliant saffron flesh to use as a side dish or as the body of a vegetable main course.

I roast the pumpkin (I often use butternut squash), tossed with olive oil or melted butter, chilli flakes and salt, until it is quite soft, then put it into small dishes and fill them up with a herb-flecked custard and lightly cooked Brussels sprouts. You could cook the vegetable-studded custard in a pastry case if you prefer. I don't, feeling there is quite enough to do already.

Makes 4, serves 2
pumpkin or butternut squash – 500g (peeled weight)
olive oil – 3 tablespoons
dried chilli flakes – 2 teaspoons
Brussels sprouts – 200g
eggs – 3
double cream – 250ml
rosemary, finely chopped – 1 tablespoon
parsley, finely chopped – 2 tablespoons
butter – a little, for the ramekins

You will also need 4 ramekins or small, ovenproof dishes approximately 9cm × 4–5cm deep. I sometimes use large Indian thali dishes.

Set the oven at 200°C/Gas 6. Cut the squash into discs about 2cm in thickness, then cut each disc into quarters or sixths depending on their size.

Put the butternut pieces into a mixing bowl, pour in the olive oil, then add the dried chilli flakes and a little salt and toss together gently, evenly coating the squash with oil and spice. Put the butternut on a baking sheet in a single layer and bake for thirty minutes, until pale golden brown and tender.

Meanwhile, cut the Brussels sprouts in half and cook them for a couple of minutes in deep, boiling, lightly salted water until they are approaching tenderness. Drain and refresh in iced water. Break the eggs into a medium-sized mixing bowl, pour in the cream and combine, then stir in the chopped rosemary and parsley and a little seasoning. Lightly butter the inside of the ramekins and place them on a baking sheet.

Divide the butternut and drained Brussels between the ramekins, then pour in the herb-flecked custard. Bake for twenty to twenty-five minutes, until the custard is lightly set around the edges, and a little wobbly in the centre.

Wrapping up Christmas

Furoshiki is the art of wrapping objects up in cloth, a beautiful bundle for you to carry home in lieu of a bag. It is how your washing comes back from the laundry in many hotels in Japan, and how they package your shopping in some of my favourite clothes shops. It is also how I would like to wrap my Christmas presents.

The abandonment of sticky tape and paper makes this a distinctly green way of dealing with the annual, last-minute palaver of gift wrapping. The soft cloths, often of simple, inexpensive cotton but sometimes of intricately patterned silk, are used year after year. Most of my dusters are rescued cheap furoshiki wrapping cloths. And another thing, it makes wrapping an awkward present as easy as tying a shoelace. I speak as someone who has on more than one occasion tried to wrap up a teapot.

The art of furoshiki is ancient. It was originally how you kept your clothes separate from other's at the sento, the communal public baths (nowadays you mostly get a wicker basket), and for centuries was used in place of carrier bags. After decades of decline, shops are reintroducing this way of wrapping purchases as a way to avoid using plastic bags.

Green gifting, the idea of environmentally friendly gifts, wrapping paper and cards is something I have inadvertently been doing for years. Surely I can't be alone in tenderly teasing the Sellotape away from the paper when I unwrap a present with the purpose of reusing the paper? Or of pressing the creases out with my hands and putting it away in a drawer for another occasion? That is why I tend to use paper that is not specifically for Christmas, in the hope it will be used by the recipient to wrap someone else's birthday present. If nothing else, it brings a whole new meaning to pass the parcel.

Much wrapping paper cannot be recycled (glitter and foil being a nightmare for those at the recycling plant), so it makes sense to use paper or cloth that you can reuse. By which I mean heavy paper that doesn't tear easily. Thin, cheap wrapping paper is difficult to use again, often being torn in the excitement. I am already spotting the presents under the tree whose covering is destined never to see the inside of the recycling bin. (Each year the United States produces four million tons of waste Christmas wrapping paper. A sobering thought.)

Tonight I sit at the table wrapping everyone's presents. As always, I start the job in a wave of enthusiasm, pretty paper and ribbon, and end exasperated and short of sticky tape. If I am completely honest, I am not exactly the best present wrapper in the world, each parcel giving the appearance of having been done with my eyes closed. The trick is to allow enough time, which isn't easy on Christmas Eve, the cook's busiest day of the year, hence my early start.

I have a healthy respect for exquisite wrapping paper, buying it even when I don't need any, just to have it there when I do need it. I do the same with cards too – it's a thing. I delight in being given a meticulously wrapped gift, especially when the paper has been artfully secured without recourse to sticky tape. Which, of course, brings me back to furoshiki and my plan for 'next' year.

Getting the blues

A wedge of blue, its veins running like a road map through the creamy curds; something soft and giving, its tendency to roam held in place by a downy white robe; a firm-textured cheese with a hard rind for eating with a Comice pear or a crisp, chilled apple. Christmas, in this house, is unthinkable without cheese.

Life is too short to stand in the Christmas Eve cheese queue, so I shop early today instead. I am not fond of cheeseboards, those 'carefully considered' collections of bits and pieces, 'something for everyone'. The scattergun approach. I prefer cheese that will be brought to the table in one large piece, or even a whole, small one, rather than a cheese's answer to a box of Quality Street.

I tend to go for quality over quantity. Three is enough. A blue-veined cheese, a sheep's or goat's milk variety and something firm and waxy-fleshed. As a kid, I looked forward to our annual slab of Danish Blue, the only one we could get in the depths of the 1960s. It sat, pongy and mysteriously exotic, next to a new moon of scarlet-waxed Edam and a block of Cracker Barrel, its red foil peeled back enticingly. I guess we move on. I don't go out with a definitive shopping list, only a vague idea that I want three cheeses. There are no rules. I simply buy a large piece of the three that are most enticing on the day.

There are hundreds of cheeses with which to grace the Christmas table, and the choice is yours, but it is the blues that are traditional. There is a reason for this. Several of the blue-veined types reach their point of perfection during the winter. Maturing for several months allows bigger flavours to develop, making them good for eating now. Their slightly more powerful flavours seem appropriate in cold weather – just as mild and milky burrata and ricotta feel perfectly attuned to a summer's day. Blue-veined cheeses also have an affection for walnuts, the autumn's harvest so good right now. The sweet wines we drink at this time of year, Marsala, Madeira, sherries and the muscats, can be a rare treat with a piece of Stilton, for instance. And all work splendidly with a glass of Champagne.

I eat blue cheeses throughout the year (Crozier Blue from Ireland, for instance, is very pleasing on a summer's day with a ripe peach or apricot). The more aggressive, salty blues are not really for me, I go for the gentler types. So, perhaps, a soft, pale-veined Gorgonzola; a tight-textured Spanish blue such as the fig-leaf-wrapped Picos or Cabrales. (Roquefort is my healing cheese, the one I head for when I have been in close proximity to someone with a cold perhaps. And no, I haven't had a cold for a decade or more.) That said, for the last few years my Yuletide Blue has been British. The character of each cheese, its flavours and texture vary reassuringly with the season. At Christmas, when they have been maturing for a while, their flavour is often a little more pungent, but never assertively so. To name names:

Shropshire Blue, a gorgeous golden blue cheese, crumbly and big-flavoured. I am exceptionally fond of the version made by the cheesemakers at Cropwell Bishop.

Harbourne Blue, that rare thing, a blue goat's milk cheese. Made in Devon, it has a delightfully crumbly texture, a clean bite and mild, sweet notes.

Beenleigh, a delicately blued sheep's milk cheese, refreshing, deliciously salty (and perfect for eating with a ripe pear), which I tend to spread rather than eat in a lump.

Devon Blue is buttery and rich and decidedly sweet, made from cow's milk.

Cashel is perhaps the best known of the Irish cheeses – it was one of the first of a new wave of small-scale, farm-produced cheeses. Moist, buttery yellow, fruity and slightly spicy.

Stichelton is a cow's milk cheese made with raw milk. It can be glorious. I find it varies more than most, according to the time of year and its maturity, a charming, even exciting quality for a cheese and endorsing the fact that these cheeses are handmade and are allowed to do their own thing.

Lanark Blue, a fine, complex, Scottish ewe's milk cheese, beautifully made, whose flavours become more powerful in the run-up to the end of the year. (The dairy stops milking in September, so a long-matured Christmas cheese has a stronger flavour than a summer one.) Their late-season batches have been described as 'a bit of kilt lifter'.

Stilton, a well-made Stilton can be a wonderful thing, especially for those who prefer a blue with a milder, creamier character. They are often the most delicate of the family. The cheeses produced in Colston Bassett – the smallest of the production centres – are a particular favourite of mine, possessing a sweet nutty quality.

Keeping your cheese

You can, despite what you have probably been told, keep your cheeses in the fridge. (That screaming noise you can hear is a thousand hysterical foodies throwing a hissy-fit at that last sentence.) The problem is that a fridge should be running at 3°C and cheese really doesn't like to be stored any lower than 5°C, so a fridge is not ideal. However, you may find, as I do, that wrapped in waxed paper and kept in a lidded plastic box in the salad crisper, your cheeses keep in perfectly fine condition. (Don't even think of using clingfilm.) Especially if you give them an hour out of the fridge in a cool place before you serve them. I leave mine, still wrapped in their waxed paper, on a marble board in the larder. It's not a perfect solution, but it works.

At the table

I serve my cheese on a rectangular willow tray lined with wax paper or a rush mat; the blues on a wavy-edged elm board. I keep them separate because no matter how hard you try, there is always someone who will use the blue cheese knife to slice a piece from the delicate, snow-white goat's milk cheese.

I offer simple biscuits, oatcakes and the like, but bread is strangely popular, even after dinner. At this point in the proceedings I am likely to prefer fruit – a pear, a russet apple or some sweet and very cold grapes. A well-seeded biscuit, crunchy with poppy seeds and oats, is suitable for mild and milky cheeses, but my preference for a blue is for something simpler.

Trifle

There has to be trifle. Our layered confection of fruit, sponge cake, cream and deep custard has come a long way since Hannah Glasse's eighteenth-century recipe, the one that included boiling calf's feet and hartshorn to extract the gelatine. I make mine without jelly, layering sponge with some sort of fruit, custard – either a classic recipe or new-fangled with mascarpone and cream – and, of course, whipped cream.

As befits its name, trifle should be adorned with frivolities, like crystallised fruits, toasted almonds, sugared flowers, in keeping with the spirit of the recipe.

Sometimes I make my own sponge. Sometimes I don't. If I have time it may be freckled with poppy seeds or nibs of candied peel. If I don't, the base of my trifle could be a shop-bought Madeira cake or some soft amaretti biscuits unwrapped from their pretty, traditional tissue. My parents preferred Swiss roll.

Summer trifles are the best, because you can use blackcurrants, damsons, plums or gooseberries to introduce a layer of tart relief among all the custard and cream. In winter the affair takes a turn for the sweeter, with a layer of stewed apple or sliced bananas. Today I found some more early forced rhubarb at the greengrocer's – slim, tender and as pink as a fairy.

It wouldn't feel like Christmas without trifle. But then, trifle is something I am quite capable of eating for breakfast. That said, I'm not making a vast bowl of it this year, because there will be other, simpler offerings too.

There probably should be something crisp crowning the top. The trifles of the seventeenth century would have been decorated with sweetmeats such as sugared aniseeds and dragees; later versions had toasted almonds and then, a century later, the unspeakable silver balls. I like crystallised rose petals or crushed praline on mine, something to bite amid the layers of pale softness. Whatever you choose should twinkle like jewels on a tiara.

The classic, no messing, family favourite (sponge, jelly (or not), custard and cream) is a crowd-pleaser but I prefer something more contemporary and without the sugar overload of jam. It is worth remembering that people can be 'very' fussy about trifle, possibly more so than any other dessert. I know those who throw a tantrum about the tiniest detail. And so they should.

Rhubarb (or apple) trifle

If you use ready-made sponge cake or ratafia biscuits, you will need about 250–300g. You will need a deep glass or china dish that will hold about 1.5 litres. If you prefer, peel and core 750g of sharp apples, then cook as below.

Makes 8 servings
For the sponge:
butter – 100g
golden caster sugar – 100g
eggs – 2
self-raising flour – 100g
an orange

For the rhubarb:
rhubarb – 750g (trimmed weight)
oranges – 2 (100ml juice)
caster sugar – 3 tablespoons

For the cream:
mascarpone – 500g
eggs – 2 separated
caster sugar – 2 tablespoons
vanilla extract – a few drops
double cream – 200ml

To decorate:
sugared rose petals

You will also need a shallow 20cm round sponge tin, lined on the base with baking parchment.

If you are making your own sponge, set the oven at 180°C/Gas 4. Cut the butter into large pieces and place in the bowl of a food mixer. Add the sugar, then beat until light and fluffy. Break the eggs into a small bowl and beat them lightly with a fork, then add them, a little at a time, to the butter and sugar. If there is any sign of curdling, introduce a little of the flour. Grate the zest of the orange and mix into the cake batter. Lastly, gently fold in the flour.

Scrape the mixture into the sponge tin and smooth the surface flat. Bake for about twenty to twenty-five minutes, until lightly springy and starting to come away from the sides of the tin. Remove from the oven and set aside for a few minutes. Turn the cake out on to a rack and leave to cool.

For the rhubarb, chop the stems into short lengths and place in a stainless steel saucepan with the orange juice and sugar. Bring to the boil, then lower the heat, cover, and leave to simmer for seven to ten minutes, or until the rhubarb is soft and just short of collapsing. There should be plenty of brightly coloured syrup.

Tear the cake into large pieces and place them snugly in the base of a large serving bowl. Pour over the rhubarb and its syrup, allow to cool, then refrigerate for an hour or two until thoroughly chilled.

Make the cream: put the mascarpone into the bowl of a food mixer. Add the lightly beaten egg yolks, sugar and vanilla and beat to a soft, pale custard. In a separate bowl, beat the egg whites until almost stiff (they should just hold their own shape), then fold into the mascarpone custard.

Spoon the custard over the top of the trifle, leaving some of the rhubarb showing in the middle if you wish. Whip the cream until thick but not stiff, then spoon over the top. Refrigerate for a good couple of hours. Overnight is even better (in which case I would leave whipping the cream until the day you intend to serve it). To decorate, crush a few sugared rose petals and sprinkle them over the cream.

Evergreens and a new fish pie

Christmas Eve, and I am bringing in the evergreens. I do this early in the day, so they have time to dry if they are, somewhat inevitably, dripping with rain. My ritual, but one that dates back to Roman times. Yew from the garden to adorn the mantelpieces. Holly and ivy to drape over the oak table. A bunch of mistletoe to hang from the old lantern above the fireplace in the hall. And, most important of all, a lichen-encrusted branch, dotted with fir cones barely bigger than acorns, a benign presence from the forest to watch over the unfolding festivities.

The yew is poisonous, but I have never worried about that. My visitors are unlikely to have to resort to tucking in to the decorations. The practice of filling the house with evergreens has been with us since Roman times, the plants chosen simply because they were in leaf or, in the case of holly and mistletoe, fruit. They show that, despite appearances, life is still present; the garden is simply sleeping. Symbols that mark not the end of the year, but the beginning of a new one.

I bring in holly too, not from the garden but in string-tied bunches from the farmers' market. Apparently holly is considered a man's plant. Ivy, a woman's. Heaven knows why. Holly is hated by witches. My childhood bedroom at home had a holly tree outside the window. I looked forward to spotting the berries, especially if it snowed. On a crisp winter's morning, the view from my room was that of a Christmas card.

The bunches of holly, their leaves glossy, almost black, are stuffed into the empty fireplaces peppered around the house. Sometimes there is enough to fill a portly jug on the study table too. I rather like the idea that in Sweden the floor used to be strewn with spruce and juniper. In Poland straw was used in a similar way. Habits that are wholly about bringing in good luck and benign spirits.

The Yule log

Fires burn in only two of the fireplaces in this old house. I would dearly love to light those in the kitchen, bedrooms and bathroom too, but running up and down the stairs with buckets of ashes is beyond me. Not to mention the risk that lies in an unattended fire. Central heating may be unromantic, but I'm all for it.

The term 'Yule log' is now associated with a buttercream-filled chocolate Swiss roll, decorated to look like the branch of a tree, the charm of which has so far eluded me. Step back fifty years or so and the Yule log is a far more interesting affair. Each Christmas Eve, a magnificent lump of wood, vast in both circumference and length, was brought into the house and partially burned over Christmas. It would be allowed to go out, leaving it somewhat charred, then it would be used to light the following year's log. During the intervening twelve months it would be kept in the house, where its magical properties would act as a talisman against lightning, hail, family ills and house fires.

My father used to bring the most splendid log he could unearth from the pile in the woodshed into the house each year. It is a deed that dates from the sixteenth century, a pagan ritual believed to have German origins. The encyclopedia of English folklore mentions it as a seventeenth-century occurrence, yet its presence was well known earlier, when it was known as the Yule Clog, and could date back to the Saxons. (Gerry Bowler, author of *Santa Claus, A Biography*, suggests that the idea could go back as far as 1184.) Whatever, the burning of a large log is well documented.

Further afield, particularly in eastern Europe, the story becomes even more delightful. Clement Miles, writing in *Christmas Customs and Traditions*, mentions a Dalmatian habit of wrapping oak trunks in red silk and adorning them with leaves and flowers. In Serbia, three oaks are felled for each household, then brought into the room and lit at twilight. In other rural areas, wine or corn is thrown as the logs are brought over the threshold. Italy and Provence have their ancient Yule log observances too, still occasionally followed. The rule is not to remove any ashes from the house on Christmas morning while some households insist that ashes could only be removed once a green leaf or twig had been brought in.

The Yule log is more than just a lump of burning wood. It is seen to represent life itself. Even in these times of centrally heated homes, it is not difficult to see the importance of a fire in the grate, and its association with warmth, good health and happiness. Whether a log of wood can have powers beyond keeping us warm depends on your way of looking at things.

The Christmas Eve dinner

The house is looking gorgeous. The tree shimmers in the corner of the dining room (a space which for most of the year doubles as my office); candles are lit on every available surface (there are no window ledges in this house, so every side table and mantelpiece becomes home to a candle or two). Every empty fireplace is stuffed with holly, and ivy hangs from every mantelpiece. The table is laid – an old sheet standing in for a tablecloth – and the lights are low.

We start with Champagne flushed with a dash of pomegranate juice, dishes of basil, mint and parsley to pick at (a habit picked up in Lebanon), and crisp pastries filled with green olive paste. We eat a fish pie, bulging at the seams like an overstuffed pillow, its filling full of herbs, cream and smoked fish oozing as we cut it. At its side a cucumber salad, tiny batons, carelessly peeled to show the bright emerald green under their skin, tossed with dill and tarragon vinegar. There will be the trifle I made yesterday if I can find the rhubarb. If not, an apple version.

Truth told, the British make less fuss of this day than the rest of Europe. For much of the continent, this is the principal dinner of the season and feasting can go on into the wee small hours. Historically, this is the night before Christians broke their long Advent fast. Fish is the most popular choice. (There is not a turkey in sight.) From Poland's carp with gingerbread sauce to America's fish pie, Christmas Eve dinner is a piscatorial feast. Most spectacular of all is La Vigilia, the Italian feast that involves seven fish dishes, from baccalà and baked cod to octopus salad and deep-fried calamari, which can go on for twenty-four hours.

My habit of serving some sort of fish dish on 24 December is unshakeable, but for reasons that are more practical than religious. Today is the last day for buying fresh fish until well into the New Year. This is my last chance to eat oysters, mussels and mackerel, and indeed anything that isn't frozen or smoked.

For years I made a fairly standard fish pie, usually of haddock, prawns and mussels in a creamy sauce topped with deep furrows of mashed potato. Served in a deep enamel pie dish, it was splendid, but a recipe that involved the most unbelievable amount of work. Not to mention using almost every saucepan in the house.

Five years ago I decided that a large pastry-based pie, a sort of fish-based beef Wellington, was both more spectacular and less of a hassle. I stuffed two whole fillets of skinned salmon with shredded cucumber and wrapped them in puff pastry. Lighter than a potato-topped pie, and quicker to produce, it was a doddle. The recipe has proved to be one of my most popular ever. (I can't tell you the number of people who come up to me after Christmas to tell me how much everyone enjoyed it. The recipe is in *Kitchen Diaries*, Volume II, if you're interested.)

This year I feel a change is needed. A dish that has the crisp and flaky crust of the latter but something of the creamy filling of a traditional fish pie. I should mention that the filling must, absolutely must, be allowed time to firm up in the fridge before you wrap it in pastry.

Hot-smoked fish and leek pie

The pie reheats well, should you need to do so tomorrow.

Serves 8
leeks – 500g
butter – 40g
double cream – 500ml
plain flour – 3 heaped tablespoons
hot smoked salmon – 250g
smoked mackerel – 250g
new potatoes – 300g
olive oil – 4 tablespoons
chopped parsley – 3 tablespoons
chopped tarragon – 2 tablespoons
puff pastry – 375g
an egg
nigella or sesame seeds – 1 tablespoon

You will need two large baking sheets and a piece of baking parchment.

Cut the leeks into discs 1cm in width, wash thoroughly, then put them into a deep, heavy-based pan with the butter over a moderate heat. Let the leeks cook for eight to ten minutes, covered with a round piece of greaseproof paper and a lid, so they cook in their own steam and soften without browning.

Gently warm the double cream in a small pan and remove from the heat. Add the flour to the leeks, stir, leave to cook for a couple of minutes (to get rid of the raw taste of the flour), then break the hot smoked salmon and mackerel into large flakes and gently stir into the leeks. Pour over the warm double cream and leave to cook over a low heat for five minutes. Remove from the heat.

Slice the potatoes into thin coins, each about the thickness of a one-pound coin. Warm the olive oil in a shallow pan, then fry the potato slices on both sides over a moderate heat until golden. They must be soft inside. Fold the cooked potatoes into the fish and leek cream, season carefully with salt and black pepper, add the chopped parsley and tarragon, then transfer to a mixing bowl and leave to cool. Chill thoroughly in the fridge. (If you skip this step it will be impossible to shape the pie.)

Set the oven at 200°C/Gas 6. Place one of the baking sheets upside down in the oven. Line the other one with baking parchment. Cut the pastry in half, then roll out each piece to a rectangle 32cm × 22cm. Place one rectangle on the lined baking sheet. Pile the cold filling on top of the pastry, leaving a border on all four sides of at least 2cm. Smooth the top of the filling so you have a deep rectangle of mixture. Beat the egg in a small bowl or cup and brush the bare edges of the pastry generously.

Place the second sheet of pastry over the filling, then press the edges of the two pieces of pastry firmly together to seal. It is important that they are well sealed, otherwise your filling will leak. Brush the top layer of pastry all over with the beaten egg, scatter with the nigella or sesame seeds, then pierce a small hole in the centre with a knife or the handle of a wooden spoon. Place in the oven, the lined baking sheet on top of the hot, upturned one, and bake for forty minutes, until golden brown.

Leave to settle for five minutes, then slide the pie off the baking sheet on to a serving board or dish and slice.

Lighting the Yule candle

Enchanted as I am by the ancient ritual and magic of the Yule log, I am more likely to follow the more modern custom of burning a Yule candle. My fascination with candlelight is no secret, but the idea of keeping a flame burning throughout the night of Christmas Eve is both a joy and a challenge. It is, of course, a fire risk and not something I would recommend, but it is one that I am happy to take, ritually, each year. It is asking too much of a nightlight – most burn for just six hours – so a large candle it must be.

Much of Europe still lights a large candle on Christmas Eve, sometimes two. They should still be burning in the morning. I remember a midwinter trip to the city of Gothenberg, where a flame seemed to glow in every wooden-framed window. There is something thoroughly 'hygge' about coming down

to breakfast on Christmas morning to find a flame burning in a jam jar. Tradition has it that the light must not go out, for fear of death in the family. But I am not one to take notice of negative traditions, only positive ones.

Some families in Scandinavia, where candles are more popular than in Britain, still let two candles burn overnight on the kitchen table. They are extinguished at sunrise. In earlier, more religious times, the candles wouldn't be snuffed until the church service, in which case it would be done by the eldest member of the family.

My own heavy, beeswax candles are lit on Christmas Eve, secured in tall, heatproof glass jars and left to burn quietly throughout the night. I have never known them not be there, twinkling and glowing, on Christmas morning.

Getting organised

You will probably have wrapped the presents and decorated the tree days ago. There are some people who leave this until Christmas Eve. All very well in Victorian times, but I find there is far too much to do on this day as it is. The idea of chasing the Sellotape or replacing the missing strings on a bauble at this late stage is not my idea of fun.

At the risk of sounding a bit do-it-and-dust-it, this is a chance to get organised for tomorrow. No matter how late you stay up, it will be time well spent.

Gravies

I make the gravies for tomorrow. I cannot recommend this too highly. One for the turkey or goose, the other for the vegetable loaf. It takes a good two hours of my day, but it is a job that I find deeply satisfying and they will both be richer, more mellow, when they emerge from a night in the fridge.

Onion gravy for the turkey

Enriched with chicken wings and dried mushrooms, this is the gravy I think worth making for the feast. The ingredient list seems endless, but they are mostly things we tend to have knocking about anyway. The crucial bits are the mushrooms, wings and giblets, responsible for giving a velvety consistency.

Enough for a medium-size turkey
a large onion
olive oil – 5 tablespoons
banana shallots – 6
whole chicken wings – 14
the turkey giblets
small carrots – 4
celery – 2 ribs
garlic – half a small head
bay leaves – 4
black peppercorns – 12
dried mushrooms such as porcini – 20g
thyme sprigs – 8
water – 1 litre
redcurrant jelly – 2 heaped tablespoons
dry Marsala or Madeira – 3 tablespoons

Peel the onion, cut it in half, then slice each half into thin segments. Warm 3 tablespoons of the olive oil in a deep pan, add the onion, then leave to cook over a low heat, stirring regularly. Let the onion cook until it is sweet, golden brown and very, very soft. A good twenty minutes.

Peel and halve the shallots. Warm the remaining oil in a shallow pan and fry the shallots for five minutes or so, until nicely browned. Remove the shallots from the pan, then add the chicken wings and let them brown, introducing any of the giblets you like towards the end.

Scrub the carrots and slice them in half. Roughly chop the celery, then add the carrots, celery and garlic to the onions, together with the shallots and wings, the bay leaves, peppercorns, dried mushrooms, thyme and water. Bring to the boil, then lower the heat so the liquid simmers gently and leave for two hours. Check regularly to make sure the gravy doesn't boil.

Strain the gravy through a sieve, then bring to the boil in a saucepan, stirring in the redcurrant jelly and the Marsala or Madeira. Leave to cool, then refrigerate. The next day, check the seasoning, adding salt as necessary, and serve, piping hot, with your Christmas dinner.

A mushroom Marsala gravy

A meat-free gravy with something of the bosky depth of a meat-based version, dark and mysterious from the addition of mushrooms. Like most of these recipes it will be better for a night in the fridge. A single heaped tablespoon of flour will give you a thinner, pouring-style gravy. Two will require a spoon to ladle it, thick and steaming, from the jug.

Enough for 6
onions, medium – 2
butter – 40g
garlic – 3 cloves
celery – 1 rib
dried porcini – 25g
button mushrooms – 200g
olive oil – 3 tablespoons
thyme sprigs – 8
plain flour – 1–2 tablespoons
dry Marsala – 125ml
fruit jelly such as redcurrant – 2 tablespoons

Peel the onions, cut them in half from stem to root, then slice each half into thin segments. Warm the butter in a heavy-based saucepan, add the onion and leave to cook over a medium heat. Peel and thinly slice the garlic, add to the onions and continue cooking until the onions have been cooking for a good fifteen to twenty minutes. Finely slice the celery and stir into the onions and garlic as they start to soften. Soak the porcini in a litre of water.

When the onions and celery are soft, golden and sweet, slice or quarter the button mushrooms as you wish, then add them, together with the oil, to the onions. Pull the thyme leaves from their stalks and stir into the onions and mushrooms. When the mushrooms are soft and nut-brown, scatter the flour over the surface, stir, and cook for a couple of minutes. Pour in the porcini stock and add the porcini and Marsala, and bring to the boil. Stirring, lower the heat, season, then leave to simmer for about fifteen minutes.

Stir in the fruit jelly, then taste for sweetness, adding more if you wish. You want a balanced gravy, savoury and sweet with a deep, wintry character.

Parsnip loaf with rosemary and mushrooms

Serves 6
parsnips – 500g
carrots – 250g
an apple
butter – 75g
onions, medium – 2
garlic – 2 large cloves
chopped parsley – 2 heaped tablespoons
rosemary needles – 2 tablespoons
hemp seeds – 1 tablespoon
pumpkin seeds – 1 tablespoon
sunflower seeds – 1 tablespoon
poppy seeds – 1 tablespoon
thyme leaves – 1 tablespoon
eggs – 2
butter for greasing the loaf tin
thyme sprigs – 8

You will also need a loaf tin measuring about 22cm × 12cm × 8cm, lined with baking parchment.

Peel the parsnips, then cut them lengthways into quarters. Grate the parsnip finely, using the coarse blade of a food processor, slightly thinner than matchsticks, then do the same with the carrot. (I don't find it necessary to peel the carrots, only to scrub them with a vegetable brush.) Grate the apple, without peeling it, and add to the bowl.

Warm half the butter in a shallow pan, then add the grated root vegetables and apple and let them cook for three or four minutes, until they are bright and approaching softness. Tip them into a large mixing bowl. Set the oven at 180°C/Gas 4.

Peel, halve and finely slice the onions. Melt the remaining butter in the shallow pan and cook the onions until they are soft and pale gold. Peel the garlic, crush finely, then add to the onions and continue cooking. Tip the onions and garlic into the bowl with the carrots and parsnips.

Add the chopped parsley to the mixture, then finely chop the rosemary needles and add them too. Add the hemp, pumpkin, sunflower and poppy seeds, thyme leaves and a generous grinding of salt and pepper. Break the eggs into a bowl, beat them lightly to combine yolks and whites, then fold into the mixture. Combine the ingredients together thoroughly.

Line the loaf tin with baking parchment, then butter it generously. Scatter a few thyme sprigs over the bottom of the tin. Transfer the mixture into the loaf tin, pressing it firmly into place. Smooth the surface level and cover with buttered baking parchment. Place the loaf tin on a baking sheet and bake in the preheated oven for about forty-five minutes, until lightly firm to the touch.

Remove from the oven and leave to settle for ten minutes, then turn out of the tin and carefully peel away the paper. Cut into slices and serve with the porcini Marsala gravy or with Cumberland or cranberry sauce.

The brandy butter

Something else to get out of the way for tomorrow. Frostily gritty with sugar and scented with finely grated citrus, we have been watching this seasonal spread slide down our pudding since the 1700s. Cold, straight from the fridge, it provides a contrast to the steaming heat of the pudding. Watching it melt into the jumble of raisins and spice is one of the tiny triumphs of Christmas.

Americans know our brandy butter as hard sauce, and sensibly bring out it for other puddings too, such as bread pudding and – excellent idea, this – gingerbread.

The recipe

Butter should be room temperature when you start, otherwise it will take an age to soften under the beaters, and will probably bounce out of the mixing bowl. Unsalted is the way to go.

Sugar needs to be caster, so the glisteningly gritty quality is preserved. White will do, but the modish golden sugar is my own preference, if only because of its colour. (However you dress it up, it is still sugar.) Icing sugar will make the sauce altogether too sweet, though it might be an idea for those who dislike the grainy quality of the original. No one wants a dollop of buttercream on their pud. The soft, damp-textured brown sugars such as muscovado add deep butterscotch or caramel notes to the sauce, bringing more to the party than just sweetness. Demerara is a tad too gritty.

Orange and lemon zest add brightness and a seasonal scent. Take care only to include the very outer zest, none of the white pith that lies underneath. Oranges do the job, but clementines, the tight-skinned flat-topped citrus fruits, feel more appropriate. The baggy-skinned, easy-peeled varieties are useless for grating.

Vanilla should be extract or seeds scraped from the pod. Often forgotten but to my mind essential, the tiny brown-black seeds add an ice-creamy note. Don't even think of using the chemical-tasting 'essence'.

Avoid the temptation to increase the quantity of brandy. It will simply make the sauce bitter.

The recipe is pretty impossible to get wrong, but I would suggest that the butter is left out of the fridge for an hour before using and that you don't over-mix it, which might cause the sauce to separate. Introduce the brandy slowly, stopping promptly at any idea of curdling.

Refrigerate the finished sauce for a good two or three hours, or overnight, tightly wrapped in paper or clingfilm. Used soft and warm there will be no contrast with the pudding.

Variations
· Sherry, rum and whisky are all perfectly acceptable alcohols to use in place of the more popular brandy.
· The dark brown sugars are worth trying, but are best mixed with white or golden caster so as not to overpower with their intense, butterscotch character.
· Ground almonds have their supporters too – add them once the butter and sugar are thoroughly creamed.
· It is worth mentioning here that Nigella Lawson has a voluptuous, take-no-prisoners version using cold caramel sauce and butter.
· Nutmeg, a little and very finely grated, will give the butter the homely quality of a custard tart. Cinnamon likewise.

The genre has its detractors, most of whom seem to prefer double cream, custard or vanilla ice cream.

A good, nicely balanced brandy butter

Serves 8
unsalted butter – 180g
soft brown sugar, such as muscovado – 90g
golden caster sugar – 90g
a clementine
a small lemon
a vanilla pod
brandy – 3 tablespoons

Take the butter out of the fridge an hour or so before you start. Cut it into small dice, as this will help it to marry with the sugar more successfully.

Cream the butter and sugars, either with a wooden spoon or, better I think, with the flat paddle beater of an electric mixer. Taking care not to over-mix, which will send the sauce 'oily', add any extras such as ground almonds (2 tablespoons).

Remove the zest of the clementines and lemon using the finest side of the grater, then add and combine. Slice the vanilla pod in half lengthways, then scrape out the seeds with the point of the knife. Stir them into the creamed butter and sugar. Add the brandy.

Make the butter a day or more in advance and store, tightly covered, in the fridge. You can freeze it too.

A few alternatives

A prune and vanilla cream for the pudding

The dark fruity liquorice note of prunes as an accompaniment to what is already a festival of vine fruits may sound like too much of a good thing, but it works. In just the same way as adding honey to already sweet roasted parsnips, it seems to flatter rather than smother. The prunes are mashed into a sticky purée, then folded into whipped cream. No other sugar. But a drop or two of vanilla extract gives a pleasing backnote.

soft dried prunes – 100g
vanilla extract – 2 or 3 drops
double cream – 250ml

Put the prunes into a bowl, then crush them to a soft, creamy purée with a fork, or using a food processor. Stir in the vanilla extract.

In a chilled bowl, whip the cream until it will just hold its shape – not stiff enough to stand in peaks. Fold the prune and vanilla purée gently into the cream and pile into a cold serving dish. Chill thoroughly, taking care to cover the cream with clingfilm.

Clementine and ginger butter

An alternative to crème fraîche or ice cream, sweeter, but with a soft citrus note that flatters the dried figs. Tightly wrapped, it will keep in the fridge for a week.

Serves 8
unsalted butter – 125g, room temperature
golden caster sugar – 100g
clementines – 2
a small lemon
preserved ginger in syrup – 3 knobs
Marsala, sweet or dry – a capful

Put the butter into the bowl of a food mixer, add the sugar and beat for three to four minutes until light and fluffy, scraping down the bowl from time to time with a rubber spatula.

Finely grate the zest from the clementines and the lemon and fold into the butter and sugar. Slice the preserved ginger into thin discs, then chop finely. Add the ginger to the butter, then slowly stir in the Marsala. Transfer to a serving bowl and set aside, in the fridge, for thirty minutes to firm up a little.

The visit from Santa

Tonight is also the night that Father Christmas is due to visit. Please don't tell me you are not excited, I know I am. The idea of Santa Claus flying across the sky on a sleigh piled with gifts, pulled by reindeer, is suspiciously like the legend of the white-bearded, long-cloaked Norse god Odin (Woden). He also travelled the night sky but on an eight-legged horse called Sleipnir, distributing gifts while people slept. Whoever turns up will need to get their descent right. Only the kitchen chimney in this house is wide enough for a large fellow to get down. (The others will barely take a chimney sweep's brush.) I shall leave a glass of sherry and a sugar-dusted mince pie.

Santa's eight reindeer – Dasher, Dancer, Prancer, Vixen, Comet, Cupid, Donner and Blitzen, first mentioned in the 1923 poem 'The Night Before Christmas' – can rest briefly on the roof. (Always worth learning their names; they come up on television quiz shows from time to time.) The head reindeer Rudolph, incidentally, is a more modern invention. He first appeared in 1939 in Robert L. May's book *Rudolph the Red-nosed Reindeer* and has rather stolen the others' thunder.

The night before Christmas

Just before bed, we shall exchange gifts. This is new, both from a personal aspect and from an historical one. Our family traditionally opened their presents on Christmas morning. Many other families waited until Boxing Day (a custom that dates from when those in service opened their presents). The wait must have felt like an eternity. I, like many others, now open mine on Christmas Eve.

Until the Reformation, December 6 was the day of gift-giving, as it still is in much of Germany, Hungary and Slovakia. Sixteenth-century Protestants moved the day to the 24th and the bringer of gifts to the Christkindl.

We have a roly-poly Santa Claus, white-bearded and scarlet-cloaked, bringing sacks of presents on a sleigh. I promise if you go out at midnight and look up at the night sky you will see his sleigh, weighed down with golden sacks of beribboned presents, being pulled by a troop of reindeer over the rooftops. (In most illustrations there will be snow too, but I can't promise that.) He stops at the homes of good children and climbs down the chimney with his sack of gifts.

It is traditional to leave a mince pie and a glass of sherry out for him to speed him on his way. It is curious that no matter how hard I have tried, and how excited I am, never once in sixty years have I actually managed to see him.

In Germany, Austria, Poland, the southern Tyrol and the Czech Republic (and much of Latin America too) the presents are brought not by Santa but by the Christkindl, the blond angel representing the Christchild. No doubt an attempt by the Lutheran church to get children to think of Jesus as a good thing. Like our own dear Santa, the children never see the Christkindl, and are warned not to stay up for fear of not being brought their presents. (Yes, that old trick.)

In Austria, so I am told, you may get Christkindl, the Archangel Gabriel and St Peter performing in a play, directly before the presents are handed round. There are gifts only for good children. In Russia, presents are delivered by Kolyáda, a maiden in white who arrives by sleigh and hands over presents in return for a carol.

Whether our presents arrive with a jolly chap in red, or a straw-haired angel with wings, they must be opened. I thoroughly dislike opening presents in front of the giver. (Which is why I prefer mine to arrive by sleigh in the middle of the night.) I feel that they can read my mind, as I pull the ribbon and wrapping paper slowly and ostentatiously from the parcel, praying that they won't be able to see my disappointment when the enclosed gift is thoroughly wrong.

The night the spirits roam

24 December is, for so much of the world, the night of the supernatural. Much more so even than Hallowe'en. Traditionally, this is the night some Scandinavians stay at home, for fear of bumping into witches and trolls. The night the dead return and are made welcome. The night not to be caught out when the cock crows.

Ghosts are much easier to imagine in winter. The dark, of course, but it is the half light, the dusk that hovers between late afternoon and early evening, that is so much more suited to seeing spirits. The bare trees, with their stripped, witchy branches, and the shadows that linger at this time of year, only add to the prospect. This may well be why the lane outside the house is so quiet tonight, and why a walk round the garden by the light of a lantern is carried out in silence.

Note to self: leave stocking out.

CHRISTMAS DAY

Ringing bells and a roasting goose

Christmas morning, and my day begins with the ringing of church bells. There is a delightful online source called Bells on Sunday, an archive of bell-ringing from churches around the country. For which I thank BBC Radio 4. You can scroll down and choose your belfry. Not only do you get the most glorious bell-ringing but also snippets of history about the barrels, ears, cannons and clappers of the bells themselves. Utter joy.

Despite the heartache of no snow, nothing can extinguish the frisson of Christmas Day. Yes, there is much to do, but I have always felt that to be a good thing. (Heaven help me the day I have nothing to do.) Much of the practical business was dealt with yesterday. The gravy is mellowing in the fridge; the stuffing awaits its fate and the plum pud is ready to be steamed. I have the bird to roast and baste, the vegetables to do (potatoes to roast, parsnips to cook and mash and Brussels sprouts to halve and sauté in butter). There are a few sausages to wrap in bacon because I love them. At some point there is the table to lay and some wine to open, which doesn't sound much but this is, above all, a day of interruptions. Well-meaning, but interruptions nevertheless.

There is a moment, late on Christmas morning, when I can feel myself start to relax. The bird is singing sweetly in the oven. The preparation, vegetables, pudding, gravy are done and dusted. The kitchen smells wonderful. A smell that is joyous, rich, full of happiness and geniality. May I suggest you sit down and take it all in, as I do. Collect your thoughts – there is still much to do – but also take in the scene. Listen to that roast sizzling calmly in the oven, the excited chatter of loved ones, the happy chaos of Christmas morning. Five minutes in which to settle your spirit.

The goose

I love the smell of a goose as it roasts, the sweet savour of its meat, the lashings of fat it gives us to play with. The flavour of the meat is magnificent. By that I mean full, deep, rich and earthy. The goose was the original Victorian Christmas bird. (The breed is indigenous to this country, unlike the turkey.) All will be well as long as you occasionally remove the fat from the roasting tray, don't overcook the bird and carve it carefully.

Goose has been my Christmas bird of choice for the last twenty years or more. Sales of geese have been slowly rising for the last few years, with all the major suppliers posting increased sales between twenty and fifty per cent on the previous year. Some butchers have told me that, for them, goose now outsells turkey.

The goose hasn't always been kept for Christmas alone. Until the Second World War, Michaelmas, September 29, was the traditional day for eating the bird in Britain, though it passed to being a Christmas event in Victorian times. The geese were mostly brought up on mixed farms, fed on grass during the spring and summer, then, come the autumn, fattened on grain and the harvest stubble, for Christmas.

They have been farmed here for centuries, particularly in East Anglia, though the most famous Goose Fair has been held in Nottingham since the thirteenth century. The fair, by the way, is held to this day, though its fame is now as an exceptional funfair, complete with rides and carousels, candyfloss and helter-skelter. No longer will you see hundreds of geese making their way on foot from Lincolnshire. Goose was once the Christmas bird of choice for the middling to well-off. Those with smaller budgets stuck to beef, while the wealthy tucked into turkey. Clearly things have changed, with goose now being the more expensive choice.

It is easy to see why some of us choose a goose, but it is not without its downside. Even the largest bird is unlikely to feed quite as many as a turkey of similar weight. The shape, long and elegant compared with the turkey's more portly frame, means you need a large oven and an equally large roasting tin. The fat that seeps out as it cooks, however delicious and useful, can be a danger. It needs removing from the roasting tin carefully if we aren't to scald ourselves. Geese are generally more expensive, partly because they cannot be reared in such a confined environment as the turkey. Another downside is that, as the flesh cools, it firms up, rendering it slightly less useful for leftovers. (The trick for sandwiches is to slice it very thinly.)

Traditionally, we pack the carcass with a stuffing of onion, breadcrumbs and sage. The most pungent of kitchen herbs (use more than five leaves in anything and you will have made chest liniment) has an affinity to fatty meats, which is why it is so often used with pork. The resinous pine notes of sage seem especially appropriate at this time of year. Fruit-based stuffings, provided they include lemon or orange zest, are worth thinking about – add cubes of quince, pear or sharp apple to softened onions and fresh breadcrumbs perhaps, or, brilliant I think, dried apricots. There is something about dried apricots and goose that just works, like pork with apple. Use pearl barley instead of breadcrumbs if you like (about 500g for a 4.5kg bird), boiled, drained and seasoned with softened onions, a little thyme and snippets of fried bacon.

The sweet, rich flesh responds to a little sourness. That balancing snap of acidity often comes in the form of apple sauce or redcurrant jelly. I toss lemon shells into the roasting tin, partly for the heavenly smell of roast goose and citrus wafting through the kitchen on a winter's morning. Others stuff an orange up its bottom. The meat of the bird, served cold the following day, will perk up at the sight of a gherkin or a vinegar-spiked dill and cucumber salad. I often serve an orange or grapefruit salad with mine.

A few notes

Buying the bird

Remember to check the size of your oven. Is it large enough for the long, flat body of a goose? Get the right weight. A 4.5kg goose will feed six. A (massive) 6kg bird will feed 8–10. It is best to order it from your butcher a good week or two in advance. It will guarantee you a bird, but may also make the matter simpler and quicker. You know how busy the butcher gets at Christmas.

Roasting your goose

Take the bird out of the fridge the night before. You need the skin to be dry if it is going to crisp properly. Ignore anything you may have read about piercing the skin.

Allow fifteen minutes in the oven per 450g, plus twenty minutes extra. Some cooks like to place the goose on a rack above the roasting tin, so the bird sits clear of its own fat. Fair enough, but I remain unconvinced of the need. You may require a large sheet of tin foil, if the skin starts browning too quickly. Have one ready just in case.

Cooking temperatures and times

As always, recipes and temperatures vary from cook to cook. In my experience, it is all too easy to over-estimate the cooking time of a goose. Ideas change. Beware that some older books and cooks suggest an unnecessarily long cooking time.

For a 4–5kg goose:

An experienced goose breeder suggests three hours at 200°C/Gas 6.

Delia insists 220°C/Gas 7 for thirty minutes, then 180°C/Gas 4 for a further three hours.

Mary Berry suggests that 220°C/Gas 7 for thirty minutes, then 180°C/Gas 4 for a further one and a half to two hours, is right.

Jamie Oliver, on the other hand, cooks his goose for three hours at 180°C/Gas 4 (he suggests cutting the bird in half lengthways first, which is an interesting idea).

Each of the above cooks is renowned for rigorously testing their recipes and clearly the results work, which only goes to show that there is more than one way to skin a rabbit. My own preference is for a high start (220°C/Gas 7), then a long, slow roasting at 180°C/Gas 4. Of course, you need to know your oven and keep an eye on the skin. If it appears to be browning too soon, drape a layer of foil over the top.

Draining the fat

You need a turkey baster to remove all the fat that comes from the goose as it roasts. I don't need to tell you (though I will) that the fat is copious and horrifically hot. Please be careful. You can ladle the fat out every forty-five minutes or so, but it is awkward and potentially dangerous if it involves tipping the roasting tin. Far easier to invest in a baster from a kitchen shop and suck the fat up. The fat is, of course, gorgeous. Keep it.

Resting the bird

The essential, though often missed, trick of leaving the roasted bird in a warm place, covered with foil, for thirty minutes after taking it from the oven. It gives you time to make the gravy, but crucially, the rest ensures the flesh is juicier and easier to carve.

Carving your goose

Those who carve a goose as they might a chicken, with long slices taken straight from the breast while still on the carcass, may struggle to get a 4kg bird to feed more than four. The route I take every time is to REMOVE THE WHOLE BREAST FIRST, a simple procedure of slitting the skin along the breastbone of the cooked bird, then carefully prising away each of the breasts in one piece, tenderly separating them from the carcass with a carving knife. You then slice each breast across into short thick slices. It is a method that magically produces far more meat than carving straight from the bird.

The gravy

There has to be gravy and lashings of it too. Much as you can make it on the day, it is often a sound idea to get it ready the day before. It's a relief, waking up on Christmas morning and knowing you have done the gravy, but, more importantly, the overnight sleep gives the gravy time to mature and mellow.

The recipe

Put a peeled and halved onion, a chopped carrot, the goose giblets (minus the liver), a handful of chicken wings, 3 cloves of garlic, a rib of celery, 10 peppercorns, a teaspoon of salt and 3 bay leaves into a pot, pour over

1.5 litres of water and bring to the boil. Lower the heat and simmer for forty-five minutes. Strain and set aside.

Peel and chop 2 large shallots and sauté them with a further chopped carrot and a chopped stick of celery in a little butter. Once the vegetables are starting to soften and have turned an appetising golden brown, pour in about 50ml of Marsala, Madeira or medium sherry, let it sizzle for a minute, then pour in a litre of the hot stock. Bring to the boil, then lower the heat and simmer for twenty-five minutes. You will have a glorious gravy, thin, rich and full of flavour.

Pour into a bowl, let it cool, then chill it overnight. Slowly heat it up the next day and serve piping hot.

Roast goose, apple sauce, lemon potato stuffing and Marsala gravy

Serves 6–8
a goose – 4.5–5kg
potatoes, floury, white fleshed – 1.3kg
banana shallots – 400g
olive oil – 3 tablespoons
a lemon
rosemary – 3 stems
thyme sprigs – 10

For the apple sauce:
large cooking apples such as Bramleys – 3
lemons – 2
a cinnamon stick
cloves – 4

Remove the goose from its wrapping and place in a large, deep roasting tin. Set the oven at 220°C/Gas 7. Peel the potatoes and quarter them, then cook

them in boiling, lightly salted water for about ten minutes, until they have just started to soften.

Peel and halve the shallots, remove the roots, then unfurl the layers. Warm the olive oil in a shallow pan over a moderate heat, add the shallots and let them cook until soft and golden.

Drain the potatoes and return them to the dry saucepan, pressing down on them lightly with a potato masher or fork to slightly crush them. Squeeze in the juice of the lemon, then cover with a lid and let the potatoes infuse with the lemon juice. Reserve the empty lemon shells.

Pull the needles from the rosemary and roughly chop them, then chop the thyme leaves. Add the herbs to the potatoes, fold in the cooked shallots, then season with salt and black pepper.

Stuff the crushed potatoes into the goose. A few may fall out into the tin – no matter. Season the skin of the goose with salt, add the lemon shells to the tin and place in the oven for twenty minutes, then lower the temperature to 180°C/Gas 4 and leave to roast for two hours. Watch the progress carefully, covering the skin with foil if it appears to be browning too quickly. When it is ready, the skin should be a deep walnut brown. (If the goose produces vast amounts of fat, and well it might, remove some carefully from the tin with a turkey baster or small ladle.)

While the goose roasts, make the apple sauce. Peel, core and roughly chop the apples. Put them into a heavy-based saucepan. Squeeze the lemons and add the juice to the pan together with the cinnamon stick and the cloves. Bring to the boil, then lower the heat and leave to simmer until the apples are soft. Remove and discard the cloves and cinnamon stick, then crush the apple sauce finely with a fork or a potato masher.

Lift the goose from the tin, place it on a warm serving platter and cover with foil. This resting is important. Carefully ladle out most of the fat into a bowl or jar, let it cool, then store in the fridge. (There should be lots of it and it will be useful over the next couple of weeks for roasting chickens and potatoes, and for sautéing vegetables.) Carve as below.

Place the goose on a chopping or carving board with a little foil underneath to catch any juices. Using a long, sharp carving knife, make an incision as close as possible to the breastbone, at the open end of the goose. Slide the knife along the length of the bird, keeping as close to the breastbone as you can. Prise the meat away from the bone and slice downwards, the blade of your knife tight to the ribcage, removing the breast in one large, long piece. Now repeat with the other breast. Move the carcass on to a serving dish, then cut the breast into short, thick slices, putting them on a warm serving dish. Cut slices from the legs, removing as much meat as you can, and serve.

The turkey

A roast turkey taken from the oven on Christmas morning is a splendid sight. The skin glistening gold, the legs lightly crisp, and the juices sizzling in the roasting tin are treasures to behold. You will need a dark feathered bird of a traditional breed that has been bred for flavour, slowly reared and properly hung. It will have had a good life, some might say pampered, some of which may have been spent outdoors. It will have cost you a small fortune and will be worth every penny. The alternative, a huge, cheap, pale mass-produced bird, reared cheek by jowl and packed like sardines in a dreary barn, is not even worth thinking about.

There is no mystery to roasting a turkey (you can effectively ignore all you have heard about wrapping the legs in foil or whatever the latest wheeze is). Simply take the bird from its box, unwrap it and leave it at cool room temperature for a couple of hours before you cook it. Season it with extreme generosity, baste it regularly during cooking, and let it rest before you carve. It really is as simple as that.

I offer no rules, but I do have a few suggestions:
· Order your turkey from the butcher in advance.
· Go for broke. This meal may well be the most memorable of the year. Investing in a higher-quality, higher-welfare bird that has been properly hung, with its guarantee of a better, deeper flavour, will be worth every penny. A cheap turkey is cheap for a reason, so you can bet that someone,

somewhere is getting a rough deal. Tragically, it may not just be the farmer, it may be the bird itself.

· Don't cook it straight from the fridge. Give the bird a good two hours in a cool room before cooking.

· Do not panic. It's only like cooking a big chicken.

· If you stuff the bird (and well you might – the chance of having those roasting juices trickling through the stuffing as it cooks is too good to miss), don't pack the cavity too tightly; leave plenty of room for the heat to get right through. Cook any extra stuffing separately.

· Use a roasting tin large enough to give the heat a chance to circulate and, just as importantly, room to put a few of the tatties and stuffing balls around the roast.

· Consider starting the bird on its breast and turning it over halfway through roasting – this will keep the breast meat deliciously moist and juicy. (I baste regularly during cooking instead, but some people swear by it. It is worth a thought.)

· Leave the cooked bird to rest for a good thirty-five to forty minutes before carving.

· Consider the carving method below – it produces more juicy slices of meat.

· The most crucial piece of advice I can offer is not to overcook it. Old roasting times, those in Granny's cookbooks for instance, are generally way too long for modern, good-quality birds.

My turkey

There are myriad ways of cooking a turkey and every cookery writer has added their own signature. I am not about to suggest that mine is the only way, but it is the way I like best, the way that produces a delicious, golden, juicy result. I choose a smaller turkey, one under 5kg in weight. Such a bird will feed ten. My personal preference is for a dark-feathered, naturally reared, free-range bird such as a Kelly Bronze.

Some cook their bird dry, others smear the breast with butter, some insist on anointing the flesh with olive oil. I, somewhat controversially, use goose fat, smearing the breast and legs generously, then basting regularly with hot fat and juices from the roasting tin as it cooks. The argument that I am using a fat from a different bird rather falls apart when you note that butter doesn't come from a turkey either, and anyway, the result – a bird of supreme savour and succulence – is worth it. I do stuff my bird, but only enough to half-fill the cavity; the rest of the stuffing is cooked separately. And yes, I do think cranberry sauce, gravy and roast potatoes are essential, cooking the latter round the bird if there's room, in a separate tin if not. Little sausages, often wrapped in bacon, are amusing, a delicious extra.

Serving

I think it crucial not to overcrowd the plate. And yes, I know that the very essence of a feast is generosity and the implication of that is there should be too much food, but there is little I find less appetising than a plate piled high with food. I navigate this by serving only a few slices of turkey and its golden skin with a little stuffing, gravy and cranberry sauce and couple of roast potatoes. Vegetables come next, with a small second helping of meat. Second helpings, and even third, being preferable to one plate piled high like a dog's dinner.

Roast turkey, sweet potato stuffing

I cook my turkey for slightly less time than most. The trick is in the resting. You can time it as I suggest below, or you can use a meat thermometer. The latter is the most accurate method to determine the readiness of your bird. Insert the point of the thermometer at the thickest part of the leg – when the temperature reads 65°C, the bird is ready to be removed and rested. (The temperature applies to a higher-welfare, traditional breed.) Resting results in juicier meat and should be for a minimum of thirty-five minutes.

For the stuffing:
sweet potatoes – 1kg
light open bread, such as ciabatta – 200g
pancetta, in the piece – 250g
olive oil – 2 tablespoons
banana shallots – 350g
sausage meat – 500g
thyme leaves – 2 tablespoons
sage leaves – 6

The turkey:
a turkey – 4.5kg
goose fat – 6 tablespoons

Set the oven at 200°C/Gas 6. Peel the sweet potatoes, cut them into large pieces, then steam, in a steamer basket or a colander over boiling water, until very soft and crushable. A matter of twenty-five minutes or so. Tear the bread into postage-stamp-size pieces, scatter over a baking sheet and bake until dry and pale gold.

Cut the pancetta into 2cm cubes. Warm the oil in a frying pan, add the cubes of pancetta, and fry until fragrant and the fat has turned golden. Peel and finely chop the shallots. Remove the pancetta as soon as it is ready, then soften the shallots in the pan. Break up the sausage meat, stir briefly into the ingredients in the pan, then set aside.

Mash the sweet potatoes roughly with a fork, then add the dried bread and the pancetta, the shallots, the thyme leaves and the sage, finely shredded. Season with salt and black pepper, mix thoroughly, then shape half the mixture into 16 balls, each slightly bigger than a golf ball. Stuff the remaining half of the mixture into the turkey, pushing it deep inside the body of the bird.

Place the turkey in a roasting tin, baste it generously with the goose fat and roast for 25 minutes. Lower the heat to 180°C/Gas 4 and continue roasting for a further two hours. Baste the breast of the turkey twice with the cooking juices from the roasting tin during this time. (Be quick, so the oven doesn't lose any heat.) Halfway through roasting, when the bird has been cooking for

about seventy-five minutes, turn the bird over and place the remaining balls of stuffing around the sides. Alternatively, and this is what I often do, bake them in a little goose fat in a separate baking tin.

Remove the turkey from the oven and let it rest for thirty-five to forty minutes. Don't skip this, no matter how much everyone pleads for their dinner. I cannot emphasise this enough.

Roast potatoes

You will not find recipes for boiled Brussels sprouts here, or even Brussels sprouts with chestnuts, but as roast potatoes are such an integral part of the meal I will repeat here my way of ensuring a perfect batch. (Details in full are in *Tender*, Volume I.)

Peel the potatoes, cut them into pieces large enough to need two bites each, then bring them to the boil in deep, generously salted, boiling water. Boil for five to seven minutes or so, until they will take a skewer with ease, then drain and return them to the pan. Take the pan with both hands and give it a good shake or two, which will have the effect of bruising the edges of the potatoes.

If you are cooking them around the roast, tip them in now, toss them briefly in the roasting juices, then cook for about forty-five minutes, turning once, until they are golden and crisp. If you are cooking them separately, get the fat hot (duck or goose or dripping is the best, butter and a little olive oil if not), then toss the drained and bruised potatoes in the fat and roast for forty minutes, turning them once to ensure a nice even crispness.

When the turkey comes out to rest, turn the oven up to 200°C/Gas 6 to get a good crisp finish to your potatoes.

To carve

When the bird has rested for thirty to forty minutes, it is time to carve. I remember the first time James showed me how to carve a bird by removing the breasts as two long, thick pieces of meat rather than carving them, traditionally, in long thin slices. It changed everything. The bird fed more, the meat stayed juicy and warm, and the whole enterprise became far less of a hassle. It should, however, be done in the kitchen, not at the table.

Get the gravy hot – it will help keep the meat warm as you carve. Securing the bird with a carving fork, and using a very sharp carving knife, remove the wings and drumsticks first and put them in a warm place. If you don't remove them first, they will just get in the way. Run your carving knife along the breastbone, slowly easing the meat away from the carcass as you go, working your knife down the body until the breast can be freed in one long, thick piece. Repeat on the other side.

Remove the brown meat, the best bits, from the legs and wings and place them on a large, warm platter. Slice the breast meat into short, thick pieces, add them to the platter, then ladle over some of the piping hot gravy.

The extras

Gravy, there simply has to be gravy, preferably made the day before to give it time to develop and you time to breathe. It must, absolutely must, be blisteringly hot. Something sweet-sharp such as cranberry sauce will go nicely with the sweet meat. Stuffing is important, though far from crucial. Oh, and roast potatoes are non-negotiable.

It goes without saying that the choice of vegetables is up to you, but they should, I think, be seasonal. Parsnips and sprouts, then, rather than green beans. To make life bearable for the cook, avoid all suggestions to try to please everyone, otherwise you'll find yourself cooking sprouts with and without chestnuts, both roast and mashed parsnips, peas, carrots and red cabbage. Oh, and someone is bound to want cauliflower cheese too. My advice is to cook one green vegetable (sprouts or cabbage), one roast vegetable (parsnips), and roast potatoes only.

By the way, those little sausages wrapped in bacon I mentioned earlier are really rather wonderful with the turkey and I do try to find time and space for them.

Steaming the pudding

The pudding, wrapped up in its china bowl, is already cooked, needing only to be reheated. The density of a plum pudding means a long steaming, the actual time depending on its size. My recipe (see page 115) is for eight, so a steaming of three hours should produce a shining orb of fruit, piping hot right through to the middle.

To reheat, get a large, deep saucepan of water on to boil. The water should come halfway up the sides. Lower the pudding, in its basin, wrapped tightly in clingfilm, foil and muslin, into the water. (Tying the corners of the muslin in a large knot on the top will make for easier lifting when the pudding is done.) Cover with a lid, lower the heat to a low boil, and steam for three hours, taking a regular look at the water level. If you need to top the water up, as you almost certainly will, use boiling water from the kettle so it never comes off the boil.

The end of the day

The aftermath of Christmas dinner is a beautiful sight. The abandoned table, jewel-bright pools left in shimmering glasses – garnet and ruby; abandoned paper crowns in shades of gold and pink; a scattering of corks and empty bottles; crumbs and crackers and ribbons and wrapping paper. A scene of jubilant devastation.

It is now, with the washing up being carried into the kitchen, that I dig my heels in. I flatly refuse to get involved in games, playing charades or trying to figure out the rules of a recently unwrapped board game. I have never been a team player and I am not going to start now. I would much rather read a book. Each unto his own, I guess.

I have an excuse. I cooked. I shopped and chopped, stirred and stuffed, roasted and toasted. I am doing nothing else now. Not a jot, not a crumb. I shall simply pour myself a drink, reach for a mince pie and watch Christmas Day television, which is never without its delights.

I should add here that there is a bi-annual tradition in this house, one that doesn't apply this year, where I start writing a book on Christmas afternoon. For the life of me I cannot remember how it even started – I only know that the first sentence of each of my books has been started on this day. It has become something of a ritual. It is what I have done every other year for the last twenty-five years and, if I'm honest, what I would like to do until I conk out. Hopefully, shortly after Christmas dinner a few years hence, collapsing silently, discreetly, into my plum pudding.

A pig in a blanket, a crisp salad

Boxing Day could, just could, be the very best day of the year. I could elaborate, but what is the point when all is said in one vast, magnificent, glorious sandwich. There is, I venture to suggest, no finer sandwich than the one built from the contents of the fridge on the day after Christmas. Thin folds of roast turkey, beef or goose, generously salted, cold stuffing, cold sausage, cranberry or apple sauce. A few sharp, possibly fiery pickles. You will need some rather good bread of course, a dollop of mayonnaise, some leaves of sprightly lettuce or a tangle of watercress. You will almost certainly want to crisp a handful of rashers of smoked streaky bacon too.

Layer upon layer, your sandwich will be the best you have had all year. The choicest bits of the meat, the bits and bobs of deliciousness left on the carving plate; the secret treasures that lie under the roast carcass; the beads of mayonnaise and sauce that peep from its crust. The accompaniments too, the reheated roasties, newly made sautéd potatoes or a generous bowl of thin, salty, plain potato crisps. Oh, and did I mention something sparkling too? Well, I really think such a treat is worth opening a bottle for.

You need no help from me to make a sumptuous goose or turkey sandwich. I will, though, offer up a couple of recipes for things that have gone down well here at home on this fine day. A coil of herby, Cumberland sausage with a sweet, sticky glaze of date syrup and crisp bacon, and a plate of potato pancakes, as a treat for slices of leftover turkey or beef, soft and warm as a Christmas kiss.

Boxing Day is the first weekday following Christmas Day. So should Christmas Day fall on a Saturday, Boxing Day is celebrated on the following Monday. Traditionally, it is the date on which gifts, usually money, or occasionally treats from the table, were handed out to household staff and tradespeople. The term 'Christmas box' was coined in the seventeenth century to describe the gratuity your employees could expect to receive. It was also when kitchen staff would prepare a buffet for the house, then take their leave to attend to their own family celebrations.

The last few years has seen this day, reserved in the past for sport and simply relaxing, become one of the most commercial of the year. Online shopping and queuing for 'the sales' has replaced the more quaint family-orientated options of watching sport and playing games. (I should also mention that the tradition of the Boxing Day hunt still exists. My father used to load his gun on this day each year in case the local hunt set foot on our land. Whether it was to put the poor, hounded fox out of its misery or to take a pot-shot at one of those in hunting pink we never got to find out.)

I can't help feeling a pang of sadness that this day has become so relentlessly commercial, but I doubt the habit is likely to change any time soon. A campaign mounted in the last couple of years to keep shops closed on the 25th and 26th of December fell at the first hurdle. It is no longer bells we hear ringing; it is tills.

Cumberland sausage, dates and pancetta

A sausage is for one. A Cumberland sausage, on the other hand, is something to share. A long roll of seasoned sausage meat, curled into a ring the size of a dinner plate, to be cut into slices like a cake. An altogether jollier affair, and one that will feed four to six of you. It has the advantage of being something you can offer as a side dish to cold cuts too. You will need a jar of hot mustard and a bowl of cranberry jelly to keep the sausage company.

The very essence of Christmas, sticky, sweet-sour date molasses is available from most large supermarkets and certainly from any Middle Eastern grocer.

Serves 6
Cumberland sausage – 500g
dates – 6
pancetta, thinly sliced – 75g
bay leaves – 6
sage leaves – 4
juniper berries – 8
date molasses – 2 tablespoons

Set the oven at 180°C/Gas 4. Place the Cumberland sausage on a baking sheet lined with foil or baking parchment.

Split the dates in half and remove their stones. Wrap the pancetta rashers around the sausage, tucking a couple of the bay leaves, sage leaves and most of the halved dates under as you go. Once the pancetta is in place, tuck some of the juniper berries underneath. Scatter the rest of the bay and juniper berries on top, then bake for twenty-five minutes, until nicely browned.

Remove from the oven, baste all over with the date molasses, then return it to the oven for a further twenty minutes, or until glossy and sizzling.

Potato and feta pancakes

Round, flat cakes, the size of a digestive biscuit – a tangle of shredded potatoes, dill and shards of salty feta to eat with slices of cold roast goose or beef. The cakes are substantial enough to offer as a vegetarian main course, in which case you would need two or three per person and they would be good with a dish of spice-studded pickled red cabbage. I turn mine only when the underside has crisped lightly.

Makes 6, serves 2-3
potatoes – 250g
carrots – 150g
olive oil – 3 tablespoons
eggs – 2
feta – 200g
dill, chopped – 3 tablespoons

For frying:
olive oil – 3 tablespoons

Peel the potatoes and carrots and coarsely grate them. If using a food processor use the coarse grating disc as you would for remoulade. Warm the oil in a frying pan, add the grated vegetables and cook for six to eight minutes, until they have started to soften.

Beat the eggs lightly with a fork, just enough to mix yolks and whites, then tip in the softened vegetables. Crumble the feta cheese into the mixture, then add the chopped dill and some black pepper.

Warm the oil in the frying pan, then divide the mixture into six patties about the diameter of a digestive biscuit. Press them flat with a palette knife or the bowl of a spoon, and let them fry until pale gold. Turn each one over carefully and brown the other side. Remove with a palette knife or fish slice, drain briefly on kitchen paper, and serve.

27 DECEMBER

The prospect of soup

Christmas used to be longer. The Twelve Days were truly celebrated with feasting and merriment right up until Twelfth Night, the feast of Epiphany on January 6.

This is worth remembering as people head frantically back to the shops on Boxing Day. It is as if the point of the whole event was about the presents and, once opened, it's back for more. Could anything be sadder? The Swedish word 'lagom' springs to mind. The idea, and it's a good one, that what we have is probably enough, sufficient for our needs, 'just right'.

I hear people describing the days following Christmas Day as 'flat'. I am of another mind. They are peaceful days, gentle days that are as much a part of Christmas as those leading up to Christmas Eve. I am not suggesting a week of feasting, but my heart does sink at the idea of 'business as usual' the minute the washing up from Christmas Day has been put away.

This is the day on which the bones from the turkey or goose should probably be used up. They will last longer under refrigeration, but so many of us can't find room in the fridge that many birds sit in the coolest place in the house, smothered in a tea towel. This means the prospect of soup, and of one of my favourite jobs of Christmastime, divesting the roast carcass of its meat.

It's a job for rolled-up sleeves and an apron. You need a bit of space too. There are thick bones good for broth and a few too thin to bother with. Bits of interesting meat stuck to the carcass but too small for soup. There will be useless bits and pieces. You also need somewhere to peel and chop vegetables.

I make a stock with the bones, a stick of celery, a leek, split lengthways, an onion and a fat, almost woody, carrot. There are whole black peppercorns and bay leaves, a few twigs of thyme. I set aside the meat I have stripped from the carcass. Nothing good will come from more than an hour's simmering, so that is what it gets. If the butcher was open, I might add some fresh chicken wings,

370

but he isn't, neither should he be. These next few days are about making the most of what is left.

A pot of stock, thin in consistency, but full of flavour from the roasted bones, is a blank canvas. Anything is possible. This year I make a soup – or to be honest James does – thick with butter beans, thyme and goose goodness. (Though it is just as easily made with turkey.)

Goose (or turkey) broth with butter beans and thyme

The bits and bones of goose or turkey that remain are treasure. A soup allows their flavour to be exploited to the maximum and the expense of the bird to be justified. The roasted wing tips are a particularly good source of flavour, as are the bits of golden jelly that lie beneath the goose.

Serves 4
goose fat – 3 tablespoons
medium onions – 3
pancetta – 200g
chicken, turkey or goose stock – 1 litre
thyme – 6 sprigs
bay leaves – 3
goose bones, wing tips, bits of meat
butter beans – 2 × 400g tins

Warm the goose fat in a deep casserole over a moderate heat. Peel and chop the onions and sauté them in the goose fat until soft and golden. Cut the pancetta into 3cm dice and add to the onion, letting it cook until the fat is golden, then add the stock, thyme and bay leaves. Tuck in any bits of goose, such as the wing tips and bits of meat, you may have to hand, then bring to the boil. Lower the heat immediately and cook for forty-five minutes.

Drain the beans and rinse them under running water, then tip them into the broth and simmer for a further ten minutes. Check the seasoning, remove the bones and thyme sprigs and ladle into deep bowls.

Using up the cheese

There's the Christmas cheese to use up. A thoroughly delectable thought or a millstone, depending on how you feel about leftovers. A cheese pudding, perhaps (beaten egg whites folded into a thick cheese sauce, a scatter of thyme leaves, then baked until you have honey-coloured clouds outside, the inside barely set). Fritters of blue cheese and mashed potato, rolled in grated Parmesan, crumbed and fried. A salad maybe, of jagged lumps of Cheddar, tossed with almonds, fat black raisins, apple, cider vinegar and shredded red cabbage. I would put some air-dried ham in there too.

You could, of course, serve the cheeses in their own right, piled on to freshly baked biscuits warm from the oven; slathered with a spiced apple purée or a single, pickled fig. Or, if there isn't really enough to do anything much with, make the cheese biscuits below.

Seeded cheese biscuits

Tender crackers, as fragile as a butterfly's wing, freckled gold and black with sesame and nigella seeds, just firm enough to support a spoonful of chutney or pickle.

Makes 14
butter – 150g
plain flour – 150g
Parmesan, grated – 1 heaped tablespoon
firm blue cheese – 75g
nigella seeds – 5g
poppy seeds – 10g
sesame seeds – 10g

Cut the butter into small pieces and add to the flour. If you are making the biscuits by hand, rub the butter into the flour with your fingertips. If you are using a machine, blend the flour and the butter briefly in a food processor. Preheat the oven to 200°C/Gas 6.

Add the grated Parmesan to the butter and flour, then crumble in the blue cheese in tiny pieces. Add the nigella, poppy and sesame seeds. Process briefly, then bring the mixture together with your hands and roll into a short, fat cylinder. Wrap in greaseproof paper and refrigerate for thirty minutes.

Cut the log of dough into fourteen equal rounds and place them on a parchment-lined baking sheet, leaving just a little space between them. Bake for nine to ten minutes, until lightly golden. Let them cool for five minutes, then, using a palette knife, transfer the biscuits carefully from the tray to a wire rack and leave to cool. (That said, they are delicious when eaten warm.)

A sweet moment

The books. There are books in the kitchen, books in the study and books in the drawing room. There are books in my satchel, books on my desk and books by my bedside. There are novels and short stories, biographies and diaries, haikus and travelogues. There are gardening books and poetry and of course there are cook books, though I am far from being what you might call a collector.

Right now, though, there are also fairy stories. If this sounds odd, it is probably because books about princes, elves and magical kingdoms are those we read as children or to children. Such collections are not generally considered suitable for adult eyes. But listen, may I suggest you think again. The fairy tales and ghost stories we read aged seven or eight are more than worthy of a re-read in adulthood. It won't take long – even the longest fairy tales are rarely more than a few pages. But the forgotten magic that lies among those yellowing pages of Garamond type will take you to a place you will almost certainly have forgotten about. A place, I argue, we could all do with visiting from time to time.

'He was never without a book.' I can see it now, carved on my gravestone. It wouldn't be accurate, of course. I usually have at least three on the go. I am currently reading four: a biography of a woman climber, which is odd considering my acute vertigo; another about a writer and her vegetable patch; a collection of columns from a gardening journalist I picked up for a pound plus postage. There is also a book of fairy stories I found in a second-hand bookshop before they were driven from the high street by absurd rents.

This time of year was made for reading, for cosying up with someone's words. I have a reading chair, comfortable, with a good light and, crucially, from which it is impossible to see the television. It is the carrot with which I tease myself on a busy day. An hour of housework, fifteen minutes' reading.

Two hours at my desk, thirty minutes with a book. It works. (And is a thought for a new year's resolution.)

Howling wind or falling snow aside, the best reading companion is the smell of something baking in the oven. A cake sweet with figs, a marrow-thickened casserole, something involving beans, onions and woody herbs. Food that gets on with business itself. Very quickly, to this end, I knock together a sponge of deep, butterscotch flavours, a treacly fruit pudding sweet enough to stop the sugar police in their tracks. This is a treat, a once-a-year gift of forbidden flavours to everyone who trudges in, chilled to their very soul, looking for magic.

Cranberry butterscotch pudding

A light, brown-sugar sponge pudding with sharp fruits and creamy, butterscotch notes. Sticky without being heavy. You'll need a jug of cream, or better still, vanilla ice cream.

Serves 6 (good cold too)
dried apricots – 180g
fresh or frozen cranberries – 50g
boiling water – 200ml
butter – 100g
plain flour – 150g
baking powder – 1½ teaspoons
light muscovado sugar – 100g
an egg

For the sauce:
light muscovado sugar – 100g
double cream – 125ml
butter – 70g
maple syrup – 1 tablespoon
cranberries, fresh or frozen – 100g

You will also need a deep baking dish or pudding bowl roughly 18cm × 15cm.

Preheat the oven to 180°C/Gas 4. Cut the apricots into small pieces and put them into a heatproof mixing bowl. Add the cranberries and pour the boiling water over. Set aside while you make the pudding.

Butter the pudding bowl with a small knob of the butter. Mix the flour and baking powder. Put the rest of the butter into the bowl of a food mixer. Add the muscovado sugar and beat until soft, pale and creamy, occasionally scraping down the sides of the bowl with a rubber spatula.

Make the sauce: put the sugar, cream, butter and maple syrup into a small saucepan and bring to the boil. Let it simmer for 2 minutes, then roughly chop the cranberries (more easily done with frozen fruit in a food processor), adding them to the sauce.

Break the egg into a small bowl and beat lightly with a fork, just enough to mix the white and yolk, then add to the creaming butter and sugar.

When the egg is fully incorporated, stir in the flour and baking powder mixture, turning slowly until there is no visible trace of flour left. Fold in the apricots and cranberries and the water they are in. Transfer the mixture to the buttered dish, smooth the surface, then bake for thirty minutes until pale gold and lightly firm on top. Remove from the oven and pour over half the cranberry butterscotch sauce, then return to the oven for a further ten minutes.

Serve hot, with the remaining sauce.

Christmas stamps and bubble and squeak

Tidying up, I find a pile of cardless envelopes destined for the recycling, and it dawns on me that I received very few cards with Christmas stamps on this year. A Christmas card without a Christmas stamp is like a birthday cake with a candle.

I can remember the very first British commemorative Christmas stamp. It was the winter of 1966 (there had been a previous stamp for use by the forces sending mail home for Christmas in 1935) and I was desperately hoping for The Beatles' *Revolver* in my stocking. In the end I couldn't wait and bought the album with my pocket money. The stamps were of children's paintings, including six-year-old Tazveer Shemza's picture of Good King Wenceslas. That delightfully wonky Wenceslas was the start of a tradition that continues to this day, sometimes religious, other times secular. At the time I was amazed that something so important as a postage stamp could be designed by a child. It put all sorts of ideas in my head and was probably the catalyst for my first cook book, written that year with watercolour pictures of food and sadly lost long ago.

Should it matter that my cards weren't accompanied by stamps depicting the Nativity (1988), a robin (latest 2016), a hippy angel (1969) or coloured birds flying from a letterbox (1983)? This year was the 50th anniversary of the British Christmas stamp and I would liked to have received more. My all-time favourite was released in the winter of 1976, a 13p stamp showing a 1330 embroidery of the Magi at the Nativity in scarlet and gold.

I am mulling over the recycling. I have been an avid recycler since it first started in my borough. The scheme was originally introduced by a non-profit-making company in 1994, for the 'domestic kerbside collection of cans, cardboard, foil, glass, paper, plastic bottles, and textiles'. There were just two paid staff and one volunteer. I signed up to have mine collected each week for the princely sum of one pound. Now of course it is dealt with by the council and the fee is included in the council tax.

I have been putting my Christmas cards and wrapping paper into the recycling for years. But this year I learn that paper or cards with glitter or gold foil cannot be recycled. There are a few of these in the pile. I tear the blank backs from the cards to use for shopping lists and pull the Sellotape from the paper which goes into my squirrel store of wrapping paper. I don't think I have bought any Christmas wrap for years.

Over the next few days there will be bag upon bag of discarded wrapping, ribbons and festive cards. There will also be naked Christmas trees, brown as berries, as the trees are thrown onto the pavement, resembling tumbleweed in a Western. The saddest of all is the one with a lone bauble still tied to its upper branches.

Shopping at the Neues Museum in Nuremberg earlier in the winter I was pleasantly surprised to see Christmas baubles made from recycled drinks cans, and brought them home, only to find the shiny tin caught the light beautifully. Most of the decorations on my tree are either second-hand or as old as the hills. The tree itself gets recycled by the council into compost.

There is nothing much edible left from Christmas now. Some pistachio Turkish delight (the rose and lemon went within hours), a box of cranberries confined to the freezer, some sugared fruit jellies and a handful of chipped Brazil nuts (there are always Brazil nuts). The waste has been next to nothing. Each bowl of vegetable became bubble and squeak; every bone was the base of a soup.

There is a particularly successful version of bubble and squeak today. The most delicious I have ever made. Its success centres on its texture as much as its flavour. Made with freshly cooked Jerusalem artichokes and vital green Brussels. The mash is on the soft side, and even after being rolled into perfectly formed ovals and chilling in the fridge it has shape-shifted in the pan. The mixture slides into the oil and butter as it fries, forming a lightly crisp crust as delicate as lace. You need the ability to leave them alone to form a crust before you gently turn them in the pan. Silky, crisp and fluffy, they work rather well with some rashers of crisp smoked bacon.

Jerusalem artichoke and Brussels sprout fritters

Serves 4
Jerusalem artichokes – 500g
potatoes – 300g
olive oil – 4 tablespoons
Brussels sprouts – 300g
garlic – 2 cloves
spring onions – 3
butter – 50g
parsley – a small bunch

Peel the artichokes, dropping them into a bowl of cold, lightly acidulated water. (A generous squeeze of lemon juice will do.) Drain, then put into a pan, covering with water. Bring them to the boil, then lower the heat and simmer for about twenty-five minutes until tender enough to crush.

Peel the potatoes (or if their skins are thin, leave them be) then put them through the coarse grater of a food processor to give thin matchsticks of potato. Warm the olive oil in a frying or sauté pan and cook the shredded potato until pale gold and approaching tenderness.

Shred the sprouts finely and add to the potatoes with the crushed garlic. Finely chop the spring onions and stir into the potatoes. When all is golden and sizzling, remove from the heat.

Drain the Jerusalem artichokes, tip into the bowl of a food mixer, add the butter and beat until thick and smooth (take care not to overbeat as they will turn gluey). Roughly chop the parsley and add it to the artichokes together with the potatoes.

Place generous spoonfuls of the mashed potato and artichoke onto a baking sheet and refrigerate for an hour.

Fry the cakes on both sides in hot olive oil until golden. They are fragile, so take care when turning them to brown the underside.

Fizz and focaccia

My father adhered strongly to the Scottish tradition of first-footing, the habit of making sure that the first person to enter the house on New Year's Day was a dark-haired male brandishing a sixpence and a lump of coal, to bestow good luck on the coming year. Just before the stroke of midnight, he would leave the house through the back door, then, once the clock had struck twelve, would enter through the front, coal and silver coin in hand. He would sing, too, though I cannot honestly remember what. I do know there was quite a fuss made of the whole charade, which I found both quaint and faintly embarrassing.

New Year's Eve is barely mentioned in our house. I don't throw a thirteen-course dinner or join hands and sing 'Auld Lang Syne' (my dear) with friends and family. Feeling that the first day of January comes too close to Christmas and is neither the start nor the end of anything much, it is not really an event I can get enthused about. To be honest, I just see it as another year gone in what I already feel is a rather short life.

And yet I wouldn't dream of not toasting the coming year with a glass of something frosty, or making everyone a bite to eat with which to 'see in the New Year'. So, as the sky over London's East End erupts with cascades of pink, gold and silver stars, we tuck into focaccia straight from the oven and glasses of fizzy, pink wine. Torn from its tin in jagged lumps, the soft loaf is sweet, with soft, golden shallots and the occasional burst of sourness from baked cranberries. A celebration, albeit on my part a somewhat reluctant one.

Note to self: get more sleep.

Cranberry focaccia

Serves 6
For the bread:
strong white bread flour – 500g
easy-bake dried yeast – 1 sachet, (7g, 2 teaspoons)
sea salt flakes – 1 teaspoon
olive oil – 1 tablespoon
warm water – 350ml

For the cranberries:
small shallots – 200g
olive oil – 2 tablespoons
rosemary – 4 sprigs
thyme – 8 small branches
juniper berries – 10
cranberries, fresh or frozen – 150g

Put the flour and dried yeast into a large mixing bowl, add the salt, finely crushed, and the tablespoon of olive oil, then stir in the warm water. Mix thoroughly until the dough will come cleanly away from the sides of the bowl. Tip the dough out on to a floured work surface and knead lightly for five minutes. Sometimes I do this in the food mixer with the dough hook.

Once the dough feels elastic, put it back into the bowl, lightly floured or oiled, then cover with a tea towel and leave in a warm place for an hour or so. It is ready when it has risen to almost double its original size.

Make the cranberry mixture: peel the shallots, halve each one and remove the root end. Separate the layers of the shallots, teasing them apart with your fingertips. Warm the oil in a shallow pan, add the shallots, and let them cook over a moderate heat for fifteen minutes, until soft. As they cook, remove the rosemary leaves from their stems and finely chop them, stirring them into the shallots with the thyme, some black pepper and the lightly bruised juniper berries. (I bash them briefly with a pestle.) As the shallots approach the palest gold, stir in the cranberries and immediately remove from the heat.

Tip the dough out on to a baking sheet measuring 24cm x 12cm, then deflate the dough by flattening it with the palm of your hand. Spoon the cranberry and shallot mixture over the surface, holding back the oil with a spoon and reserving it. Cover the dough and leave to rise for about thirty minutes. Set the oven at 200°C/Gas 6. When the dough has risen once again, press holes deeply into its surface with your finger or the end of a wooden spoon, then trickle over the reserved oil from the shallots.

Bake for about twenty-five minutes, until the bread is cooked right through and the cranberries are puffed up and starting to leak juice here and there on to the surface of the bread. Remove from the oven and allow to settle for fifteen minutes, then tear into pieces and serve.

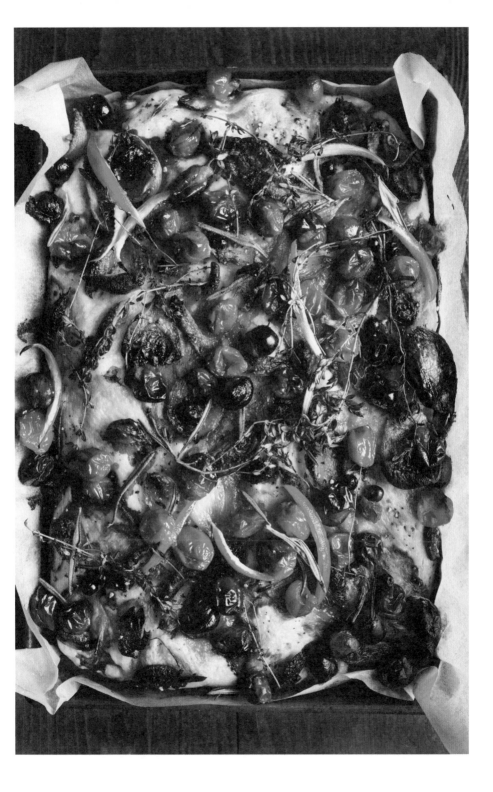

A new loaf, soup and salad

The comfort of ritual, the reassurance of the familiar, is important to me. Doing repetitive, domestic things – kneading bread, stirring soup – on the same day each year helps me feel grounded. But that repetition must be seasoned with the new. I don't want ever to stand still. That way lies a score of missed opportunities, not to mention a certain atrophy, physical, emotional and culinary.

Today I make a New Year loaf with the malty, toasted notes of rye flour and inspired by the seeded breads I ate last year in Finland, Germany and Denmark. There is soup too, sweet, sour and hot, scarlet-ochre with chillies and mustard seed. A soup to blow away the cobwebs.

Legend has it that lentils, eaten on this day, bring good fortune for the coming year. It is not by chance alone that I have a large squirrel-store of orange lentils in a jar on the top shelf, the ones that look like tiny coins. They produce a bland soup until you introduce the punch of ginger, the warmth of yellow mustard seeds and cumin and the vivid sourness of tamarind paste or lime. Either will introduce a flash of acidity to the warm, dusty notes of the spices.

The New Year's Day table is spare but not bare. There is the loaf, that rust-coloured soup and a wooden board of smoked salmon, cut thicker than is usual. The smoked fish aside, it is humble but I don't think ungenerous. But there is butter too, soft, whipped like ice cream, scented with dill, smoke and juniper. A salad of watercress and raw Brussels sprout leaves and cool, pale lettuce sits in a china bowl. Tucked inside the mound of greens are thick slices of avocado. The dressing, white as snow, has a spring in its step.

There are crumbs of fruit cake left from Christmas, and pears whose progress I have been monitoring, hawk-like. One minute a pear is ripe, its flesh cool and juicy, like sorbet, then in a heartbeat it is gone, like snow. Today I see a fox at the top of the garden, its fur the colour of sand, the bushiest tail I have seen in an urban specimen, a flash of white at its tip. No matter how often the handsome scavengers visit, it always evokes a few moments of excitement from the kitchen window. Later, I find an abandoned pizza box in the garden.

Last year was heavy with travel. My suitcase barely closed. Japan, Finland, Denmark, Iran, Lebanon. Then there were the city visits, Cologne, Copenhagen, Nuremberg, Oslo, Bergen and Vienna. Turning the pages of my new diary, I vow this will be a 'home year', where I hunker down and do domestic things, settle I suppose, and concentrate more on the side of my life that is homemaker, gardener and cook. At least, that is the plan.

A loaf for the New Year

I begin the year with flour on my hands. The kneading of dough is the way I have started the New Year for as long as I can remember. This time though, a change of step. A dough that requires mixing, cake-like, in a voluminous bowl, rather than pummelling on a wooden board. One that requires little kneading, only one proving and keeps like an old friend.

This is a sticky dough, too wet to push and stretch with your hand. The texture is akin to Christmas cake and almost as generously stippled with fruit and seeds. The bread itself is sweet with sultanas, has the soft crunch of pumpkin and sunflower seeds and is as dark as a ginger cake.

A dose of black treacle ensures the loaf is a keeper. Four or five days if wrapped tightly. The pebbledash of seeds suggests not only an interesting texture to each cut slice, but a sprinkling of fibre and a handful of the sort of good things you find listed on the side of a multivitamin jar. The golden linseed, especially when lightly crushed with a pestle and mortar, brings with it the gift of omega-3 fats.

Once the fruit-freckled dough has risen to almost twice its size, I lift it carefully from its bowl, trying to interfere with its dumpy, dome-like shape as little as possible, then place it straight down on to a hot baking stone and then into the hot oven. Its shape returns like a plumped-up cushion. Use a loaf tin if you like your toast neat.

As much as I like trickling olive oil over black-crusted sourdough, for the densely textured, slightly sweeter breads such as this it has to be butter. A pale, unsullied butter is ointment enough, but this time I go to town, seasoning a pack of sweet, almost white unsalted with onions cooked to a deep bronze, snipped dill, juniper and crystalline flakes of smoked sea salt. A butter that stands up well with a breakfast kipper, melting sweetly over the mahogany surface of the smoked flesh and is just the job to fork into the fluffy heart of a baked potato on a frosty night.

Rye, linseed and treacle bread

Using a hot stone or baking sheet makes a substantial difference to the base of the loaf, and helps the bread to cook through more evenly than a loaf baked on a cold baking sheet. I heartily recommend putting one or the other in the oven to heat up first.

Makes a medium-sized loaf
rye flour – 200g
strong, white bread flour – 200g
barley flakes – 50g
sea salt – 1 teaspoon
black treacle – 2 tablespoons, lightly heaped
warm water – 350g
dried, fast-acting yeast – a 7g sachet
rolled oats – 40g
golden sultanas – 75g
pumpkin seeds – 35g
sunflower seeds – 25g
golden linseeds – 30g

Warm a deep, wide mixing bowl. The warmth will help your dough rise more quickly. Combine the flours and barley flakes, then lightly crush the sea salt flakes in the palm of your hand and stir them in.

Put the black treacle into a jug and stir in the warm water, dissolving the treacle as you stir. Tip in the yeast, let it dissolve, then pour it into the flours and barley. Using a wooden spoon rather than your hands – the dough is sticky – stir in the rolled oats, sultanas, pumpkin and sunflower seeds and golden linseeds. Mix for a full minute, so the flour, liquid, seeds and fruits are thoroughly combined. The texture of the dough should be very moist, poised between that of a bread dough and a cake mixture.

Dust the surface with a light sprinkling of flour, cover with a clean tea towel and place in a warm place for an hour or so. I find the back of the Aga useful for this, but any warm, draught-free spot will work. Check the bowl occasionally to make sure it is warm but not too hot.

Get the oven hot – it will need to be at 220°C/Gas 7. If you have one, place a bread or pizza stone, generously floured, in the oven to get hot. Failing that, a baking sheet will do. When the oven is up to temperature and the dough has risen to almost twice its original volume, transfer the dough to the hot baking stone or sheet, reshaping it into a round loaf as you go. Bake for thirty-five minutes, until the crust is lightly crisp and the base sounds hollow when tapped with your fingers.

Transfer the warm loaf to a cooling rack and allow to rest for a good thirty minutes before slicing. The loaf will keep, wrapped in clingfilm and foil, for three or four days. It toasts well too.

Smoked salt, dill and juniper butter

Uses for this smoky, aromatic butter go well beyond spreading on a loaf. Melt slices over potatoes, served unpeeled and hot from the steamer; use it to sauté salmon steaks or pieces of snow-white haddock; toss wedges of lightly cooked, piping hot cabbage in it.

Makes 250g and freezes well
a small onion
unsalted butter – 250g

juniper berries – 8
dill – 10g
smoked salt – to taste

Peel the onion and cut into quarters from root to tip, then slice each piece thinly. Melt 30g of the butter in a shallow pan, stir in the sliced onion and let it cook over moderate heat for fifteen to twenty minutes. The onion should be sweet, deep gold in colour and translucent. Remove the onion from the pan and allow to cool.

Place the rest of the butter in a mixing bowl and beat to a soft, lightly whipped consistency with a wooden spoon. Bash the juniper berries with a heavy weight, such as a pestle, so they release their fragrance, and add them to the butter. Remove the dill fronds from their stems, chop them finely and add to the butter.

Add the salt, tasting as you go, then the cooled toasted onions, and combine gently, taking care not to overmix. Serve with the bread.

The butter will keep for several days in the fridge. You can freeze it too. Roll into a fat cylinder shape, then place on a piece of clingfilm, wrap and seal. Freeze until needed. Alternatively, and to make defrosting particularly straightforward, refrigerate the butter until cold enough to slice, then wrap and freeze in individual slices.

Spiced red lentil soup

Possessing a fiery hue, hot with chillies, sour with limes or tamarind, this soup is frugal, quick, warming, energising... I could go on. This is my version of the southern Indian 'rasam', in which I include tomatoes (not everyone does), because that is how I first met it in Cochin, Kerala, at a beautiful, unlicensed hostel overlooking a green. Their version was considerably hotter than mine (we drank cold beer with it, disguising the fact by shrouding our glasses in napkins to hide them from passing police), but this is as much chilli as I want nowadays. It is good.

Enough for 4
red split lentils – 175g
cumin seeds – 1 teaspoon
black peppercorns – $\frac{1}{2}$ teaspoon
ginger – a 30g lump
garlic – 2 cloves
a medium-sized, moderately hot chilli
groundnut or vegetable oil – 3 tablespoons
yellow mustard seeds – 1 teaspoon
tomatoes – a 400g tin or 4 medium fresh
tamarind paste – 3 teaspoons, or 2 limes
coriander leaves, if you wish – a handful

Wash the lentils in cold running water. Put the cumin seeds and peppercorns into a mortar or spice mill and grind them to a coarse powder. Tip the ground cumin and peppercorns into the bowl of a food processor, add the ginger, cut into large pieces (no need to peel), the peeled garlic, and the chilli. Pour in a tablespoon of oil and process to a coarse paste. Should the mixture stick, add a little more oil.

Pour the remaining oil into a deep saucepan over a moderate heat, then add the mustard seeds and let them cook for a minute, shielding with a lid should they start to pop. Stir in the spice paste and fry for a minute or two, moving it round the pan with a wooden spoon, until fragrant.

Chop the tomatoes and add them to the paste in the pan. If you are using tinned tomatoes, add them, crushing them with a spoon as you go. Continue cooking for two or three minutes, add the drained lentils, then either the tamarind paste, or the lime juice and spent lime shells. Pour in 750ml of water, add $\frac{1}{2}$ teaspoon of salt and bring to the boil. Lower the heat immediately and leave at a low simmer for twenty-five minutes. An occasional stir will stop it sticking.

Blend half the soup, removing the lime shells as you go, then stir back into the rest. Check the seasoning, adding salt, and more tamarind or lime as you think fit, then ladle into deep bowls, stirring in the torn coriander leaves if you wish.

A salad of young kale and avocado

The small heart leaves of kale have a sweet tenderness missing in the coarse, outer plumes. (I feel rather like a donkey chewing the hard-going, outside leaves of kale.) They introduce a robustness to a salad whose other leaves are of a softer, more delicate texture.

A salad stands or falls by its dressing. This first salad of the year has a refreshing piquancy to it, delivered by the addition of a yoghurt and herb dressing. The basil that I also include, though unseasonal and not of this climate, comes as a green and peppery change, a respite from the richness of so much of our seasonal eating. I regard its addition here as crucial.

Crisp, green and light, I have kept this coarse-leaf salad raw and simple, but you could also include fat, salted almonds, a little goat's or sheep's cheese crumbled in at the table, or maybe some crisply fried bacon or pancetta.

Serves 4-6
For the salad:
Brussels sprouts – 200g
watercress – 100g
a little gem lettuce
young kale or chard – 2 large handfuls
an avocado, or 2 smaller ones
sprouted seeds such as radish or beetroot – a handful

For the dressing:
natural yoghurt – 6 tablespoons
olive oil – 6 tablespoons
basil leaves – 10g

Trim the base of each Brussels sprout, then remove the leaves layer by layer as far as you can go. Cut the hearts in half and put them and the leaves into a large bowl.

Wash the watercress, remove the toughest stems and add the leaves and fine stalks to the sprouts. Halve the little gem lettuce lengthways, then trim the stalk and separate the leaves. Finely shred the kale or chard leaves. Toss together the sprouts, watercress, lettuce and kale or chard.

Make the dressing: mix the yoghurt and olive oil together with a small whisk or fork, then add the basil leaves, finely shredded, and season with salt and freshly ground black pepper. Halve, stone and peel the avocado, then cut the flesh into thick slices.

Transfer the leaves to a salad bowl, tuck the slices of avocado gently among the leaves, add any sprouting seeds you may like, then trickle over the dressing and toss gently before serving.

4 JANUARY

Pear and pickled radish

A ripe pear is a lovely thing, and they are still with us. Tubby as a cherub, their flesh butter-soft, especially if you watch over them as carefully as you might a sick child, and have the patience to wait for the day they reach perfection. It is a fleeting moment, more so than even an avocado.

I probably take more care over ripening a plate of pears than I would a dish of peaches at the height of summer. (The pear's window of perfection is open for a shorter time than that of the stone fruits.)

And so it is today – four cossetted, perfect pears that need using while they are at their most heavenly. Two of them are eaten at breakfast, slowly, with the sort of respect you might reserve for a piece of lovingly sliced sashimi. The other two are translucent with juice, their flesh almost pure white, and should be dispatched as soon as possible.

I have never done this before, but I have a fancy to match them to some sweet-sour pickles. Radishes, contrastingly crunchy and peppery, take rather well to modern pickling, the sort that is less about preserving and more about making something to shake other flavours from their shyness. I have a feeling they will form a beautiful partnership with the pears. And so they do.

Serves 2
pears – 2, perfectly ripe
walnuts – a handful
coppa – 125g, thinly sliced

For the pickled radishes:
salt – 2 teaspoons
juice of a large lemon
white wine vinegar – 300ml

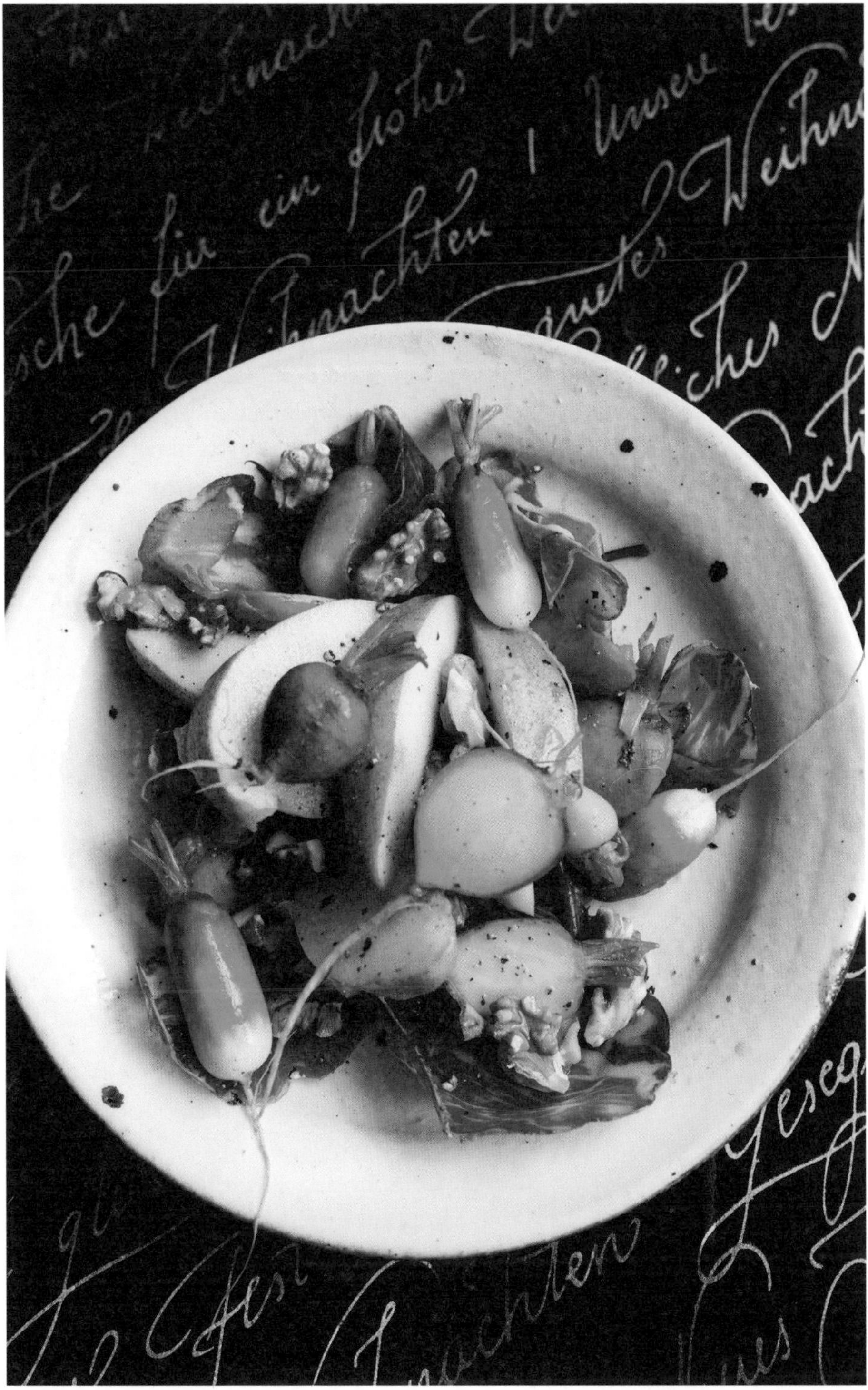

sugar – 75g
black peppercorns – 12
dill – 6 sprigs
radishes – 350g

Put the salt into a stainless steel saucepan, squeeze in the juice of the lemon, add the vinegar, sugar and peppercorns and bring to the boil. Tear the fronds of dill from their stems. Trim the radishes and cut each in half lengthways.

Pack the radishes and dill fronds into a sterilised jar, then pour over the hot brine and tighten the lid. Leave to cool, then chill in the fridge overnight.

To make the salad, cut the pears into quarters, remove their cores, then cut them into thick slices. Remove about half the radishes from their brine and add to the pears, together with 3 tablespoons of pickling liquor. Toss the radishes and pears gently together. Lightly toast the walnuts.

As you transfer the salad to plates, tuck the thinly sliced coppa among it.

We eat this crisp, luscious salad after a bowl of chicken soup plumped up with orzo, the tiny pasta shaped like rice, handfuls of radiant green parsley, lemon, and the last of the chicken torn from the carcass.

The New Year comes at an odd time. Just when we feel a pulsing need for salads and fruit, we have little to play with, and the weather makes us yearn for warmer alternatives. We just have to be a little ingenious in the kitchen, that is all. But I can't help feeling the New Year should start in September, when our shops and markets are lush with the good ingredients that match our good intentions.

Epiphany or Twelfth Night

I am constantly on the lookout for celebrations, personal, public or local. If necessary I will borrow them from other cultures. (I would happily celebrate Hanukkah if I didn't feel, as a non-Jew, that it might be seen as rather inappropriate.) My enthusiasm is only an excuse to bake a cake. Epiphany is the twelfth and last day of Christmas. It is, for some, a religious celebration, that of the coming of the Magi, bringing gifts to the baby Jesus. Truth told, the date is more on my calendar for being the day the decorations are supposed to come down. If they are not removed by midnight, folklore has it that bad luck shall descend upon the house. Well, I'm having none of that.

I find packing away the decorations both unbearably sad and something of a relief. The tree is looking somewhat tired; the branches have begun curling inwards like dragon's claws, the result of which has been that one or two balls have slipped off and smashed. Needless to say they were some of my favourites.

And so it is, a day of wrestling with cotton strings that have wrapped themselves inexplicably around the bristles of the Nordmann fir; wobbling on steps trying to reach bunches of emasculated mistletoe; wrapping up each and every glass bauble, separately, like the precious cargo they are. Precious not for their value, but for the memories held in their reflections, often of those who gave them to me, some of whom are no longer with us.

The decorations, whether of mercury glass, painted enamel, intricate foil or wood, live in crates and cardboard boxes and warrant their own place in the bottom of the airing cupboard. Three shelves under the towels and my siege-like squirrel-store of white loo roll. (If ever you're stuck, you know where to come.) The decorations live here purely because it is regarded as a safe place, somewhere where, after being dazzled by fairy lights for three weeks, they can sleep in heavenly peace until next year.

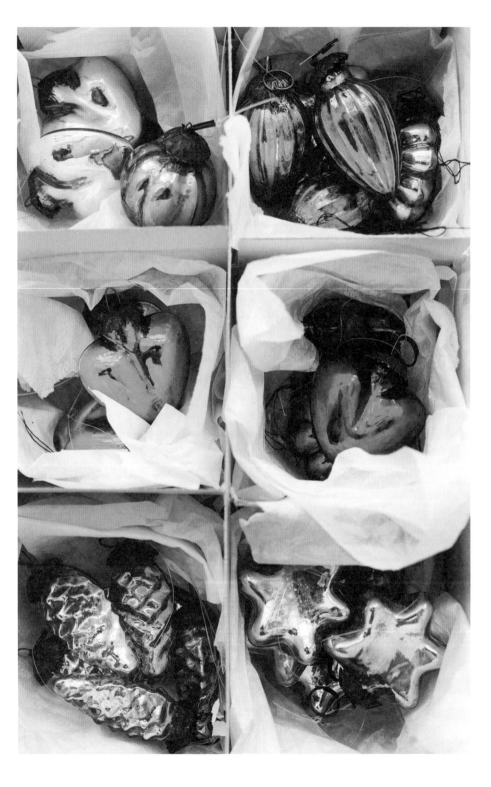

Each bauble is tenderly wiped and wrapped in bubblewrap; the painted enamels are returned to their brown envelopes; the fairy lights are wound with OCD-like concentration around three long cardboard rolls. (Poster tubes from the art shop on Holloway Road.) I start with almost military precision, each box filled as its label decrees. I end, several hours later, with a mysterious shortage of bubblewrap and some of the 'decs' being shoved anywhere there is a gap in a box.

I then sweep the floor, theoretically removing every last sprig of dead fir tree. In practice, I shall be finding them until next autumn.

Three Kings' Day, as Epiphany is also known, is a busy day for biodynamic farmers, allotment holders and gardeners. Jane Scotter, of Fern Verrow farm in the Black Mountains, reminds me that this is the day they mix the Three Kings preparation, 'an offering to the elemental world and a blessing for the earth', and anoint the land with it. It is quite a recipe. Gold, frankincense and myrrh are ground to a powder using a pestle and mortar, then stirred quietly for an hour into a barrel of rainwater. They then wrap up warm and walk the boundaries of the farm with bucket and brush, sprinkling the mixture as they go. 'All the while wishing good things to manifest on the farm and a feeling of gratitude towards the elemental world.' It is, in essence, a thank you, but also a good luck charm for the coming year's planting.

You may not believe in such magic, but as someone who carries a small lump of frankincense, worn smooth and the colour of a piece of ancient netsuke, wherever I go, I am in no position to judge.

Dinner this year is a quiet event. Perhaps non-event would be more accurate. A dish of hot-smoked salmon (very) successfully married to Brussels sprouts, and then, later, we eat spoonfuls of dense and utterly gorgeous chocolate mousse. The latter ends up lasting for three days, a feat that involves some serious restraint.

Salmon and sprouts

Serves 2
a large onion
olive oil – 3 tablespoons
Brussels sprouts – 300g
butter – 30g
hot-smoked salmon pieces – 300g
chopped dill – a handful

Peel and finely slice the onion. Warm the olive oil in a shallow pan, add the onion and fry until soft and pale gold. Shred the sprouts, add the butter to the onions, let it melt, then stir in the sprouts. Fry for another three or four minutes, until the leaves soften, then break up the pieces of salmon and fold them, gently and without mashing them, into the sprouts and onions.

Toss in the dill, season and serve.

Chocolate hazelnut mousse

The thickest chocolate mousse, with a fine layer of crisp chocolate and praline on top. The trick is not to let the mixture get too hot, and to fold the egg yolks in quickly but lightly.

Serves 6
dark chocolate – 250g
butter – 40g
hot espresso – 3 tablespoons
eggs, separated – 5

For the praline:
hazelnuts – 50g
caster sugar – 75g

To cover:
dark chocolate – 100g

Break the chocolate into pieces and melt in a small bowl balanced over a pan of simmering water. When it has melted, add the butter and stir, very lightly, to mix. Pour in the espresso.

Separate the eggs, and beat the whites until they are almost stiff. Remove the chocolate mixture from the heat, then fold in the egg yolks. Work quickly, stirring gently and firmly. Fold the beaten egg whites into the mixture, making sure there are no lumps of unincorporated egg white.

Transfer the mixture to a serving bowl approximately 20–22cm in diameter, or into four small dishes. Place in the fridge, covered with clingfilm, for at least four hours, to set.

Meanwhile make the praline: toast the nuts in a shallow pan until golden. Scatter over the sugar in a single layer and leave to melt. When the caramel is golden, pour on to a baking sheet and leave to cool. Break into pieces and process to coarse crumbs.

When the mousse is set, break the remaining 100g chocolate into small pieces and melt in a bowl over a pan of simmering water. Scrape it out of the bowl with a rubber spatula, smoothing it over the surface of the cold, set chocolate mousse. Scatter with the hazelnut praline and return to the fridge until the chocolate has set.

The Twelfth Night cake

It has become rather fashionable to buy a Twelfth Night cake (the French galette des rois) from a posh pâtissier's and bring it home in a golden box wrapped with skinny golden ribbon. The cake – it is more of a pastry really – involves a moist almond sponge filling, the sort you find inside a Bakewell pudding, within a puff pastry crust. Some contain a bean or good luck charm. Your cake is likely to come with a twee golden crown too.

Britain's own Twelfth Night cake has rather fallen out of favour. Generally a deep fruit cake, sometimes risen with yeast, it contains a dried pea and haricot bean known as the 'favours'. Whoever found the bean became King of the Revels (the Lord of Misrule) for the night, the finder of the pea, the Queen. We have made these rich fruit cakes since medieval times, though the first printed recipe seems to have appeared in 1803. The cake was the fruit-studded centrepiece of elaborate Twelfth Night parties, given in celebration of the last day of Christmas. An evening of fun that involved not just cake but characters. Each person present chose a card from a pack, each card illustrating a 'character' which the holder then 'played' for the night.

Players took their chance on whether they might be Sir Benjamin Bounce or Delia Do All, Madge Mayflower or Lord Lollipop, the Countess Flyaway, Madame Mandoline or Fanny Fandango. The cutting of the cake and the acting out of an assortment of comic characters marked the last chance to celebrate Christmas. A few still celebrate by baking a cake of sorts, though the 'character cards' will now be museum pieces. As usual, I make do with the skinny French pastry.

7 JANUARY

A breakfast of silence and solitude

Six thirty. Not a soul stirs. Just me, a pot of coffee, and the golden flame of a flickering candle in an old marmalade jar. The kitchen is millpond calm. The boiler chugs away. The muffled scraping of a spoon on a cereal bowl.

I recommend the solitary, silent bowl of porridge before the mayhem of the day starts. Time to gather your thoughts. Time for your spirit to be at peace. Oats, softened with water, milk or both, stirred over the heat; some berries, a trickle of maple syrup, honey, and, occasionally, a spoon of yoghurt. This is my recipe for a winter's morning.

Porridge, in my house at least, is often as simple as oats, salt and water, eaten without fruit, syrup or sugar, and there is nothing wrong with that. But there are other grains, such as rye, barley and spelt, each one lending a different, more interesting texture. The cooking times will vary a little. The consistency will be knubbly or smooth, depending on the firmness of the grains. Rye flakes are a hearty chew. Spelt is softer and more delicate. I change my grains as the mood takes me, but I invariably include some fine or medium oatmeal in the mix, for its ability to bring the large flakes and liquid together into a smooth, cosseting mass.

The trick is to keep stirring with either a wooden spoon or a traditional spurtle. (That's the wooden stick at the back of the gadget drawer with one end shaped like a thistle.) After seven minutes or so, your porridge will have progressed to a creamy, silken paste.

I have also taken to toasting the oats before adding them to the water or milk. The smell, similar to that of freshly made toast, will waft up as you stir. It takes five minutes, with the occasional half-asleep stir to warm the oats to a pale, nutty brown in a dry pan. The flavour becomes deeper, and when a pinch of sea salt is added (something I feel is quite crucial) you have a bowl of porridge that is about so much more than comfort and sustenance alone.

Toasted spelt and barley porridge with berries

Enough for 2
medium oatmeal – 35g
spelt flakes – 35g
barley flakes – 30g
milk – 200ml
water – 200ml

For the berries:
blackberries or blueberries, fresh or frozen – 300g
maple syrup or honey – 150ml

To finish:
jumbo oats or barley flakes – 2 tablespoons
yoghurt – 4 tablespoons

Sprinkle the oatmeal, spelt and barley flakes into a dry, shallow pan and toast over a moderate heat for five to seven minutes, until they smell warm and nutty. Pour the milk and water into a small, deep, non-stick saucepan and bring to the boil. Lower the heat, scatter the toasted cereals over the warm milk, then simmer, stirring almost continuously with a wooden spoon, for seven to ten minutes. As the grains soften, beat firmly. The porridge should be thick and creamy.

Tip the berries into a small, stainless steel saucepan and add the maple syrup or honey. Bring to the boil, then lower the heat and leave for a couple of minutes until the berries start to burst and their juice colours the syrup.

To finish, toast the jumbo oats or barley flakes to a deep nutty brown. Tip the porridge into bowls, spoon in the warm fruits, add a spoon or two of yoghurt, then the honey or maple syrup from the fruit, and then, finally, the toasted oats or barley.

Breakfasting like a king

I have eaten yoghurt every day of my life since I was a teenager. At home or away, there is always yoghurt on the breakfast table. A little glass pot of sheep's milk yoghurt, a bowl of goat's milk yoghurt or, if those aren't available, I will eat the cow's milk variety. The big, commercial brands are not on my shopping list. Too bland, too sweet. Much of the well-known yoghurts are now so sweet they taste like pudding. Yoghurt for people who don't really like yoghurt.

This particular type of dairy produce should have an acidic freshness to it, a faint tang of sharpness on the tongue. The most regular breakfast in this house is a bowl of fresh or dried fruit, a pool of fruit purée or compote, and a scattering of seeds and yoghurt. There may be oatmeal, some blue-black poppy or pumpkin seeds, golden linseeds or crunchy hemp.

Yoghurt aside, the most essential elements of my breakfasts are fresh fruit and fruit compote. The fruit changes with the rhythm of the season. Peaches, mango or apricots in summer; autumn brings blackberries and raspberries, russet apples and crisp pears; in winter and spring I include sliced persimmons, slices of grapefruit, or jewelled chunks of pomegranate.

The purée or compote that is stirred into the yoghurt is a regular round of stewed apple, icily chilled, and purple fruits such as blackcurrants, blueberries or damsons, often cooked from frozen with a little water (and a little sugar for the damsons and currants). Forced rhubarb, poached in orange juice with star anise and cloves, is a New Year treat, just as gooseberries are in summer. I make no bones about using frozen fruit for my compotes – nothing comes close to a deep purple ribbon of blackcurrants or damsons swirled through a bowl of cool yoghurt.

At the weekend, when time is less critical, such bowls will just be part of the story. There may also be porridge of some sort, toast or a bacon sandwich. Either way, the yoghurt remains a standard. Unshakeable, reassuring, steadfast.

Other good things to add to your breakfast porridge

· The apricots, figs and prunes saved from the Christmas liqueurs (see page 29).
· Apples, peeled if you wish, then stewed and seasoned with cinnamon, cloves and lemon juice.
· A compote of frozen blueberries cooked with apple juice and a little sugar.
· The marmalade pears, chilled, from page 43. (They will keep for a week in the fridge.)
· Freezer fruits – the damsons, gooseberries and blackberries you froze in summer with good intentions, and that you now find need using up. Simmer them with a little sugar and water (remove any stones once the plums and damsons are cooked), then spoon them and their juices into the hot porridge.

A baked potato for dinner

The baked potato with cheese has been with me pretty much all my life, indeed at one time I seem to remember almost living on them. They have taken various paths, from the simplest Aga-baked King Edward with grated Cheddar to the Maris Piper with Wigmore oozing into its flesh. I have smashed them open with my fist, squashed them with a vegetable masher and served them just cracked open, the floury flesh peeping temptingly from the walnut-brown skin. There have been baked new potatoes with rosemary and juniper, salt-crusted Arran Victory, split and mashed with Mrs Appleby's Cheshire, and baked Jersey Royals with a blue cheese dip.

Baked potatoes suit this time of year rather well. They just get on with things while we do other stuff. They need no stirring or basting, turning or tweaking. They warm and cosset us, are cheap and incredibly cheerful. Last Christmas I rolled tiny maincrop potatoes in salt, baked them, then piled

them, sparkling with salt, in a dish and served them with a little bowl of melted Shropshire Blue. The salt crust brushed off, leaving the skin crisp and savoury. Just give me a plate of these, and the garlicky cheese dip beside them, and I'll be just fine, thank you.

Salt crust potatoes with blue cheese and goat's curd

Serves 4–8
smoked sea salt flakes – 5 tablespoons
sea salt flakes – 5 tablespoons
thyme leaves – 2 tablespoons
potatoes, floury, medium – 8
thyme – 6 whole sprigs
garlic – 6 large cloves

For the dip:
goat's curd – 175g
blue cheese – 100g

Mix the smoked and natural sea salt flakes and tip them into a roasting tin. Set the oven at 200°C/Gas 6.

Chop the thyme leaves, then toss them with the salts. Wash the potatoes thoroughly, then, while they are still wet, roll them in the thyme salt, pressing them down so the salt adheres to their skins. Set them well apart in the roasting tin, on the bed of salt. Tuck the whole thyme sprigs and cloves of garlic, unpeeled, among the potatoes and bake in the preheated oven for an hour, until the potatoes are crunchy outside, soft and fluffy within.

Warm the goat's curd in a small saucepan, then crumble in the blue cheese. Remove the garlic from the roasting tin, slice each clove open and squeeze the soft, sweet flesh within into the cheese. As the blue cheese starts to melt, give it a quick stir, then pour it into a small, warm bowl.

Remove the potatoes from the oven and wipe off most of the salt – it has done its job. Split the potatoes open, and serve with the cheese and garlic dip.

8 JANUARY

A celebration of sprouts and citrus

To read the press, watch television and certainly to scan the endless press-releases that infest my inbox, post-Christmas dinners are supposed to be different. A casting off, a release from relentlessly rich and sweet festive fodder. Food that will take us from sloths lying imprisoned by our own greed on cushioned sofas to being energy-packed titans of the gym. Follow their suggestions and we will emerge flushed from our workouts and 'superfoods', pumped with energy, glowing with vigour and New Year positivity. At least that is what we are told.

I have never changed what I eat just because I have opened the last window on the Advent calendar. As I wrap up the mercury baubles from the tree in their bubblewrap and wrinkled tissue, I never think about a change of diet, food for a new 'me'. Christmas is a feast, a wonderful, glittering festival of food-and-family love. The sharing of vast birds, nut roasts and pork pies the size of cake tins, of boxes of cellophane-wrapped 'chocolates' and glasses of sticky drinks we wouldn't normally go within fifty feet of. It is what it is. A feast.

Except mine isn't quite like that. I doubt yours is either. It is festive, thoughtful and not without joy. It has generosity and bonhomie and heart-warming love. But it is not the grotesque force-feeding of family and friends that the advertisers and newspapers try to suggest. There is no need for me to rethink my diet, or detox or reboot or any other ridiculous cliché they try to guilt-trip us with. And anyway, I go to the gym all year, thank you.

Post-Christmas food is different because the weather is colder, the ingredients in the shops are different and our budget is probably a little tighter. Yes, there is a slight change of step, a tweaking of our everyday eating, but that is to do with the shifting seasons. It is neither an act of repentance for food enjoyed nor a desire to change our lives. It is the media, the publicists and the health food business that needs the colonic. Not us.

Salads punctuate my everyday eating regardless of the time of year. A simple bowl of lovingly washed lettuce and watercress after my main dish, or a more complex, composed version eaten as a main course. If I make a salad of greens and fruit and seeds it is because that is what I feel like eating, because it sits comfortably into the season.

A salad of Brussels sprouts, clementines and russet apple

I know a salad of Brussels sprouts sounds mirthless, but I urge you to give it a chance. It has enough citrus, almonds and rough-skinned apple to be interesting. A dressing made with liquid honey and clementine zest removes any notion of worthiness. There are a few sesame seeds and some flat-leaf parsley, but it's not complicated with unnecessary ingredients. It has a certain simplicity to it.

I tend to think if you can smell a sprout then you've overcooked it. In this recipe the leaves are given a hot bath rather than cooked. A brief two-or-three minute dunking in boiling water. It sets their colour to a vital, lively green. It tenderises without softening. This is the sort of salad you could eat with grilled bacon. Sprouts and bacon fat is a fine marriage.

The sprouts seem sweetest when cut straight from the stalk. It's an infuriating way to buy them. The stalk is ridiculously long and weighs far more than you expect. Initially, I wrote off the sprouts-on-the-stalk thing as a greengrocer's gimmick. An attempt to make your shopping bag feel like it had been to the farm gate. Wrong. They do stay perkier when bought on the stalk. Though in my defence the bloody things are virtually impossible to shoehorn into the fridge.

Serves 4
Brussels sprouts – 175g
clementines or other small citrus – 2
a russet apple
sesame seeds – 1 tablespoon
olive oil – 2 tablespoons

almonds, skinned – a handful
flat-leaf parsley leaves – a large handful

For the dressing:
a clementine
a lemon
olive oil – 2 tablespoons
white wine vinegar – 1 tablespoon
liquid honey – 1 tablespoon

Put a large pan of water on to boil. Trim the sprouts, then remove the outer leaves and put them into a bowl of cold water. Slice what is left of the sprouts into quarters and add to the leaves. Rinse thoroughly, then drain. Lightly salt the boiling water, then lower in the sprouts. Leave them to cook for a maximum of two minutes, until their colours are bright.

Have ready a bowl of water with ice cubes in it. Failing that, a basin of very cold water. Drain the sprouts and put them into the iced water. This will stop them cooking.

Remove the peel from the clementines. Slice the fruit in half, then into thin slices, and place in the salad bowl. Halve the apple, then cut each half into thin segments, removing any pips as you go. Toss the apples with the clementines.

In a dry pan, toast the sesame seeds to a rich golden brown, then tip half of them into a small bowl and the remainder into the clementines and sprouts. Return the pan to the heat, and add the oil and then the almonds. Leave them to cook, moving them around the pan every few minutes, until they are golden and fragrant. Salt lightly, then remove and place on kitchen paper.

Drain and lightly dry the sprouts and their leaves, then toss them gently with the apples and clementines. Squeeze the clementine and lemon and stir their juice into the reserved sesame seeds. With a fork or a small whisk, beat in the olive oil, white wine vinegar and honey. Season with salt and black pepper, then use to dress the salad.

We eat soup tonight too – shallow bowls of leek and potato, smooth and deceptively creamy. Fish, leeks and potatoes quietly, frugally, ticking every box.

Leek, potato and mackerel soup

Serves 4
leeks – 4 (about 500g)
butter – 30g
chicken or vegetable stock – 1 litre, plus 3 tablespoons
potatoes – 1kg
bay leaves – 3
olive oil – 3 tablespoons
mackerel fillets – 4 small

Trim the leeks, discarding the roots and only the very toughest part of the green, and slice them into 3cm rounds. Wash, then put the sliced leeks into a large pot together with the butter and the 3 tablespoons of chicken or vegetable stock. Place a piece of baking parchment or greaseproof paper over the top of the leeks, pushing it down into the pan so it touches them. Place a lid on top and cook over a moderate heat for five minutes, until the leeks have softened.

Cut the potatoes into small, 2cm cubes, then add three-quarters of them to the softened leeks. Pour in the litre of vegetable or chicken stock, add the bay leaves and a little salt and bring to the boil. Lower the heat and simmer for about twenty minutes, until the potatoes are soft.

In a shallow pan, warm the oil, then fry the reserved potato cubes until tender and golden. Remove the potatoes from the pan and put them on kitchen paper. Place the mackerel fillets in the pan and fry quickly, turning once, until they are golden and the skin side is lightly crisp.

Ladle half the soup into a blender or food processor and process until smooth and velvety, then stir back into the rest of the soup. Ladle the soup into warm bowls, divide the fried potatoes between them, and place a fillet of mackerel on each.

9 JANUARY

A fry-up for a rainy day

I am envious of the north, of Scotland and Scandinavia, with its Arctic air and drifts of snow. The winter of 2016 brought Scotland twice as many days of frost as it did to England, the west of Scotland even more. Further south, the months of December, January and February often seem to consist of little more than rain. In truth, England had forty-eight days of rain in the winter of 2016, compared to sixty-six in Scotland. Almost fifty days of rain out of ninety-three. To put it another way, it rained virtually every other day.

The total days of frost, just eighteen compared to Scotland's thirty-three, point to the picture of winter that we carry in our heads, our books and greeting cards, our paintings and films, as being something of a myth. Winter, it would seem, is not white, but wet.

I will take the rain. The steady patter on the kitchen skylights, or torrential rain beating, drum-like, on the flat roof; the rich, sweet sound of a downpour; the smell of petrichor, of wet earth, once the showers stop and the sun breaks through. Yes, I will take it. Driving sleet is another matter. Caught in the hinterland between snow and rain is to be soaked through, numbed, hampered. Give me crisp, give me cold, give me wet, but don't give me sleet.

As rainwater pours from the roof of the house it collects in a vast black butt in the back garden. Not a thing of beauty, but there is always a plant pot or two soaking in it, a way of getting water deep down to the roots, so it is more of a vast plant container than a water butt. I water some of the plants even in January, in areas of the garden that never seem to get watered despite those forty-eight days of rain. Those with an impenetrable canopy or whose circumference shields the pots they are in from the rain need help if they are not to dry out. The water is also used by the sparrows, who use it to wash their feathers. It is extraordinary that so many of us don't save rainwater when we have so much. One day we will have no choice.

No matter how vast your umbrella, how tight the strings on your hood, rain is probably best observed from indoors. Listening to the rain is entrancing. I recommend taking a minute or two, eyes closed, totally still, just to listen. It is a sound that refreshes the soul.

Dinner is a fry-up, of sorts. The smell of apples and smoked bacon frying on a damp day brings everyone into the kitchen, plate in hand.

Apples, potatoes and bacon

Serves 2
potatoes, large – 2 (450g)
juniper berries – 6
apples, large – 2
butter – 30g
olive oil – 2 tablespoons
smoked back bacon – 6 rashers
parsley, chopped – a small handful
crème fraîche – 150ml
grain mustard – 1-2 teaspoons

Put a pan of water on to boil. Scrub the potatoes and cut them into large pieces, drop them into the boiling water and cook for ten minutes, then drain. Roughly crush the juniper berries. Cut the apples into quarters and remove the cores.

Warm the butter in a shallow pan with the olive oil, then add the crushed juniper berries, apples and drained potatoes. Keep the heat low to moderate and the pan partially covered with a lid. Baste from time to time. As the apples and potatoes edge towards tenderness, add the back bacon to the pan and let it cook in the appley butter. Season with salt, coarsely ground black pepper and half the chopped parsley.

When the potatoes are golden and the apples soft, remove everything from the pan on to warm plates. Tip away any fat, but not any delicious crusty bits stuck to the pan, then spoon in the crème fraîche and mustard. Bring to the boil, stirring constantly, then spoon over the bacon and apples.

Jars of joy and the marmalade dragons

A winter afternoon, just getting dark, the scent of hot citrus and sugar climb the stone steps that lead up from the kitchen. Marmalade Day – it is actually two days – will always be up there with Stir-up Sunday as the best of kitchen days. If I'm honest, I didn't really need to make marmalade this year. There is some Seville orange left from last time, much of which was used in ice cream with dark chocolate shards, to frost an almond cake and to coat chicken wings with a sticky, ginger-spiked glaze. I just like making marmalade; the sweet, frosty scent of citrus zest, the slow 'all's-well-with-the-world' bubble of the sugar, juice and shreds of fruit on the stove, the tinge of smugness at the sight of the row of neatly labelled, glistening jars as you perch them on top of one another in the larder.

I take my time, slicing pink grapefruit peel into matchstick strips by hand. Marmalade is not something to hurry. The details are personal – cut the peel too thin and it is like eating a tangle of cotton threads. Too thick and eating your breakfast toast will resemble a dog chewing gum. And yes, I know you can prepare your fruit in seconds in a food processor, but to do that is to miss the point of making marmalade. A do-it-and-dust-it attitude that is only about the finished product. I love pulling the pith out of the orange shells with my fingers, the slow, methodical slicing of the peel. The cascading pile of shredded, orange-rimmed pith.

Yes, making a batch of marmalade will take a day of your life. You need the right fruit, a razor-sharp knife, some muslin and a row of spotlessly clean glass jars. Your kitchen will receive a faint sticky film over its surfaces, your thumbs will ache, your cuts will sting. But you will have had the most rewarding time you can spend in your kitchen. The uplifting, reveille call of sliced citrus zest, the sheer hands-on joy of cooking – oh, and a collection of shimmering, translucent preserves on a bright winter's morning. Marmalade is a glowing reminder that cooking is about so much more than the end result.

Its hue will vary from rose to amber, saffron, tangerine and bronze-like treacle toffee. It can be made with oranges, kumquats, lemons, grapefruits, limes and thin-skinned mandarins. We have stirred this citrus jelly for hundreds of years. The word was in use – usually to describe a jam made of quinces, marmalada – three hundred years before the first printed recipe for the orange preserve with which we are familiar. The common usage now means a soft preserve made from citrus fruits, using their peel. I would like to add the word translucent, but that might upset those who like theirs as dark as a stormy sea, thick with chunks of coarse-cut peel and as brown as maple syrup. Marmalade is different things to different people.

You can make marmalade from sweet oranges, but to capture that bittersweet tingle, that spritz of freshness, and surely the reason you want marmalade rather than jam, you will be best served by Seville oranges. They have that elusive breath of bitterness that rises above the sweetness.

The Seville orange season, like Advent or Easter, is a movable feast. I have seen the knobbly, flat-topped 'marmalade oranges' as early as the first week of January. Towards the end of the season, in late February, they rarely make a good batch, since their pectin seems to disappear as they ripen. You can navigate this by adding more lemons, but your precious preserve may lose its point.

I should mention that marmalade-making brings out both the best and the worst in people. The best, those who share their recipes, and give much of their golden bounty away, are the open-minded band who understand that the perfect marmalade is the one you like. But there are those I call the marmalade dragons, the self-styled guardians of marmalade. What my dad would call 'a bit up themselves'. They insist theirs is the only recipe worth using, even though generally it is both too stiff and too sweet. Their recipes read less like a chat with a friend, more like a slap across the face. What they fail to understand is that there is no perfect recipe, only a recipe that you personally like. I have friends who like theirs firm and full of peel, while I prefer a marmalade that is lightly set, rather than one that wobbles like a jelly at a children's party. Have no truck with the dragons – a pot of marmalade should be a golden, beaming joy, not a test to be marked.

Some useful stuff

The clock

This is not the time to show off your multi-tasking skills. Choose a 'marmalade day' rather than trying to squeeze it in with everything else. Otherwise you will find the peel-shredding frustrating and the simmering pan a harridan.

The jars

You really do need newly sterilised jars. Put them through the dishwasher, pour boiling water into them, bake them. Anything. Just don't stint on the cleaning of your jars. A less than spotless jar will make your marmalade go mouldy.

The overnight soak

The peel, pith and pips are essential to the character and setting of your orange jam. In fact, it won't set without them and won't taste much like marmalade either. Leave the pulp and pips, tied in a muslin bag, soaking overnight with the juice and shredded peel. The nocturnal soak will produce softer shreds of peel and a more successful set.

Setting

If your marmalade doesn't set you can tip the contents of your jars back into a clean pan and boil it up again. The downside of that is that you can lose the freshness of the fruit, which is after all what you are trying to preserve. The mixture may darken and caramelise too, giving you a toffee backnote. The result will be fine for cooking with – tarts, cakes and the like – but is unlikely to fill your early mornings with happiness.

Shop early

Get your Seville oranges early in the season. Once they start to soften they lose their pectin, and therefore your preserve will lose its structure.

Pink grapefruit marmalade

Making sure your jars are sterilised is essential, as it will prevent mould from forming. I put the jars and their lids on a baking sheet in the oven for ten minutes, but you can also pour boiling water from the kettle into them if you prefer, drying them with a spotlessly clean tea towel afterwards.

Makes 5 jars
pink grapefruits – 700g
lemons – 2
water – 1.8 litres
granulated sugar – 1.5kg

You will also need a large square of muslin.

Cut the grapefruits in half horizontally. Squeeze the juice into a large, deep saucepan, catching the pulp and pips in a sieve balanced over the top.

Turn each half grapefruit shell inside out and tug out the flesh and skins with your fingers. It will peel away from the white pith quite easily.

Put the pips, flesh and skins on to the piece of muslin. Cut the lemons in half, squeeze the juice and add to the grapefruit juice. Place the lemon shells in the muslin, then pull up the four corners to form a pouch and secure tightly with a piece of string. Place the pouch in the pan.

Using a very sharp knife, cut the grapefruit peel into long, thin strips. The thickness is up to you but I would aim to cut it as thin as possible, just slightly thicker than a match. Add the shredded peel to the pan, then pour in the water. Set aside to soak overnight.

Put the pan over a high heat and bring to the boil, then lower the heat, cover with a lid and leave to simmer gently, for two hours.

Heat the oven to 140°C/Gas 1. Remove the bag of pulp and seeds from the marmalade mixture. Place a sieve or colander over the pan, then put the bag into the sieve and press down firmly with a wooden spoon to extract as much of the liquid as you can (there is a surprising amount in the bag and it would be wasteful not to use it). Discard the bag.

Pour the sugar on to a baking tray and smooth flat, then place in the oven. Leave for ten minutes, until warm, then remove and tip into the grapefruit mixture. Bring to the boil, skimming off any froth with a metal spoon or a piece of kitchen paper, then leave to cook at a sprightly simmer for eight to ten minutes, until the temperature reaches 105°C on a sugar thermometer, testing as you go. (I test mine by dropping a teaspoonful of marmalade on to a fridge-cold saucer. If it forms a skin within a minute or two and is slow to move when tipped, it is ready.) Pour into warmed jars and cover each one tightly with a lid.

Seville orange and pomegranate marmalade

Put the jars and their lids on a baking sheet in the oven for ten minutes to sterilise them, or you can also pour boiling water from the kettle into them if you prefer and dry them with a clean tea towel afterwards. Don't be tempted to omit the overnight soak of peel and pith, as it softens the peel and helps the set.

Makes 5 jars
Seville oranges – 750g
a lemon
pomegranate juice – 400ml
water – 1.2 litres
granulated sugar – 1.5kg

You will also need a large square of muslin.

Cut the Seville oranges in half horizontally. Using a reamer or an orange squeezer, squeeze the juice into a large saucepan, catching any pips in a sieve balanced over the top of the pan.

Turn each half orange shell inside out and scrape out the flesh with your fingers or a teaspoon, letting it fall into the sieve with the pips.

Transfer the pips, flesh and skin on to the piece of muslin. Cut the lemon in half, squeeze the juice and add to the orange juice. Put the lemon shells on to

the muslin, then pull up the four corners to form a pouch and secure tightly with a piece of string. Place the pouch in the pan with the juice.

Using a very sharp knife, slice the orange peel into long, thin strips no thicker than a match. Add the shredded peel to the saucepan, then pour in the pomegranate juice and water. Push the pouch of pith, pips and pulp under the surface and leave to soak overnight.

Next day, put the pan over a high heat and bring to the boil, then lower the heat, cover with a lid and leave to simmer gently, for one and a half hours. Check regularly that the heat is not too high and the liquid isn't evaporating.

Heat the oven to 140°C/Gas 1. Remove the bag of pulp and seeds from the marmalade mixture. Balance a sieve or colander over the pan, put the bag in the sieve and press down firmly with a wooden spoon to extract as much of the liquid as you can. Discard the bag and its contents. It has done its work. Place a saucer or small plate in the fridge to get cold.

Tip the sugar on to a baking tray, smooth it flat, then put it into the oven to warm for ten minutes. Tip the sugar into the pan. Bring to the boil, skimming off any froth that appears on the surface with a metal spoon or a piece of kitchen paper. Leave to simmer for eight to ten minutes, or until the temperature reaches 105°C on a sugar thermometer.

Test to see if the marmalade is ready by dropping a teaspoonful on to the chilled saucer. Put the saucer back into the fridge for a minute. If the test sample is slow to move when the saucer is tipped and forms a skin within a minute or two, the marmalade is ready. Pour into warmed jars and cover each one tightly with a lid.

Ribsticker bread pudding

For all the excitement of bringing home a freshly baked loaf, its crust dark and crisp enough to shatter messily under the bread knife (a chewy piece of which is usually removed, buttered and devoured before I even have my coat off), there is inevitably some left after a day or two that is beyond toast.

The weather was so cold this week I layered half a loaf, toasted and lavishly buttered, in a baking dish with cheese, ham and the sort of creamy custard you might use in a quiche. The result, a sort of savoury bread and butter pudding, had a deep, soul-warming quality second only to tartiflette. Custard-soaked sourdough, strings of cheese, thyme-scented ham and a crisp Parmesan crust, the sort of dinner you dream about when you have come in numb with cold.

Like quiche, this is a recipe that is improved by being given a while to calm down. A good ten minutes in a warm place after baking will allow the juices to soak into the bread and the texture to settle. Make no mistake, it is best eaten hot, but it will retain the heat like nothing else.

In practice there is rarely any bread thrown away in our house, or even given to the robins. Probably because we eat so much soup. Even the stalest crust is often resuscitated by a ladleful of chicken and leek broth. The uses of a past-it loaf, though, are never-ending. A favourite is a mixture of crumbs fried in butter until crunchy, flavoured with orange zest, black pepper, chopped parsley and pine kernels, as a crust for baked tomatoes, aubergines or mackerel. Another has become something of a habit, that of putting a thick slice of bread under a small roast, a pheasant or piece of pork loin perhaps. The bread soaks up the roasting juices as it crisps. I tear it to pieces and eat it while carving the meat.

I like biscotti or shortbread with poached fruit, an apple fool or a syllabub. The joy of the crisp and the soft. But bread, cut into long thin soldiers, as you might slice it for a boiled egg, can do splendidly too. Butter the bread,

sprinkle it with caster sugar and grill until the sugar melts, or do as I did this week, spreading the toasted bread generously with marmalade and caramelising it under the grill. Something for stewed apple, mango fool or poached rhubarb.

Bread pudding with ham, Comté and Taleggio

Don't feel tied to tracking down Comté or Taleggio, even though they feel perfect for this. You need a firm-textured, punchy cheese for slicing and another that will melt into strings, such as Fontina. (Mozzarella will work, but it is a bit on the mild side for this.)

Serves 4-6
crusty white, rustic bread – 400g
butter, softened – 150g
Comté – 300g
Taleggio – 200g
roast ham – 400g
thyme – 12 small sprigs
Parmesan – 50g
egg yolks – 4
double cream – 250ml
full cream milk – 300ml

You will also need a baking dish measuring approximately 20cm × 24cm, lightly buttered.

Set the oven at 200°C/Gas 6. Cut the bread into slices, leaving the crusts on, about 1cm in thickness. Lay the slices flat on a baking sheet and place in the oven for ten minutes, turning once, until lightly crisp on the surface.

Remove the bread from the oven and spread generously with the butter. Cut the Comté and Taleggio into 1cm thick slices. Tear the ham into large bite-sized pieces. Pull the thyme leaves from their stems.

Place a single layer of the buttered bread on the bottom of the dish, tucking the slices together snugly. Place some of the cheese and ham on top, grind over a little black pepper, add a scattering of thyme leaves, then another layer of buttered bread and more of the cheese and ham. Continue until the ingredients are used up.

Finely grate most of the Parmesan into a small mixing bowl, add the egg yolks, then mix in the double cream and milk with a fork or small whisk. Season with a little salt, then pour over the bread, letting it trickle down through the layers. Grate the reserved Parmesan over the surface.

Cover the top of the dish with foil and bake for thirty-five minutes. Remove the foil and continue baking for a further ten minutes, until the top is golden. Remove from the oven and leave to settle for ten minutes before serving.

After such a hearty affair, you will want something (if you want anything at all) that is effortless, cool, refreshing.

17 JANUARY

Toasting the trees, roast pork and apple cake

Those sad souls who fail to appreciate the cold months might feel better when they remember that the winter solstice was once the time of much making merry. The festivities lasted from harvest until Candlemas. Drunkenness, debauchery and feasting were the rules of the day. A far better idea than sitting around moaning about the cold and the rain.

The single word that seems to sum up the joyous spirit of the cold months is surely 'wassail'. An ancient word – the Anglo-Saxon greeting 'waes hael' means 'be healthy' – that is the bringer of much jollity. In the twelfth century the meaning was extended from a simple greeting to that of a party, a joyous occasion where men would sit around drinking each other's health.

The term wassailing is believed to have first appeared in the cider-producing counties of England and the earliest record was in Fordham, Kent, in 1585. The word refers to the ceremony, still carried out to this day, in Somerset, Devon, Gloucestershire, Suffolk and Herefordshire, of drinking the trees' good health. The night of revelry was Old Twelfth Night, January 17.

Imagine the scene: a frosty night in the orchard, the lichen-covered branches decorated with ribbons and sprigs of rosemary. Villagers attending the 'Apple Howling' carry lanterns and horns, others banging trays and pans to wake the apple trees from their winter sleep. A wassailing carol is sung. (Many villages have their own distinctive verses.) Bonfires are lit, shotguns are fired. The rollicking well-wishing scares away evil spirits and ensures a good harvest next autumn. A favourite tree, holding the spirit of the 'Apple Tree Man', is blessed.

A king and queen are chosen. They are lifted into the branches to offer a piece of wassail-soaked toast or cake as a gift to the robins, the guardians of the trees. In some ceremonies, the trees are sprinkled with cider, in others their roots are drenched and a communal bowl of the hot apple drink is invariably passed around.

The vessel from which the hot cider is drunk is known as a wassail bowl, of which there are examples in several British museums. The example in Birmingham Museum and Art Gallery in Chamberlain Square is 29cm in diameter, and there is a rather fancier ivory embellished cup in the V & A. They pop up for sale at auctions now and again. An early eighteenth-century one made £8,000 at Christie's in 2013. Made mostly from dense, and thus waterproof, lignum vitae wood or simply ash or maple (I have read of elderberry too), they are sometimes finished with pewter or silver. You take a sip (or probably more), then pass it to the next reveller. The carved bands around most bowls are there to help you grip and tip the bowl.

The contents of the wassail bowl vary from place to place but mostly involve hot cider. The oft-mentioned concoction known as Lamb's Wool, a mixture of ale, crab apples, sugar, eggs and cream, with floating pieces of toast to represent the lamb's wool, sounds rather too much of a good thing to me.

It is worth remembering that this ceremony dates from a time when labourers' wages were partly paid in cider. The health of the trees was essential to a good crop, and to attracting workers to the farm. The ceremony was as much insurance as it was convivial. Nowadays wassailing is enjoying something of a revival, though there are often family or village events held on small farms and orchards. I am tempted to, though I never have, bless my own apple tree, the Discovery. Perhaps I should. However you wassail, it sounds far more interesting than a night in front of the television.

All this revelry sounds like an excuse for a roast. And, better still, an apple cake.

Pork belly with sausage and lemon thyme stuffing

Serves 6
medium onions – 2
celery – 2 ribs
olive oil – 2 tablespoons
lemongrass – 2 sticks
good-quality sausage meat – 500g
fennel seeds – 2 teaspoons
lemon thyme leaves – 2 tablespoons
pork belly, skin scored, bone in – 2kg
cider, medium to sweet – 500ml
redcurrant jelly – 2–3 tablespoons

Set the oven at 220°C/Gas 7. Peel the onions and chop into small dice, then trim the celery and cut into pieces of the same size. Warm the olive oil in a wide, deep pan and cook the onions and celery until translucent, stirring regularly.

Remove and discard the outer leaves of the lemongrass, then shred the rest very finely and add to the pan. Remove from the heat and mix in the sausage meat, some salt and black pepper, the fennel seeds and lemon thyme. Shape the mixture into 20 balls roughly the size of a golf ball and set aside.

Season the piece of pork belly. Place it in a large tin skin side up and roast for twenty minutes, then lower the heat to 160°C/Gas 3 and leave to roast for one and a half hours. Place the stuffing balls around the roast, rolling them in the fat in the pan, then return to the oven. If there is no room in your pan, cook the stuffing separately. Turn the stuffing balls over after twenty minutes and continue cooking for another twenty.

Remove the pork and stuffing from the roasting tin to a warm dish and cover lightly with foil. Pour off most of the oil from the pan, leaving behind the sediment and meat juices that will form the base of your gravy. (You can use the resulting fat to roast potatoes or to butter a chicken another day.) Place the roasting tin over a moderate heat, then pour in the cider and bring to the boil. Scrape at the crusty bits in the roasting tin with a wooden spatula, stirring them into the bubbling cider. Stir in the redcurrant jelly, then taste for seasoning, adding salt, black pepper and a pinch of sugar as necessary.

Slice the pork into thick pieces, and serve with the stuffing and some of the cidery juices from the roasting tin.

Wholemeal apple cake, spiced frosting

Serves 8
apples, small – 500g
butter – 30g
unfiltered (cloudy) apple juice – 250ml

For the cake:
butter – 200g
light muscovado sugar – 75g
golden caster sugar – 75g
hazelnuts, skinned – 100g
eggs – 4
self-raising wholemeal flour – 150g
baking powder – 1 teaspoon
ground cinnamon – $\frac{1}{2}$ teaspoon
salt – a pinch

For the icing:
icing sugar – 150g
lemon juice – 3 teaspoons
ground cinnamon – a pinch
cardamom pods – 6
sesame seeds – 2 teaspoons
poppy seeds – 2 teaspoons
dried rose petals – 2 teaspoons

Set the oven at 160°C/Gas 3. Line the base of a 22cm springform baking tin with baking parchment.

Peel and core the apples, then halve them if they are very small, slice them if large. Melt the butter in a shallow pan and add the apples, cut sides down. Pour in the apple juice and bring to the boil. Lower the heat and cook for ten to fifteen minutes, until the apples are translucent and tender to the point of a knife. The apple juice will have virtually disappeared. Watch the fruit carefully towards the end of cooking, making sure it doesn't burn. Remove from the heat.

Make the cake: dice the butter, then put it into the bowl of a food mixer with the sugars and beat for a good five minutes, until light and fluffy; the colour of latte. Regularly push the mixture down from the sides of the bowl with a rubber spatula to ensure even creaming.

While the butter and sugar cream, toast the hazelnuts in a dry pan, watching carefully and moving them round the pan so they colour evenly. Grind to a fine powder in a food processor.

Beat the eggs lightly with a fork, then add, slowly, with the paddle turning, to the butter and sugar. Combine the flour, ground hazelnuts, baking powder, cinnamon and salt, then add to the batter, mixing it together thoroughly. Scrape the batter into the lined cake tin and gently smooth the surface.

Place the apples evenly on the surface of the cake. They will sink into the base of the cake as it bakes. Bake for fifty-five to sixty minutes, until the cake is spongy to the touch. (Test for doneness with a metal skewer after fifty minutes – it should come out moist but without any uncooked cake mixture sticking to it.)

Remove the cake from the oven and leave to settle for twenty minutes. Run a palette knife around the inside of the tin to loosen it from the tin, then carefully undo the sides of the tin and place the cake on a plate.

Make the icing: sieve the icing sugar into a bowl, stir in the lemon juice and add a little water if required to bring it to a thick, pouring consistency. Stir in the ground cinnamon. Crack open the cardamom pods, remove the black-brown seeds and grind them to a fine powder. Stir the cardamom into the icing. Lightly toast the sesame seeds in a dry pan until golden, then mix them with the poppy seeds and dried rose petals.

Transfer the cake to a plate and trickle the spiced icing over the surface. Scatter with the sesame seeds, poppy seeds and rose petals.

Crumbs

At first glance, a visitor might think my long, thin, green-upon-green garden wouldn't be especially friendly to wildlife, but listen and you will know better. The birdsong in this little urban space is relentless and delightfully so.

Look out of the kitchen window any time of year and it is rare not to spot several species at once. Wrens that play tag, endlessly, with one another through the holes in the gateposts; blackbirds busily nesting in the ivy; thrushes washing themselves in the water bucket; tits just having fun. And that's without the manic woodpecker three doors down. But the most common visitor to this garden is the robin. I only have to set foot outside, let alone pick up the garden fork, and he is there, barely six feet away, proud as punch.

Does his presence seem more common in the winter because his scarlet breast feathers are all the more visible or because I expect him to be there? Robins have long been associated with the season, on greetings cards and stamps, tree decorations, in carols and on wrapping paper. The redbreast likes human company, is cheeky, apparently argumentative and territorial, but above all I think the word is jolly.

I don't normally feed the birds. (Shake the crumbs from a napkin in my garden and prepare to be besieged by pigeons.) The other birds seem happy enough with the berries, and whatever wildlife they find in the dried seedpods I leave unpruned, to sway and rattle in the winter winds. But this morning is one of those when I feel the birds need some help. It is cold, the water pail frozen, the seed heads picked bare.

I'm looking at an unopened panettone in its red box and wondering about putting the whole thing, crumbled into gravel-sized pieces, out for the blackbirds. In the depths of winter a supplementary food source can help them survive. I know the rules. I know to feed them at the same time each day; not to give them dried coconut or salty cereals and not to put down white bread. I have picked up too that birds need hard fat to get them through the winter, and seeds, except for robins, who prefer berries, chopped grapes and bits of apple. Most birds love sunflower seeds, approved food bars and balls, dry cereals such as oats and soaked currants and raisins. (Water, that is, not brandy.) They also need water, especially when the ponds and puddles are frozen over. Robins, I hear, are partial to a bit of grated cheese.

Birds can cope with a few cake crumbs, though there are better things to give them. I decide the panettone is too much and do something with it for us instead.

We also finish off last night's roast pork, cold, in thin slices with pickled figs, crisp pieces of fennel and, crucially, some of its crackling with extra salt.

Cold roast pork, fennel and fig salad

Serves 4
cold roast pork – about 150g per person
pickled figs – 4 (see page 281)

For the pickled onion:
red onions, medium – 2
lemons, large – 2
a clementine
white wine vinegar – 50ml
fennel – 1 bulb
olive oil – 3 tablespoons

Peel the onions, cut them into thin rings, then put them into a medium-sized preserving jar. Squeeze the juice from the lemons and pour it over the onions. Grate the clementine and add the zest to the jar with the juice. Pour in the vinegar and set aside for an hour in a cool place.

Trim the fennel, reserving any young fronds. Halve lengthways, then thinly slice and place in a mixing bowl. Pour over the olive oil and add any reserved fronds.

Slice the pork thinly and place on a serving plate together with some of the figs. Toss the fennel briefly with the pickled red onion and serve with the pork and figs.

Here is an idea for getting rid of any spare panettone.

Mincemeat, apple and panettone pudding

By halfway through January it is time to say goodbye to the scrapings of dark, brandy-drenched mincemeat lurking in their jar, even though I know they will keep for weeks. I am not fond of bits in jars. It has to be the right day to eat mincemeat. If not Christmas, then at least the sort of day when you can't leave the house without a woolly hat.

I take the bowl of stewed apple from the fridge, the one I was planning to eat for breakfast tomorrow, stir in the last of the mincemeat and look around for a suitable crust. A crisp, sweet rubble under which the soft, sour apple and sweet mincemeat can hide. I could make crumble, but the panettone on the breadboard catches my eye. The soft, vanilla-scented cake is now a little dry around the edges. Time to go. Blitzed to coarse crumbs in the food processor and tossed in melted butter, it kills two birds with one stone. I have no dying panettone and I have a crust for my apple pudding.

Useful as this light pudding is for using up the last dab of mincemeat and the final, slightly stale wedge of panettone, I like it enough to buy the ingredients specially. It is one of the fastest winter puddings I have ever made. (It takes five minutes to peel and chop a couple of Bramleys.) A cold weather pudding that is neither too filling nor too much trouble. A winner.

I do think 100g of mincemeat is enough, though. More than that and its lightness will be lost. The deep, nostalgic whiff of Christmas becomes altogether too heavy and rich. You will probably need cream or ice cream for this. At least, I do.

Serves 4
apples, preferably sharp – 500g
water – 2 tablespoons
mincemeat – up to 100g
butter – 60g
panettone – 250g
demerara sugar – 1 tablespoon

To serve:
vanilla ice cream, crème fraîche or cream

Set the oven at 180°C/Gas 4. Peel and core the apples, then cut into large pieces. Put them into a saucepan, add the water and bring to the boil. Lower the heat, leaving the apples to soften and collapse to a purée. Remove from the heat and stir in the mincemeat, taking care not to overmix. A craggy ripple of glossy mincemeat running through the creamy white of the apple is preferable to turning the whole thing pale brown. Transfer to a baking dish.

Melt the butter in a medium-sized pan. Run the panettone through a food processor until you have coarse crumbs. Stir the crumbs into the melted butter and mix thoroughly, but not so much that you compact the mixture. You should have a loose, moist jumble of crumbs and dried fruit.

Tip the crumbs over the apple, leaving the surface rough. Sprinkle over the demerara sugar and bake for about twenty minutes, until the top is a deep golden brown.

Candlemas, Japan and the best present of all

The feeling you have on Christmas morning. That there is something special about this day, even before you are awake enough to realise what day it is. Well, that.

There is something different. My room is cooler than yesterday. Almost icy. There is a soft, chalk-white light coming through the shoji paper blinds. I look at the time. It should still be dark outside. I lie in bed and listen. Today is Candlemas, the day that officially marks the end of Christmas.

I am first up; I put on my padded coat, a sort of patchwork duvet of blue and brown, slide my feet into the oversized slippers that make me feel like a yeti, and pad downstairs on the slippery wooden floors. I sneak like a burglar into the curtained shoe room to retrieve my walking boots. Once out of the sliding door, carefully and without disturbing the wind-chimes that will have staff running to greet the intruder, or bow to the escapee, I am into the gardens, thick snow coating every branch and tree.

The hanging lanterns, glowing warmly in a forest of green, black and white, have been lit, the lights in the stone houses too. There is a trail of smoke coming from the open fire in the hearth around which we sat drinking sake until the wee hours last night. I can hear muffled footsteps, the sort of hushed padding of feet you only get when it has snowed. The slow, rhythmic swish, swish, swish of a brush as a man in an oversized duffel coat sweeps the path, the soft, long bristles flicking the snow into the undergrowth.

I have always loved the snow, but never so much as now. This morning, in this tiny village in Japan. Bamboo weighed down to the ground by snow, straggly camellias allowed to grow tall and open, with single flowers. I shuffle along, the snow still falling. What appeals is the other-worldiness of this place, the feeling that I have woken in a fairy tale. Snowfall was not forecast. This is the best gift of all.

Suddenly, the warm, toasted scent of buckwheat tea, then it disappears, ghost-like, as quickly as it came. The sound muffled by the snow, each slow, precarious footstep becomes a quiet joy. Each step is a whisper, a soft voice repeating 'hush' over and over. I take photographs with my phone, curious that the gardener is laying tattered raffia mats on the paths, as snow still falls.

I wander through the gardens, ducking the low-hanging branches with their white cargo, shuffling along the narrow paths, stepping gingerly from stone to stone. The tiny lanterns, like pixie houses, are still glowing, a pool of ghostly light around each one. Everything I have ever wanted is here, right now.

The cold is making me hungry. I head in, pausing to warm myself by the wood-burning stove in the hall. My request for coffee is sweetly but firmly refused, and I drink green tea from deep cups instead; and breakfast on agedashi-dofu, pieces of silken tofu, fried crisp and served in a pool of glossy ponzu broth. A little pile of grated radish, as white as the snow outside my window, flakes of katsuobushi, the fine slivers of bonito that move as if alive, and a pinch of freshly grated ginger. A salad of translucent pink radish and white lettuce in a glass bowl, crisp as ice. A fragile dish of thick yoghurt, a teaspoon of scarlet fruit purée, a single green leaf.

Strangely, illogically, I want ice cream. There is no explanation for this, other than perhaps that I often find myself wanting ice cream whenever I'm truly deeply happy. A request brings a yuzu jelly, served in its hollowed-out shell. Not quite what I want, but it will do.

The outdoors beckons once more. I shuffle out again. I find a spot in the deserted coffee room hidden in the ryokan gardens. It's early, they are not open yet, but the door is. I gingerly enter, sit down at the window, at a little wooden desk, and look out at the white world around me.

The owner arrives, surprised but apparently unbothered by my having 'broken in'. She makes me coffee and brings hazelnut cookies shaped in unruly lumps like fat pebbles. A blue woollen blanket for my knees. And then a wafer-thin ginger biscuit, coated in the thinnest white icing. Like frost on a roof tile. She lights a small wrought-iron stove. I write.

At home, a few days later, I make an ice cream whose flavours of pink grapefruit and orange are reminiscent of that jelly. The first icy spoonful, intensely citrus with a hint of pepper from the basil leaves, takes me back to that morning in the snow. Opening the shoji paper shutters, staring at the snow in disbelief at my good fortune.

Lemon, orange and basil ice

A winter sorbet, pure as a winter stream. Clean as ice, almost spicy. A tang of citrus softened by the addition of cream.

I remember my first trip to Japan, a decade ago now. Icy fingers tingling with cold, I stood at an ice cream stand, as excited as a schoolboy with a handful of pocket money. All my favourites were there, green tea, vanilla, lemon, but I knew what I had come for. Yuzu. The citrus fruit I love, like the calamondin orange, that has all the notes of lemon and grapefruit but also an elusive spiciness. Yuzu are expensive here and often come from Europe and lack the magic of their Japanese cousins. Yuzu juice in bottles doesn't work for me either. It lacks purity. There is an unwanted back-note that comes from the processing.

You can play with mixing grapefruit and lemon juices, tweaking until you get something approaching the perfumed juice of the yuzu. But I miss the whiff of pepper that seems to inhabit freshly squeezed yuzu juice.

Enter basil leaves with their notes of pepper and aniseed. Infused with citrus, stirred into cream, they offer something of the magic of the rare Japanese citrus that I can't get enough of. I have long wished oranges and lemons were treated here with the reverence that they are in Japan. Here, they are thrown around by greengrocers and supermarkets alike, as if they were rubber balls. Their zest contains the essence, the spritz of the fruit, its sweet refreshing juice. They deserve better treatment.

We are short-changed by the growers, who offer so few varieties, and by those who destroy the point of much of our fruit by breeding ever sweeter varieties. The modern grapefruit has been robbed of its essential sourness, castrated by breeders desperate to turn it into an orange. In turn, the orange itself has become dull and lifeless as a glass of squash. Until we see something of the range of citrus fruits the Japanese have, perhaps the best thing is to mix them, like a cocktail, a splash of lemon, another of grapefruit, blood orange, lime or clementine or, as I have done today, introducing the gentle spice notes of basil.

Enough for 8
double cream – 250ml
milk – 125ml
basil – 75g
caster sugar – 125g
water – 150ml
a clementine
a large lemon
a pink grapefruit
natural yoghurt – 150g

Pour the double cream and milk into a small saucepan and bring to the boil, then immediately turn off the heat. Tear the basil into pieces and push down into the milk and cream. Cover with a lid, then leave to cool and infuse.

Put the sugar and water into a small pan and bring to the boil, stirring until the sugar has dissolved. Remove from the heat and allow to cool.

Grate the zest from the clementine and the lemon. Squeeze the juice from all three citrus fruits. Stir the zest and juices into the sugar syrup, cover and refrigerate.

Strain the basil, squeezing the leaves and stems over the cream in the palm of your hand. Stir together the syrup, cream and yoghurt, if necessary whisking lightly to remove any lumps. Sieve, then pour into the bowl of an ice cream machine and churn until smooth and almost frozen. Transfer to a freezer box and freeze until needed.

Index

Note about the type

This book is set in Chiswick, designed by Paul Barnes in 2017. It is based on the vernacular style of lettering found in the British Isles from the eighteenth century onwards, created by craftsmen and artisans. It is the letterform that would adorn shop fascias, gravestones, buildings, horse carriages, market stalls; in fact anywhere and everywhere letters would appear. Painted, written or carved it remained in use for as long as people made letters by hand.